Foundation Flash CS3 Video

Tom Green
Adam Thomas

friendsof

DESIGNER TO DESIGNER™

an Apress® company

Foundation Flash CS3 Video

Credits

Lead Editor
Ben Renow-Clarke

Production Editor
Liz Berry

Technical Reviewer
David Stiller

Compositor
Dina Quan

Editorial Board
Clay Andres, Steve Anglin,
Ewan Buckingham, Tony Campbell,
Gary Cornell, Jonathan Gennick,
Matthew Moodie, Joseph Ottinger,
Jeffrey Pepper, Frank Pohlmann,
Ben Renow-Clarke, Dominic Shakeshaft,
Matt Wade, Tom Welsh

Proofreader
April Eddy

Indexer
Becky Hornyak

Artist
Kinetic Publishing Services, LLC

Project Manager
Richard Dal Porto

Cover Image Designer
Corné van Dooren

Copy Editor
Nancy Sixsmith

Interior and Cover Designer
Kurt Krames

Associate Production Director
Kari Brooks-Copony

Manufacturing Director
Tom Debolski

*To Lindsay Green (my daughter and best friend in the universe)
and her husband-to-be, Phil Darling.
May your marriage be as joyful and adventurous as
the one I have with your mother, Keltie.
—Tom Green*

*To my Dad and Grandpa; I pray I can be half the husband
and father you exemplified.
—Adam Thomas*

CONTENTS AT A GLANCE

CONTENTS

ABOUT THE AUTHORS

Tom Green is professor of interactive multimedia at the Humber Institute of Technology and Advanced Learning in Toronto. When not in class, Tom is a partner with Community MX, a regular columnist for Digital-Web.com, and a frequent contributor to the Adobe Developer Center. Tom has written four books for friends of ED, including *Foundation Flash CS3 for Designers*, which he coauthored with David Stiller. He is also an "Adobe community expert"; participates in several advisory boards at Adobe; speaks at user group meetings and conferences around the world; and is one of the founding members of FlashinTO, the largest Flash user group on the planet. Tom has also regularly lectured at universities and colleges in Germany, the United States, Canada, and China. His web site can be found at `www.tomontheweb.ca`.

Adam Thomas's career can best be defined as a successful hobby. Having an early interest in computers and being mostly self-taught, he decided to go to Humber College in Toronto, studying computer information systems. Soon after his graduation in 2001, Adam was invited back to his school to be a professor of rich media and web development. Besides teaching, he runs a successful web studio called Robin Hood Tech. Adam takes pride in employing former students and gives them the opportunity to gain experience and excel in a competitive field. Adam is cofounder of the Robin Hood Business Model, which advocates for justice in business. Adam strives for integrity and simplicity, but his true motivation is his wife and family who are daily reminders of love, faith, and blessing. Adam's web site can be found at `www.adambenjamin.com`.

ABOUT THE TECHNICAL REVIEWER

David Stiller is an independent contractor whose portfolio includes multimedia programming and design for NASA, DOT, Adobe, Nickelodeon, Wendy's, Saatchi & Saatchi, and dozens of clients across the United States and Canada. David gets a kick out of sharing "aha!" moments with others through consultation, mentoring, and regular contributions to the Adobe Flash and ActionScript forums, his blog (`http://quip.net/blog/`), and articles for CommunityMX.com. David coauthored *Foundation Flash CS3 for Designers* (friends of ED) with Tom Green, contributed the interactivity chapter to *How to Cheat in Adobe Flash CS3* (Focal Press) by Chris Georgenes, and is currently working on *ActionScript 3.0: The Quick Answer Guide for Flash Professionals* (O'Reilly). In his off hours, his interests include unicycling, anaglyph 3D photography, finely crafted wooden game boards, Library of Congress field recordings, and Turkish coffee. David lives in Virginia with his amazing wife, Dawn, and his beguiling daughter, Meridian.

ABOUT THE COVER IMAGE DESIGNER

Corné van Dooren designed the front cover image for this book. After taking a brief from friends of ED to create a new design for the *Foundation* series, he worked at combining technological and organic forms, with the results now appearing on this and other books' covers.

Corné spent his childhood drawing on everything at hand and then began exploring the infinite world of multimedia—and his journey of discovery hasn't stopped since. His mantra has always been "The only limit to multimedia is the imagination," a saying that keeps him moving forward constantly.

Corné works for many international clients, writes features for multimedia magazines, reviews and tests software, authors multimedia studies, and works on many other friends of ED books. You can see more of his work and contact him through his web site, www.cornevandooren.com.

If you like Corné's work, be sure to check out his chapter in *New Masters of Photoshop: Volume 2* (friends of ED, 2004).

ACKNOWLEDGMENTS

The path to this book has been one "long strange trip" that started over hamburgers in 2005 with Flash product manager Mike Downey. He showed us a pre-Alpha version of Flash 8 and this really cool codec (VP6) from On2 technologies. The journey continued in the late spring of 2007, when a very small group of us were shown an HD video running in the Flash Player and learned that this capability would be in a Flash Player release later that year. This explains why I have been writing about this fascinating subject for so long. I sometimes feel like a kid in a candy store and I also get to meet some amazing people along the way.

This is the fourth book I have written for friends of ED and is the first one involving my new editor, Ben Renow-Clarke. The relationship between an editor and a writer is an odd one; it can either be very satisfying or an utter horror show. Thankfully it was the former with Ben, and for that I am thankful. I should also acknowledge the work of Richard Dal Porto, the project manager who somehow managed to juggle the schedule as Adobe kept introducing new technologies almost up to the day I write this.

Finding a coauthor of Adam Thomas' caliber also helps. Adam and I shared a lot of laughs over the past year, and he exhibited the patience of a saint as I kept coming up with examples and project ideas and he brought them to life. This also marks the second collaborative effort between David Stiller and me. We regard ourselves as "Tom and Jerry" because we both share a whacked sense of humor. Anybody who can bring Puppetji to a book is okay by me. Thanks, buddy.

My students, especially the first-year students, are my harshest critics and unwitting quality-control participants. They get to work through the exercises in the book and don't hesitate to tell me when something doesn't make sense or a project or exercise simply "sucks." Thanks, guys.

Finally I want to acknowledge the support and understanding of my wife and life partner for the past 30 years, Keltie. She greets the start of each new book with stoicism and patience as I move into and out of "writing moods." It will be great to get out of my office as I try to get a life.

Tom

INTRODUCTION

In 2003, I was in Seattle getting ready to do a presentation on Flash video at Digital Design World. Jim Heid, the conference organizer, saw the title slide of the presentation and mentioned that I might be facing a rather tough crowd. I looked out over audience members, sized them up, and told Jim I had his back covered. He said he wasn't too sure about that and pointed to the title on my screen: "QuickTime is dead." Looking out into the darkened room, I watched about 200 people in the audience open their PowerBooks; hundreds of bright white Apple logos stared back at me. It was indeed going to be a tough crowd.

Nobody really expected the stranglehold that Apple, Microsoft, and Real had on the web streaming market in 2003 to be broken. Yet by spring 2005, just 18 months after that presentation, that is exactly what happened. Those three web video delivery technologies practically vanished and were replaced almost entirely by Flash video. This is not to say QuickTime and Windows Media are dead technologies. They aren't by a long shot, but when it comes to putting video on the Web, the Flash Player has rapidly become the only game in town. Before I get going, you have to understand how Apple, Microsoft, and Real "lost" the market.

How video players "got dead"

QuickTime, Windows Media, and Real essentially lost the market when they were blindsided by the growth of the Web, fast Internet connections, and the "standards movement." When practically everyone had an Internet connection, and the cost of bandwidth to the consumer was plummeting, the web standards movement—led by Jeff Zeldman, Molly Holzschlag, and Eric Meyer—started taking hold, and web designers and developers began to look at the web page as a space they controlled. Content went where they said content should be, and that was the end of that discussion.

The upshot was that consumers, with more bandwidth than ever before, were unwilling to wait for video to download before it played, and the guys who designed the sites realized that they controlled the web space. Their attitude was the following: if a video was to be content in a page with text running around it, there was no way they were going to let Apple's QuickTime plug-in tell their viewers to "upgrade to pro," or let Microsoft's video player move the video off the page into another area of the screen. This was a profound shift in perception for the design community. Up to that point, video was a "cool" technology, and cool won out over control every time. When developers and designers started looking at video not as "video" but as "content," we started our move toward the Flash Player and Flash video.

This move in perception from video to content is still occurring, and you can still see examples of the bad old days. For example, I am sure you've had the experience whereby you arrive at a video page only to see this message: "To use this product, you need to install free software."

Another favorite of mine is hitting a site and being told I don't have the codec. The browser is really nice and asks me whether I want to locate it. I click OK, and I am told, "Your codec is here. You are a smart fellow; go find it." Safari will tell me a plug-in is not supported. Windows Media tells me that the "specified octet stream is not recognized." And more often than not, when there is a video I really want to watch, I can (as long as I am prepared to sit through a bazillion ads). I use these examples not to point an accusatory finger at the designers, the companies, or even the technologies. I use them because they are prime examples of what makes the experience of watching web video such a profoundly negative experience. We are awash in a world of video thanks to TV. We bring our TV mindset to this technology on the Web and, when we want to watch a video, we expect "play" to mean "play."

Further, we expect "play" to mean "play on whatever device we are using to watch the video." Web video is being delivered to desktop computers with an Ethernet cable stuck into the back of the box. Web video is being delivered to portable computers in coffee shops and parks outside Macy's in New York that are connected to a wireless network. Web video is being wirelessly delivered to my PDA. Web video is being delivered to my Nokia cell phone. These are heady times for us and I suspect that this is just the start. If you told me five years ago that video would sweep the Web and that the Flash Player would be the delivery platform, I would have thought you were more optimistic than pragmatic.

A short history of Flash video

The rise of Flash video from relative obscurity to a web standard is a fascinating tale. There is no one date we can point to and say, "This is when it happened." Some would point to Flash MX and the inclusion of the Sorenson Spark codec. Others will claim it was Flash Professional MX 2004 that really got things started, and a valid case can be made for the current iteration of Flash (Flash CS3) and the improved FLVPlayback component, which seems to be so ubiquitous in today's video experience.

For me, Flash video became real in 2000. I was in New York, attending the inaugural meeting of the New York Macromedia user group, and the evening's speaker was Hillman Curtis. This was just before Hillman became famous, and the room was filled with Director guys who were there to listen to Hillman talk about motion graphics in Flash. During the course of his presentation, Hillman played some video in Flash. To say he got my attention would be an understatement. Up until that point, video in Flash was a pipe dream. Many of us hanging around the forums would have long discussions regarding the "theoretical" use of video in Flash. Here I was—a few stories up in New York City—and theory had become reality.

How Hillman did it was to apply an old video technique to a new technology. He simply exported the video out of QuickTime as a series of frames (the technique is called *rotoscoping*, and we cover it in this book) and placed those images on the Flash timeline sequentially. Needless to say, the word got out; suddenly a lot of rotoscoped video started appearing in Flash. I'm not claiming that it was Hillman who invented the technique and kicked off the video revolution; he simply was the first person I encountered who could get video working in Flash.

The next big event in the Flash video timeline was the release of Flash MX and the adoption of the FLV format as the video standard in Flash. When you installed Flash MX, a built-in encoder was included that used the Sorenson Spark codec to convert a variety of video formats into the

FLV format. What caught everyone's attention was how small these FLV files were compared with the original. (I cited the example of a 5.4MB video file being compressed down to around 40KB in a book I wrote about MX Studio.)

At the same time Spark was on the street, Sorenson Media, which had developed the Sorenson codec (regarded as the standard for streaming video at the time) also developed a standalone FLV encoder called Squeeze. This product offered even more power and flexibility than Spark, and many Flash video developers started regarding Spark as being nothing more than "Squeeze Lite" and shifted to Squeeze to create their videos for Flash.

In these early days, we rapidly discovered there was a huge problem with Flash video. It still had to be embedded on the Flash timeline, and the result was a rather massive SWF file. The odd thing was that users were quite content to wait for the SWF file to load simply because video was such a novelty. The other issue was that video longer than two minutes in length experienced image and playback degradation.

The next iteration of Flash, Flash Professional MX 2004, solved those issues. Instead of embedding video into the Flash timeline, developers and designers could stream video from a web server. Those new to video could use drag-and-drop video behaviors to get into the game, and, most important of all, the FLV format became an output format for all of the major video-editing applications, including QuickTime. While all of this was going on, the On2 Technologies company developed an amazing codec, TrueMotion VP6, which could be used for broadcast purposes. Macromedia was also paying attention to Flash developer community members and started talking to them about a Flash version of the codec.

While all of this was going on, Flash video was seriously catching on, thanks to the rapid adoption rate of the Flash Player 7. The rate was the fastest in Flash history, and Macromedia would tell anybody who would listen that more than three million Flash Players were installed each day. Microsoft, Apple, and Real also found themselves caught in the perfect storm. Bandwidth became cheap, users were demanding an easy install, and these same users regarded the platform as irrelevant—video content should play equally well on both the Mac and the PC platforms.

Netscape lost the browser war, and RealPlayer was a part of the Netscape browser. Once Netscape went south, Real's potential—at the time it was the best streaming video solution out there—followed Netscape. The sad part of the decline of Real is that it supported the SMIL language, which allowed it to do more than just video. Real never developed good tools for SMIL authoring and it's still trying to play catch up. Windows Media Player was OS-dependent, which cut out a lot of Mac users (there is a Mac version, but it never really caught on). The fact that Microsoft had 90 percent of the operating system market, but only a 70 percent market share in the streaming media arena, tended to indicate that its clients were not exactly happy campers. QuickTime, thanks to the adoption of the technology by a variety of media companies, became a de facto standard for broadcast-quality streaming, but it failed to catch on with the general public. Today, Adobe can claim that the Flash Player is on 97.3 percent of all the Internet-enabled computers in use today. Microsoft's Windows Media Player is on 83 percent of computers, QuickTime is on about 66 percent, and Real is hovering at 56 percent.

The deal with the users was sealed when Flash Professional 8 hit the market. The On2 VP6 codec provided superior video quality and the use of Alpha channel video. The FLVPlayback component reduced the inclusion of video in a Flash video into a web page to a series of mouse clicks, and Adobe bought Macromedia shortly thereafter. If you were to ask people from Adobe why they bought Macromedia, the answer was succinct: Flash.

Flash video takes over

In 2004, Flash video was still a bit of a novelty. Two years later it was a standard. It is the video format of choice for two of the most popular sites on the Web: YouTube and MySpace. Those two sites are classic examples of that old business adage of "being at the right place at the right time with the right product." As the Web evolved from a static, page-based format to what the pundits are calling social networking, the market realized that video is a more powerful communications medium than words and images. YouTube and MySpace have also become outlets for video captures from cell phones, digitized videotape recordings, and webcams. The market has caught onto the fact that if you can digitize a video, you can broadcast it. The odd thing about this is that video is the least interactive media format out there.

Many of the major media companies, the *Washington Post* and the *New York Times* among them, are recognizing that web video is a great value-added and economical feature that supplements their print efforts. They can get into the broadcast game without the major-league expense of creating a TV network.

When the tsunami devastated the East Indies, the *New York Times* could broadcast audio, video, and photographic records of the disaster in both the paper and the multimedia section of the site within hours of its occurrence. In fact, video has become so important to the *New York Times* that there is an entire multimedia section on its web site, and the front page of the web site contains a Flash video broadcast that changes on a regular basis. Obviously, it is no longer "all the news that's fit to print;" it is "all the news that's fit to print and broadcast." Even so, the broadcasters aren't missing a beat.

At a recent online marketing conference, Ross Levinsohn, president of Fox Interactive Media, talked about Fox's recent promos for *The Simpsons* and the start of the show's 18th season. In the three days that *The Simpsons* clip was available on Fox, it kicked out 1.4 million streams. What's more, 80 percent of MySpace users watched 5 minutes of the clip, he added, while 50 percent of visitors who streamed the clip from Fox.com saw the entire video. Those are numbers that will yank advertising executives out of their chairs and get them running for their interactive divisions.

News organizations and broadcasters aren't the only ones getting in on the web video game. Retailers are adopting this technology big time. Vodaphone is one of the best retail examples where video is treated as content.

A few years back, in answer to questions about where it thought its technologies might be heading, Vodafone created its future vision site. In this series, Vodafone makes extensive use of Flash video. The thing that really caught my attention was the fact that the video was content. Through a clever use of masking and other techniques, video appeared in watches, rolled-up pieces of plastic, and futuristic screens. The video was used in context. There were no controls, and you felt that you were peeking over people's shoulders as they engaged in a video conference, found directions to a club in London, or interacted with their parents.

Where is all this heading?

Businesses now realize that video is a powerful marketing tool. One of the most common questions I hear is this one: "The boss wants to take the stuff from our corporate DVD and put it on our web site. How can we do that?" Two years ago, that sort of thing was in the realm of sheer wishful thinking. The advertising industry is now crazy about this technology because it can now measure its impact using real numbers; 80 percent of MySpace users and 1.4 million streams over 3 days for an 8-minute clip of the *The Simpsons* makes a rather powerful business case for media buyers.

From my perspective, I find the shift from "video as video" to "video as content," especially on the Flash stage, to be rather fascinating. Experimenting with After Effects, I have come to the conclusion that the boundaries are blurring between "Flash content" and "video content" in a Flash movieclip. I have been bending video around objects, putting the FLV file in a movieclip, and applying Alpha transparency and the Blend modes to the movieclip. The upshot is what I call a "meta movieclip," which is content in a Flash movieclip that is a hybrid of Flash and video content. Even simple things, such as using a video with an Alpha transparency and embedding it in an HTML page, are no longer in the realm of advanced web video tricks. It will become more and more commonplace when designers and developers discover that it really isn't that hard to do. Toss in HD video and the capability to play an FLV file on a cell phone and you can pretty well say that Adobe has all the bases covered.

What I am really looking forward to, though, is the day I can stand on a stage at a conference somewhere and when I watch the Apple logos wink on in the darkened auditorium or the iPhones light up, I know they will be able to see exactly what I see when they want to see it.

(This article, written by Tom Green, originally appeared on Digital-web.com. We want to thank them for permission to use it here.)

What's in it for you?

So now that you know why you are here, you should also know that this book is a continuation of the journey we started together in the first edition of this book, *Foundation Flash 8 Video*. When the book was written two years ago, the authors claimed not to be experts in the field "because the field is too new." We can still make that claim because even though there is a growing body of knowledge out there, the community is finding creative uses for web video, and Adobe is continuing to provide the new software and platforms for its delivery. In two years, we have gone from simply creating and playing with video to being able to do the following:

- Deliver HD video to a web page (see Chapter 12)
- Create an FLV file for cell phone playback (see Chapter 12)
- Record a video and stream it live in the FLV file or in the H.264 format (see Chapter 10)
- Deliver video directly to a desktop AIR application known as the Adobe Media Player (see Chapter 3)
- Create a Flash video application using only ActionScript and nothing in the library (see Chapter 7)

The amazing thing about this is that these were the technologies that hit the street when we started writing this book.

The first three chapters of the book are a primer. They are designed to get you up and running with Flash video and cover the fundamentals of the workflow from concept to encoding to upload.

The rest of the book explores the creative uses of video from creating a custom video player to playing an HD video through the FLVPlayback component. In between those two techniques, we explore a number of techniques:

- Working and playing with Alpha channel video
- Using filters and blend effects
- Masking video
- Ageing video
- Working with multiple videos
- Using a webcam
- Working with cue points and captions

We hope you learn something from this book and (most importantly) that you have the same amount of fun that Adam, David, and I had as we worked our way through the book. Playing wonderful "what-if "games and having fun with this technology is what has made the past several years so exciting. We can hardly wait to see what's in store in the next seven years.

Layout conventions

To keep this book as clear and easy to follow as possible, the following text conventions are used throughout.

Important words or concepts are normally highlighted on the first appearance in **bold type**.

Code is presented in fixed-width font.

New or changed code is normally presented in **bold fixed-width font**.

Pseudo-code and variable input are written in *italic fixed-width font*.

Menu commands are written in the form Menu ➤ Submenu ➤ Submenu.

Where I want to draw your attention to something, I've highlighted it like this:

> *Ahem, don't say I didn't warn you.*

Sometimes code won't fit on a single line in a book. Where this happens, I use an arrow like this: ➡.

```
This is a very, very long section of code that should be written all on ➡
the same line without a break.
```

Chapter 1

CREATING AND PLAYING FLASH VIDEO

Let's start this book in an odd place. Let's learn how to swim.

There is a school of thought that claims the best way to learn to swim is to jump into the deep end and figure it out. That is sort of where we are starting this book. You will dive right into the deep end of creating a video for Flash CS3 Professional, but we will be there helping you along every step of the way.

Before you step off the deck and into the deep end, there are a couple of things you need to know:

- You are not creating a video; you are encoding a video. This means you will be simply converting a video from one format—MOV—to another—FLV—which is the Flash video format. This conversion process is referred to as **encoding**.

- FLV files can be encoded using the Import Video Wizard built into Flash CS3 Professional. The wizard is really nothing more than a series of panels that carefully walk you through the process of creating the FLV.

- FLV files can also be encoded using the standalone Flash CS3 Video Encoder. When you installed Flash CS3 Professional onto your computer you also installed a separate application called the Flash CS3 Video Encoder. The Encoder is found in \Program Files\Adobe\Adobe Flash CS3 Video Encoder on the PC and in \Applications\Adobe Flash CS3 Video Encoder on the Macintosh.

With two encoding choices, you might be wondering which way to go. Either one is acceptable, but if you are new to using the video features of Flash CS3 Professional, we suggest you start with the wizard. Once you start moving into more complex video use and special effects, the standalone Video Encoder will become your tool of choice.

We'll start with the Video Import Wizard built into Flash CS3 Professional, but before that you need to know a bit about the file that is being encoded.

What we'll cover in this chapter:

- Video formats used by Flash CS3
- Importing a video into Flash using the Video Import Wizard
- Encoding a video using the Flash CS3 Video Encoder
- Using the Flash CS3 FLVPlayback component to play video

Files used in this chapter:

- tortoise.mov (Chapter01\ExerciseFiles_Ch01\Exercise\tortoise.mov)

Before you import

Flash can import video only if you have QuickTime 7, QuickTime 6.5, or (for Windows users) Direct X 9 or higher installed on your computer. If you don't have them, things might not work as expected, so you might need to visit the Microsoft or Apple sites to download and install the software.

If you have QuickTime on your Mac or PC, it must be installed to import the following file formats:

- **Audio Video Interleave (AVI)**: The AVI format is very common on Windows systems.
- **Digital Video (DV)**: DV is the format used by your camcorder.
- **Motion Pictures Experts Group (MPEG)**: This is the organization that devised the MPG or MPEG standard. The most common type of video using this format are MPG, MP4, and M4A formats.
- **QuickTime (MOV)**: This standard, developed by Apple in the early 1990s, is the one used by most video professionals.

If you are a Windows user and have Direct X 9 or higher installed, you can also use these formats:

- **Windows Media File (WMF or ASF)**: WMV or ASF is commonly used by the Windows Media Player.
- **Audio Video Interleave (AVI)**
- **Motion Picture Experts Group (MPEG)**

Knowing the formats you can use makes life easier all around. If you are creating the video, you know which file format to use; if someone else is producing the video file for you, you can tell them which format to use to create the video.

> *Throughout this book we will be using the terms **video** or **digital video**. Both refer to a document using one of the formats listed previously. Files produced by a video camera will be referred to as a DV file.*

The other thing you need to do is to make sure the video you are using is as uncompressed as possible. That might sound odd, but it really has a lot to do with the quality of the final product. The encoders used by Flash actually compress the file. Video that is compressed has already lost some information, which is why video compressors are called **lossy**. If you compress an already compressed file, you will lose a lot of information, which will have a direct impact upon the quality of the finished product. What does the compression job is a **codec**, which is short for **enCOder—DECoder** or **COmpressor—DECompressor**, depending upon who you are talking to.

> *In this chapter we will be focusing on creating an FLV that—until this update of Flash Player (Flash Player 9)—was the standard format for video in Flash. In fact, much of this book (right up to Chapter 12) will work with this format. In the final quarter of 2007 Adobe handed us the ability to work with H264, M4A, and MOV formats directly within the FLVPlayback component and a video object. This will be the subject of the final chapter of this book.*

Importing a video with the Flash Import Video Wizard

The source video for this exercise is a music video named "Tortoise." It is a QuickTime video that is 3 minutes and 43 seconds long, and has a file size of 41.3 megabytes, which puts it in the realm of really big web files. You can download the .zip version of this file from www.friendsofed.com or, if you have some footage you would rather use, feel free to substitute.

When importing video, it is important that you closely match the frame rate and physical dimensions of the source video. These two values are easily obtained by opening the video in QuickTime and selecting Window ➤ Show Movie Info. The Movie Info window, shown in Figure 1-1, will open, and all the information you need will be presented. Matching the values here will ensure smooth playback later on.

Now that you know what you're working with, let's go swimming.

Figure 1-1. The sample video is opened in QuickTime, and the Movie Info window is displayed.

1. Open Flash CS3 Professional and create a new Flash File (ActionScript 3.0) document. The first thing to check is the frame rate of the Flash movie. It should closely match that of the video. In this case, it is 15 frames per second, which just happens to closely match the default frame rate of 12 frames per second on the Flash timeline. If the video is shot using the North American NTSC standard, you obviously won't have Flash play at 29.97 frames per second. In this situation, setting the Flash frame rate to 24 or even 30 frames per second will work.

2. The next step in the process is to select File ➤ Import ➤ Import Video, which will open the Import Video Wizard.

The Import Video Wizard is a rather clever series of screens that walks you through the entire video-encoding process, starting from locating the video to actually placing it on the stage and having it ready to play. You will be asked some rather interesting questions along the way, such as "Is the video to be played from your web server?" and "What style of video controls would you like to use?"

3. The first screen that opens—Select Video—simply asks you to locate the video to be encoded. There are only two places where the video can be located: in a folder on your computer or on an actual server used to stream media. This means you have a Flash Media Server (FMS), Flash Communication Server (FlashComm), or a FlashComm account with an Internet Service Provider (ISP). The other server location is a Flash Video Streaming Service (FVSS), which is a company that charges you a monthly fee to store and deploy Flash video on the Web.

4. Click the Browse button shown in Figure 1-2; when the Open dialog box appears, navigate to the folder containing the video to be encoded. Click it and then click the OK button. If you have a FlashComm or FVSS account, you only need to enter the URL where the video file (which has to be an FLV file) is located. Click the Next button.

5. Now that Flash knows where the video is located, you need to decide where it will be sent for playback. The next screen you see, the Deployment screen, determines how the FLV file will be created. Your choices are the following (as shown in Figure 1-3):

   - Progressive download from a web server: This option assumes that the FLV file will be sitting in a directory on your web server and playing from that server. When you select this option, Flash understands that the video data must be streamed into the SWF file in a slightly different manner than it would if you were to use an FMS or FVSS. This "slightly different manner" is called a **progressive download**. What happens is enough data is "streamed" into the SWF file to enable it to play smoothly from start to finish. When that point is reached, the video starts to play. This means there might be, depending on the size and length of the video, a very slight delay before the video starts to play or during playback if there is some heavy network traffic.

   - Stream from Flash Video Streaming Service: This option assumes that you have an account with one of these companies.

   - Stream from Flash Media Server: This option assumes that the FLV file will be located in your FMS account.

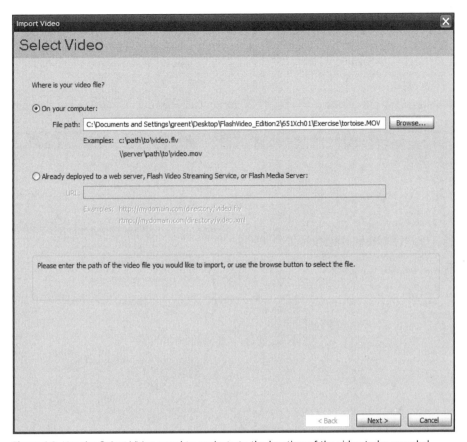

Figure 1-2. Use the Select Video panel to navigate to the location of the video to be encoded.

- Embed video in SWF and play in timeline: Essentially this option will move the FLV file into the Flash library and put the video on the main timeline or (if the video is in a movieclip) on the movieclip's timeline. In many respects, this is not recommended. When a video is placed on a Flash timeline, the timeline will expand to the full content of the video. In this case, the video will require thousands of frames to play. That might not seem like much, but when a SWF file loads in a web page, it won't start playing until a large portion, if not all, of the video has loaded. The other nasty aspect of this option is a corresponding increase in the size of the SWF file to accommodate the video. Still, if the video is short—five to ten seconds—or if you want to play with it in some manner, this option works.

- Linked QuickTime video for publishing to QuickTime: In the early pre-video days of Flash (Flash Player 5 and lower), you could actually convert the Flash movie to a QuickTime video with a Flash track. This feature is more of a "legacy" feature than anything else because Flash Professional CS3 has greatly improved the ability to export your Flash movie as a QuickTime video. This explains why it is available only in Flash 5 format or lower.

In Chapter 12 we will show you a brand-new feature in Flash CS3 Professional that actually allows you to turn your Flash movie into a QuickTime file. You still lose interactivity, but wait until you see what this feature can do for you.

Select the Progressive download from a web server option (see Figure 1-3) and click the Next button.

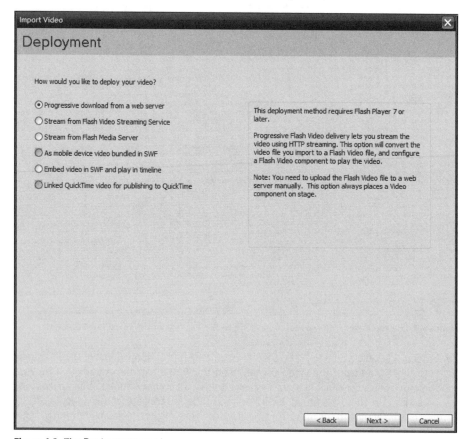

Figure 1-3. The Deployment panel

6. The next screen, shown in Figure 1-4, is the Encoding panel, in which you have to decide which codec will be used to create the FLV file, the streaming rate, the frame rate, and a number of other choices that will have an impact on playback. The decisions you make here will have a direct impact upon your viewer's experience, so let's spend some time looking at the panel.

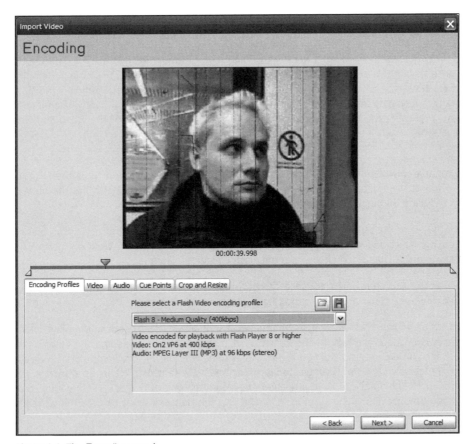

Figure 1-4. The Encoding panel

The first thing you see is the default encoding profile. If you click the drop-down menu, you will see ten presets, each targeted at the Flash 7 or Flash 8 Players or at a DV capture. If you select a preset, the settings are outlined in the Information area directly below your choice. Essentially the choice of Flash Player comes down to a choice of codec. Flash Player 7 uses only the Sorenson codec, and the new On2 VP6 codec can be used only in Flash Player 8 or higher.

> *If you are one of the 90 percent of Internet users who use Flash Player 9, there will be no problems in choosing the Flash Player 8 presets. The On2 VP6 codec is designed for use in Flash Player 8 or higher.*

The default you are looking at essentially says that the video will be playable only in Flash Player 8 or higher because it is encoded using the On2 VP6 codec. The rest of the information tells you that the video will stream at a rate of 400 kilobytes per second (kbps), and the sound in the video will be converted to an MP3 stereo format and streamed out at 96kbps.

At the top of the screen you see the first frame of the video and three sliders under it. The top slider lets you move forward and backward in the video. The two sliders under it set the In and Out points.

The top slider is commonly called a **Jog Control**, and if you move it to the right you will see that you can advance through the video. The other important thing that happens is the time under the image changes to show you exactly where you are in the video. This time measurement is quite precise: hours: minutes: seconds: milliseconds. This measurement will come in very handy later in the book when you create a movie that triggers events based on the current time of the video and when you create captioned video.

The In and Out points are also quite useful. They establish the start and end of the video, and can be used to remove unwanted footage at the start or end of the video—or even to extract a short piece in the middle of the video. Using the In and Out sliders to remove footage also has the pleasant side effect of reducing the final size of the FLV file.

The bottom half of the screen contains a number of tabs that allow you to precisely control many of the streaming values and other properties used when a video is encoded. We'll dig deeper into this area later on in this chapter when you use the Flash CS3 Video Encoder.

> **7.** Click the Next button to advance to the Skinning panel. When the panel opens, select the SkinUnderAllNoFullScreen.swf option from the drop-down menu.

The Skinning panel has a rather confusing name because it allows you to choose the playback controls used to play the video. The look of the controls, such as the buttons used and the color of the controller, is called a **skin**. In this panel you actually determine whether playback controls will be added to the video. Previous versions of Flash treated skinning much the same way Henry Ford treated the color of Model T cars: "[People] can have any color they want as long as it is black." Previous versions of Flash let you use any skin you wanted as long as it was the Halo skin used to determine the look and feel of Flash components.

Flash CS3 Professional offers you 35 different controller styles or skins that come in a variety of button combinations. In addition, you can even create a custom skin—put your client's logo in the controller or whatever—or click the Color chip and add the client's corporate color to the controller. When you select a skin style, you can see what it looks like in the preview area of the panel. The various skins, shown in Figure 1-5, appear either over the video or under the video. You can't place them at the top or to the sides of the video.

> **8.** Click the Next button to open the Finish Video Import panel. Carefully read the instructions and click Finish.

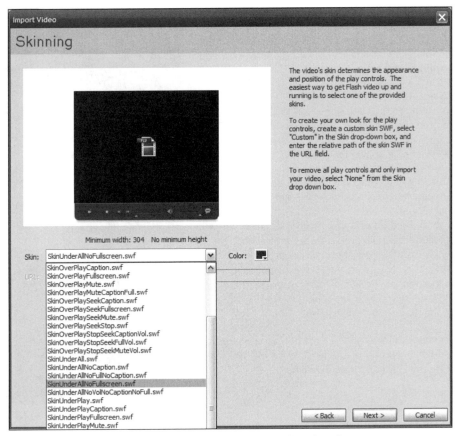

Figure 1-5. The Skinning panel with the various skin (or control) options shown

You will be prompted to save your Flash file. Navigate to the folder where this file is to be saved, name the file, and click OK. The window will close and, as shown in Figure 1-6, you will see the progress of the video-encoding process as well as a review of the options chosen in the Encoding panel.

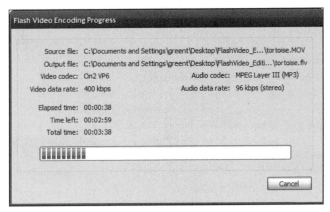

Figure 1-6. You see the progress of the encoding process.

The encoding process actually does two things: it creates the FLV file used in Flash and places it in the same folder as the Flash file you just saved. It also places a copy of the SkinUnderAllNoFullScreen.swf skin (or whatever skin you have chosen) in that folder.

9. When the encoding process finishes, you are returned to the Flash stage, and the video is placed on the stage in the FLVPlayback component. Press Ctrl+Enter (PC) or Cmd+Return (Mac) to preview the video, as shown in Figure 1-7.

Congratulations and welcome to Flash video. You have just encoded a video, chosen the skin, put it on the Flash stage, and played the video. All this in eight rather simple steps. If you have used previous versions of Flash, you will see that Adobe has pulled off a rather interesting feat. It made what was a complicated process even more complex—but easier to use. If you have never used Flash video or created an FLV file, or have regarded the entire video in Flash "thing" as being a bit over your head, welcome to the shallow end of the pool.

Take a moment to towel yourself off because we're going back into the deep end of the pool. Now you will learn how to use the Flash CS3 Video Encoder application.

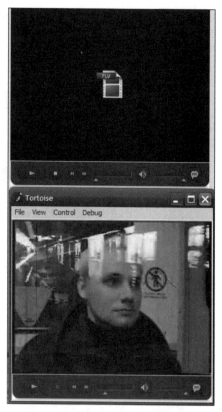

Figure 1-7. Playing back the video that has been imported into Flash

Using the Flash CS3 Video Encoder

The Video Encoder and the Import Video Wizard are somewhat similar, but are also completely different. The purpose of the Encoder is to create the FLV file and nothing more. Skins and so on are added in Flash.

The Encoder shown in Figure 1-8 is available in both Macintosh and PC versions of the application.

1. Navigate to the Flash Video Encoder. The Encoder is found in \Program Files\Adobe\Adobe Flash CS3 Video Encoder on the PC and in \Applications\Adobe Flash CS3 Video Encoder on the Macintosh.

Figure 1-8. Flash Video Encoder icon

2. The first screen that opens, shown in Figure 1-9, is where you add the video to be encoded. Click the Add button and navigate to the folder containing the video you'll be using. If you are using the materials supplied by this book, navigate to the tortoise.mov file in your Exercise folder and click Open. When your video appears in the dialog box, click the Settings button to open the Encoding Settings panel.

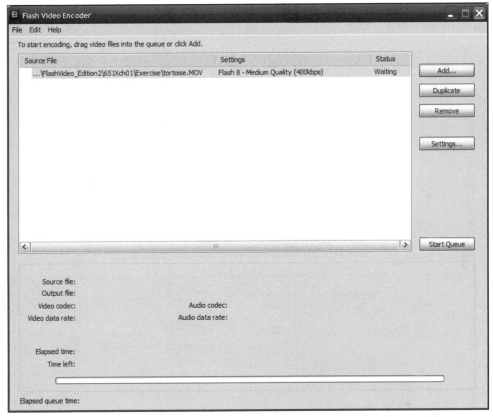

Figure 1-9. The first screen of the Flash Video Encoder is used to locate the video to be encoded.

You don't have to use the Add *button to navigate to videos in the Encoder. When the Encoder opens, you can open the folder containing the video or videos and simply drag them into the* Source File *area. Notice the use of the word* videos. *This handy little application can be used to batch process the encoding of any number of videos.*

3. The first reaction you might have to the Encoding Settings panel is this: "Hey, haven't I seen this before?" You have. It is the same panel used by the Flash Video Wizard you used to encode that earlier FLV file. We will use settings that are quite different from the presets. Name the video to be created Tortoise. In fact, the first thing you should always do is name the file. This is a great way, for example, of creating a video targeted at a variety of bandwidth situations. You could have a copy of this video aimed at users who have dial-up and limited bandwidth named TortoiseLow and another aimed at the high-speed user named TortoiseHi.

The first things to note are the tabs, which give you a tremendous amount of control over the video-encoding process and even what the viewer sees. The four main tabs—Video, Audio, Cue Points, and Crop and Resize—quite succinctly state their purpose. The default selection is, of course, Encoding Profiles.

4. Click the Video tab to open the video-encoding settings area at the bottom of the panel shown in Figure 1-10.

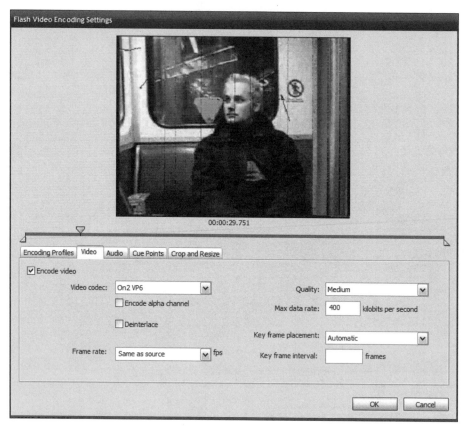

Figure 1-10. The video-encoding settings

In this chapter we will stay in this area of the Encoder. We'll use the Cue Points and the Crop and Resize features later on in this book.

The video-encoding window contains a lot of mysterious stuff. Here's what each one does:

- Video codec: This drop-down menu allows you to choose between the Sorenson Spark or On2 VP6 codecs. If your movie is targeted at Flash Player 7 or lower, you must use the Sorenson Spark codec. If you have a "Talking Head" video containing an Alpha mask, select Encode alpha channel. This feature—alpha channel video—works only with Flash Player 8 or higher and you can only use the On2 VP6 codec. If you select Sorenson Spark, this selection will be grayed-out.

- Frame rate: This choice gives you seven selections. The frame rate determines how fast—in frames per second—the video will play. A good rule to follow is this: match the frame rate of the FLV file to the FLA file. If your FLA file has a frame rate of 12 frames per second, use that number as the frame rate for the FLV file. Another good rule of thumb is to set the frame rate of the FLV file to half that of the video being encoded. If the video frame rate is 30 frames per second, the FLV rate would be 15.

- Key frame placement: Key frames in video are, in many respects, similar to key frames in Flash. In video, a key frame contains all the data in that frame, but where they part company is in what happens between the key frames. In video, the frames between the key frames are called **difference frames** or, if you are really "techie," **delta frames**. Difference frames have the stuff that doesn't change between key frames removed. For example, if you have a video of a piece of paper moving across a wall, only the paper will be in the Difference frame because it is the only thing different between the current frame and the previous frame. The wall doesn't change, so for the purposes of illustration it is removed. This means the file size is reduced. Be very careful because a bad decision here can ruin your work.

  If you were to stand at the side of a major city intersection and film cars and people walking by, there would be a lot of change and very few difference frames. Now take your camera into a farmer's field and shoot some footage of a tree. There won't be a lot of change, meaning a lot of difference frames. This explains why a 30-second video of a Formula One race is a lot larger in file size than that of a 30-second video of a tree in a field. Fewer difference frames means larger file size. The problem is that if you spread out the key frames in the Formula One video, the image quality degrades and looks blurry. We wish we could tell you that there is a hard-and-fast rule about key frame frequency, but there isn't. Before you encode the video, watch the video and see whether there is a lot of movement, both in the video and with the camera. This will determine the key frame frequency. If you are at all unsure about what to do, select Automatic from the drop-down menu and let the software do the work for you.

- Quality: This drop-down menu, shown in Figure 1-11, has absolutely nothing to do with the "quality" of the final output, but it has everything to do with the quality of the user's experience. This is where you set the data rate for the video stream into the user's computer.

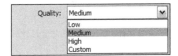

Figure 1-11. The four quality options available to you

If you select one of the three presets, the Max data rate value in the input box below the Quality choice will show 150kbps, 400kbps, or 700kbps. What this means is that a video using the High Quality setting will be fed into the computer at the rate of 700,000 bits per second. This is great for T1 or high-speed Internet connections, but fatal for the dial-up user. If you can form a mental image of trying to push a grape through a common garden worm, you can see what your user is in for.

The modem simply won't be able to keep pace; and the video will start, stop, start, stop, and so on. The result is one seriously upset user. If you select Custom (see Figure 1-12), you can enter your own value in the Max data rate text box. We tend to use a data rate of 300kbps for most situations and use a relatively low number—100kbps to 125kbps—for dial-up.

Figure 1-12. Setting a custom quality/data rate value

■ Resize video: Ignore this area. Changing the dimensions of a video will only make it really fuzzy if you increase the dimensions and less fuzzy if you reduce them. The most common dimensions for video are 320 x 240, 240 x 180, and 180 x 120. This option uses the standard 4:3 aspect ratio established by Apple when it unleashed QuickTime on an unsuspecting world. If you must resize a video, make sure to always have the Maintain aspect ratio check box selected. We highly recommend that if you must resize a video, do it in a video-editing application, not here. We'll show you how to do that in the next chapter.

5. Click the Audio tab to open the Encode audio settings for the FLV file, shown in Figure 1-13. You really only have a single decision to make here: what data rate will be used to stream the audio portion of the video?

Video is composed of two tracks. One is a video track, which we just dealt with, and the other is the audio track. This area allows you to manage the encoding of the audio track. Actually. . . audio stream.

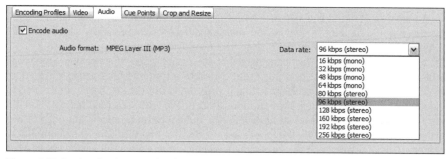

Figure 1-13. Setting the data rate for the audio track

If you click the Data rate drop-down menu, you will be presented with several choices. The bottom line is that the larger the data rate, the larger the final file size. The choice you make here is added to the video data rate for a total data rate for the FLV file. For example, if you select the 400kbps rate for the video and 256kbps for the audio, the total data rate for the FLV file will be 656kbps, which, for many users, will result in a "grape through the worm" experience. Unless there is a compelling need for stereo (okay, the train rumbling from one speaker to the next or the THX soundtrack are very cool effects, but are they really necessary?), you can knock the audio back to 64kbps mono and the user will never know the difference.

6. When you click OK, you are returned to the main Video Encoder window. Click the Start Queue button.

The video-encoding progress and the video itself will appear, as shown in Figure 1-14. You will also be shown the location of the source file, the location of the encoded file, and the settings chosen in the Encoder.

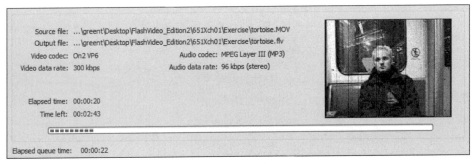

Figure 1-14. The video is encoding, and you will see a preview.

The other thing that happens is the Start Queue button changes to a Stop Queue button. If you have made a mistake, click the Stop Queue button; a dialog box will appear and ask you if you really want to do this. If you click the Yes button, the process stops, and an Errors dialog box will appear (Figure 1-15). Don't get upset. You didn't make a mistake. All this dialog box does is show you the settings and inform you that you interrupted the process.

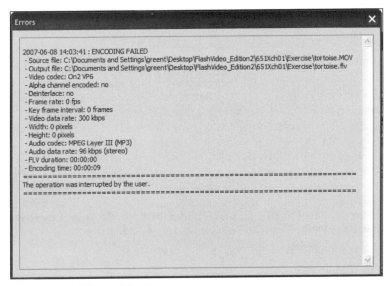

Figure 1-15. The Errors dialog box

When you close the Errors box, you are returned to the Encoder.

What you can't do at this point is say, "Well, I didn't mean to do that," and then select the video and click the Start Queue button. Nothing will happen. If you check the Status column you will see your encoding status has been changed to Skipped. To address this, select Edit ➤ Reset Status (see Figure 1-16).

When you release the mouse, the status will change to Waiting and at this point you can return to the Encoder and change the settings or click the Start Queue button. When the encoding process is finished, close the Encoder by clicking the Close button.

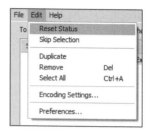

Figure 1-16. Restart the encoding process by selecting Reset Status.

Playing an FLV file in Flash CS3 Professional

The first thing to understand about the FLV file you just created is that you really can't play it anywhere but through Flash Player. In fact, you really can't play any FLV file in a web page unless it is played through a Flash SWF file.

Flash CS3 Professional makes the addition of video to a Flash movie even easier and more intuitive than in the past. This is accomplished through the use of the FLVPlayback component found in the Video Component list.

> *Before you get started, all documents you will be creating throughout this book will be ActionScript 3.0 documents. It is extremely important you understand this because there are two versions of the FLVPLayback component you will be using in this and other chapters. The Flash 8 version is the one that appears when you open a new ActionScript 2.0 document. Choose this and you will be e-mailing us to tell us that the instructions "suck." If you really want to make sure you have opened the right version, take a look at Figure 1-17. If you don't see the Captioning component, you are not working with an ActionScript 3.0 document.*

1. Open a new document in Flash CS3 Professional. Save the file to your Exercise folder. Select Window ➤ Components (Ctrl+F7 on a PC or Cmd+F7 on a Mac).

2. Drag a copy of the FLVPlayback component onto the stage.

When you release the mouse, depending on what you have done, you might or might not see a skin. Don't worry about that. The important thing is to notice that the component resembles the FLV player created using the Import Video Wizard. The major difference is that the wizard knows where the FLV file is located and which skin to use. This component needs to be given that information.

> *The FLVPlayback component does not work with Flash Player 8 or lower.*

3. Select the component on the stage, and select the Parameters tab in the Property Inspector to open the component's parameters. You can also select the component and open the Component Inspector by selecting Window ➤ Component Inspector. Regardless of which method is chosen, the information required by either one is identical.

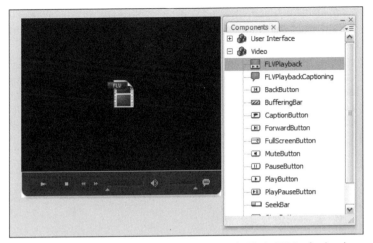

Figure 1-17. Selecting the FLVPlayback component in Flash CS3 Professional

You will be using the Component Inspector *(see Figure 1-18) only because we can show you the values in a single screen shot. The* Parameters *pane on the* Property Inspector *can't be expanded. You have to scroll to get at some of the areas needed.*

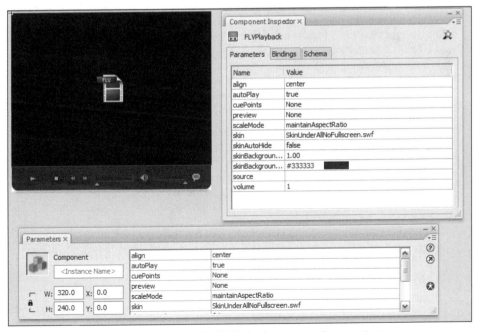

Figure 1-18. There are two ways to access the FLVPlayback component's parameters.

4. Click once in the autoPlay parameter and select false from the drop-down menu, which ensures that the movie doesn't start playing as soon as it loads. This is a good habit to develop if you use skins that have Pause and Play buttons.

5. Click once in the source area. When you see the file folder—it is a Browse button—click it to open the Content Path dialog box and navigate to the folder where you saved the encoded video. Before you close this dialog box by clicking OK, be sure to click the Match source FLV dimensions check box. This ensures that the component matches the exact dimensions of the encoded video. If you see a path to the video, this tells you that you haven't saved the FLA to the same folder as the FLV file. At this point you would click the Cancel button and save the FLA.

Figure 1-19. The Content Path dialog box

6. Click the Skin parameter and click the magnifying glass to open the Select Skin dialog box. Select SkinOverPlayCaption.swf, as shown in Figure 1-20. Click once on the Color Picker and select #990000 (**Deep Red**) as the skin color. Click OK.

You will notice there are only two types of skin: Over and Under. The Over series of skins is dependent on user interaction to become visible if skinAutoHide is set to true in the parameters. If it is true, the controls appear only when the user rolls over the video. This is a good thing and a bad thing. The good thing is that the controls aren't visible. The bad thing is that by setting the Autoplay parameter to false and the skinAutoHide parameter to true, the user sees only the first frame of the video and doesn't have a clue that it can be played. It could easily be mistaken for an image on the page.

If you select SkinUnderAll.swf you see that there is a minimum width requirement—330 pixels—for the video. What this means is the skin will be about 10 pixels too wide for the video because it is 320 pixels wide. Although the skin won't trim to fit, consider either using another control with one fewer button or using your own custom controller, meaning that you would select None in the Skin pop-up menu.

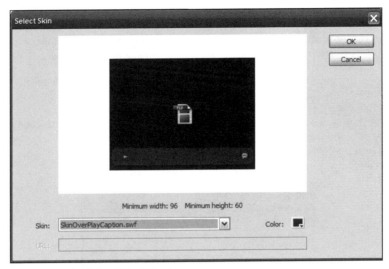

Figure 1-20. The Select Skin dialog box

7. You now have all the information necessary, as shown in Figure 1-21, for Flash to play the video. Close the Component Inspector.

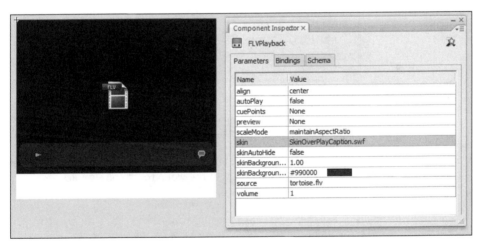

Figure 1-21. The completed FLVPlayback component parameters

For you ActionScript junkies: yes, you can control all these parameters using ActionScript. We'll get to how this is done later in the book.

If you now press Ctrl+Enter (PC) or Cmd+Return (Mac), you can test the movie in Flash Player.

Obviously, there is a bit of an issue here. There is a lot of wasted space on the stage, which only serves to increase the file size and nothing else. Close the preview; let's fix it right now.

8. Click once on the stage and click the Size button in the Property Inspector to open the Document Properties dialog box.

In Flash CS3 Professional, Document Properties has been seriously improved over earlier versions of the application. The Title and Description areas of the dialog box, shown in Figure 1-22, now allow you to enter metadata into the SWF file. This means that your Flash content is now searchable by web search engines—they can find your Flash work.

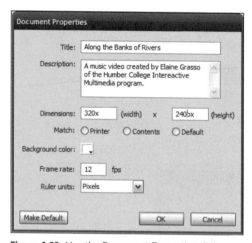

Figure 1-22. Use the Document Properties dialog box to remove the wasted space on the stage, add metadata, and set the Flash movie's frame rate to closely match that of the video.

9. Set the width of the document to 320 pixels, which matches the width of the video. Set the height value to 240, which allows for the height of the video to 240 pixels. Click OK.

> *The Flash junkies just rolled their eyes. You can simply click the* Contents *radio button, and the stage will shrink to fit the video. This doesn't work if the* Under *series of skins is used. You need to leave at least 35 to 40 pixels of stage space for the placement of those controls under the video.*

10. Select the video on the stage and make sure that its X and Y coordinates in the Property Inspector are set to 0. Test the video. The video will open in the SWF file and start playing when you click the Play button (see Figure 1-23).

If you publish the movie, just be aware that the FLV, SWF, and controller SWF files should all be in the same directory before you upload to your web site.

Figure 1-23. The video, with skin, playing in the component

So your clients saw YouTube . . . and now they want online video

It's rapidly becoming a commonplace scenario in 2007.

The Web has surpassed other forms of media as the most ideal platform for delivery of media, especially when you take into account that younger demographics are spending more time online than they do in front of the television. A high percentage of sites now incorporate Adobe's Flash video, and it's undeniably the fastest and easiest way to serve fluid video content, surpassing all other players. I judged the 2006 FlashForward Video category and was not surprised to see how many big news corporations had made the switch to Flash video.

The times they are a-changin'. The advertising world has awakened to the power of Flash video. Influencers such as Kevin Roberts (CEO of Saatchi & Saatchi worldwide) are predicting mass migration to alternative "screens" and suggesting that agencies should be putting one-third of their overall budget into interactive/digital.

As clients are becoming educated about the endless possibilities of integrating video into their online marketing mix, it's very easy for those same clients to look at the success of the YouTube phenomenon and want a piece of that action. Let's face it; who hasn't yet heard of YouTube?

Two facts I tell all my clients are these:

- *YouTube is worth more than the Manchester United Football club. Who hasn't heard of Beckham?*
- *YouTube is worth more than Sir Paul McCartney. Who hasn't heard of The Beatles?*

But do clients understand the ramifications and involvement needed to produce engaging and compelling Flash video content? Do they really comprehend the difference between optimizing existing assets and actually staging, producing, filming, editing, and compressing custom-built video content for an online audience?

I'm not suggesting that a digital media team should suddenly become the next Kurosawa or Lucas/ILM (or maybe I am), but clients need to be educated on what is involved in the whole process; i.e., preparations, locations, subject matter/content, shooting, editing, and post-production. After all, there is no magic Ctrl+F13 *button that suddenly makes their web site have instantaneous stunning motion video and bring with it a massive increase in viewers.*

So, let's go beyond the intricacies and technicalities of RTMP, FMS, VP6 CODEC, frame rates, audio synchronization, or shooting in HDV or DVCPRO HD to understand online video. Even if we boil it down to actual video content (embedded into a native SWF file), there are still issues with preplanning.

Recently, I was consulting on a big-budget production based around a series of traditional cinema/television commercial spots. I had to advise a "big-time" ad director from California on how I essentially needed the subjects/actors to return to the exact same positions after each section. This was to ensure smooth and seamless jumps when implementing simple interactivity in Flash video. Small nuances such as avoiding rapid and large movements (to avoid pixilation and blur) were also "considerations" that were discussed.

Regrettably, he proceeded to do what he thought was best. He was the "Hollywood-salary-director," and what did a "web designer" know about shooting video? Needless to say, the online component of the campaign was compromised; the smooth and natural scene jump effects were lost; a substandard "transition" was introduced as a last-minute quick fix; and the online video needed additional editing and audio enhancements adding stress, costs, post-production time, and delayed launch dates.

The yard mark for Flash video, at least for me, is Dove's "Evolution," winning the most prestigious advertising award in the world: the Grand Prix at the Cannes Lions International Advertising Festival.

Flash video is here to stay, and the world is watching.

—Simon Conlin is a digital sherpa, e-strategist, and Toronto-based interactive media consultant.

What you've learned

Okay, towel yourself off and climb up to the pool deck. Congratulations! What you have just done in this chapter is perform the very tasks that will get you into the Flash video game. In this chapter you learned

- How to create a video using the Flash Import Video Wizard
- Best practices of using the Flash CS3 Video Encoder
- How to create the FLVPLayback component
- How to test a video

This chapter covered a lot of ground, but you have also seen just how easy it can be to add video to Flash CS3 Professional. Whether you choose to use the Import Video Wizard or the Flash CS3 Video Encoder to create the FLV file is really irrelevant because they both use the Encoder. The only difference between the two methods is that the Flash CS3 Video Encoder only creates the FLV file. The skin needs to be entered using the FLVPlayback component's parameters.

The next chapter will show you how to create your own video using video-editing software.

Chapter 2

EDITING VIDEO FOR FLASH

Before we dive into creating Flash video, it is important that you understand where the content you will use comes from and how the video being encoded and used in Flash is created.

Video is prepared in an editing program of some sort. The more popular professional video-editing tools include the following:

- Premiere Pro CS3 (Adobe)
- After Effects CS3 (Adobe)
- Final Cut Pro (Apple)

They are industrial-strength tools that come with an industrial-strength price tag. In fact, each one of them has quite a number of books dedicated specifically to the application or effects that they can produce.

For the rest of us, two tools are available—and free—and come with practically every computer on the market these days:

- Windows Movie Maker
- Apple iMovie

By the time you reach Chapter 6, you will have been exposed to all five of these applications.

We will start with the last two—Movie Maker and iMovie—because we'll work with some rather simple source footage that doesn't require a lot of power under the hood.

> *You should download the files used in this chapter from* www.friendsofed.com *before you get going.*

What we'll cover in this chapter:

- Using Windows Movie Maker
- Exporting a Windows Movie Maker file for use in Flash
- Using iMovie from Apple
- Exporting an iMovie project for use in Flash

Files used in this chapter:

Movie Maker:

- CD_TT384K_Stream.wmv (Ch02_Exercises\Exercise\MovieMaker\CD_TT384K_Stream.wmv)
- club1384K_Stream.wmv (Ch02_Exercises\Exercise\MovieMaker\club1384K.wmv)
- Copyofclub1.wmv (Ch02_Exercises\Exercise\MovieMaker\CopyofClub1.wmv)
- dancing1384_Stream.wmv (Ch02_Exercises\Exercise\MovieMaker\dancing1384_Stream.wmv)
- drive_fast384K_Stream.wmv (Ch02_Exercises\Exercise\MovieMaker\ drive_fast384K_Stream.wmv)
- exit34K_Stream.wmv (Ch02_Exercises\Exercise\MovieMaker\exit34K_Stream.wmv)
- fwd_rev384K_Stream.wmv (Ch02_Exercises\Exercise\MovieMaker\fwd_rev384K_Stream.wmv)
- hand384K_Stream.wmv (Ch02_Exercises\Exercise\MovieMaker\hand384K_Stream.wmv)
- mirror384K_Stream.wmv (Ch02_Exercises\Exercise\MovieMaker\mirror384K_Stream.wmv)
- traffic384K_Stream.wmv (Ch02_Exercises\Exercise\MovieMaker\traffic384K_Stream.wmv)
- traffic2384K_Stream.wmv (Ch02_Exercises\Exercise\MovieMaker\ traffic2384K_Stream.wmv)
- TT_colour384K_Stream.wmv (Ch02_Exercises\Exercise\MovieMaker\ TT_colour384K_Stream.wmv)
- NiteLife.mp3 (Ch02_Exercises\Exercise\MovieMaker\NiteLife.mp3)

iMovie:

- CD_TT.mov (Ch02_Exercises\Exercise\iMovie08\NiteLifeProject\Videos\CD_TT.mov)
- club1.mov (Ch02_Exercises\Exercise\iMovie08\NiteLifeProject\Videos\club1.mov)
- dancing1.mov (Ch02_Exercises\Exercise\iMovie08\NiteLifeProject\Videos\dancing1.mov)
- dancing2.mov (Ch02_Exercises\Exercise\iMovie08\NiteLifeProject\Videos\dancing2.mov)
- drive_fast.mov (Ch02_Exercises\Exercise\iMovie08\NiteLifeProject\Videos\drive_fast.mov)
- exit.mov (Ch02_Exercises\Exercise\iMovie08\NiteLifeProject\Videos\exit.mov)
- fwd_rev.mov (Ch02_Exercises\Exercise\iMovie08\NiteLifeProject\Videos\fwd_rev.mov)
- hand.mov (Ch02_Exercises\Exercise\iMovie08\NiteLifeProject\Videos\hand.mov)
- mirror.mov (Ch02_Exercises\Exercise\iMovie08\NiteLifeProject\Videos\mirror.mov)
- traffic.mov (Ch02_Exercises\Exercise\iMovie08\NiteLifeProject\Videos\traffic.mov)
- traffic2.mov (Ch02_Exercises\Exercise\iMovie08\NiteLifeProject\Videos\traffic2.mov)
- TT_colour.mov (Ch02_Exercises\Exercise\iMovie08\NiteLifeProject\Videos\TT_colour.mov)
- NiteLife.aiff (Ch02_Exercises\Exercise\iMovie08\NiteLifeProject\Audio\NiteLife.aiff)

Before we start, we have created a separate tutorial for each of the applications. Let's face it: we don't know which platform you use, so we are covering all the bases. Although we don't recommend skipping exercises, in this case feel free to go to the app you plan to use. In either case, it is a relatively simple three-step process:

1. Capture video from a camera or import footage.
2. Edit the footage.
3. Export the footage in a format that can be encoded for Flash.

The footage you'll use for this section was shot by Alex Guhlushkin, a multimedia student in Toronto. Alex was asked to grab a video camera and shoot some clubbing footage for this chapter (see Figure 2-1). We were handed a bunch of short clips, and, after trying to figure out what Alex had given us, we suddenly saw that the club scene was trendy. That got the creative juices flowing.

Figure 2-1. Let's go to a club.

Before we get going, here's a quick bit of background.

Nonlinear editing

Maybe this makes me sound like an old fart, but you have it easy these days. If you have never had the pleasure of using an analog video-editing system, you aren't missing much. Analog editing involves using X-Acto knives and razor blades to cut and splice tape. It was an exacting process that required an enormous degree of organization and patience. Video edited on a computer—a process called **nonlinear editing (NLE)**, in which you can jump around the "film" at will—can be done quickly. And because it is nondestructive—razor blades and X-Acto knives are things of the past—it is also very forgiving.

In fact, most video production today is done using the NLE process, and the footage shot is captured by everything from cell phones to professional-grade cameras. That footage, ranging from your child's birthday party to earthquakes in Pakistan, is saved in a format—usually DV, which is digital video—that can be easily placed in an NLE system, edited, and then put on the Web, sometimes in less than an hour. In many respects, anyone with a DV camera and a computer can make a video.

Windows Movie Maker

Movie Maker is a small NLE application that is installed when you install Windows XP or Vista. If you are an advanced video developer or have quite a bit of experience with Premiere or Final Cut Pro, for example, you will find this application a bit rudimentary. Even so, it does give the average user the tools necessary to create and export a video.

Getting started is not at all difficult. Select Start ➤ All Programs ➤ Accessories ➤ Windows Movie Maker. Double-click the application and you will see the window shown in Figure 2-2. Although your screen is blank, the image shows content in the various areas of the interface.

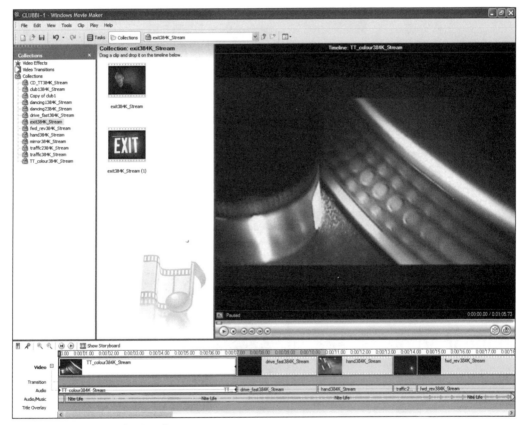

Figure 2-2. The Movie Maker interface

As you can see, there isn't much complexity to this application; it is designed for ease of use and quick editing. Instead of getting into how to use the features of the application, we'll explain many of the important aspects as we move through this exercise.

Although Movie Maker allows you to capture video directly from your camera, we will focus on creating a video compiled from a series of clips. This is likely to be the most common way you will work with the application because you will be bringing in footage for use in the application. In addition, you can import images and audio files into Movie Maker.

1. Open Movie Maker and click the Import Video link in the Tasks pane to open the Import File dialog box. Navigate to the Exercise folder for this chapter and open the Movie Maker folder (see Figure 2-3). The video clips inside the folder will be visible. If you press the Shift key and then click the first and the last clip, you will select them all. Click the Import button and the clips will be added to the Clip library, which is called a **collection** (see Figure 2-4).

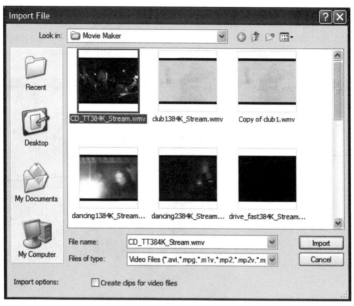

Figure 2-3. Clips are imported into Movie Maker.

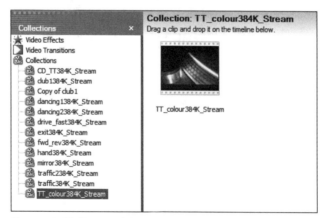

Figure 2-4. All clips are added to a collection.

> *This is a Microsoft product we are dealing with here, so Movie Maker cannot import a QuickTime movie that contains the MOV extension. If you will be using a bunch of QuickTime clips, they will have to be converted to a WMV, an AVI, or even an MPEG-4 format before they can be brought into Movie Maker.*

2. Click a clip and it will appear in the central pane.

3. After you are happy with your collection, select File ➤ Save Project and save the project to your Chapter 2 Exercise folder or some other location on your hard drive.

This video also has a sound track associated with it, and you need to bring the audio file into Movie Maker as well. Here's how:

4. Click the Tasks button to open the Movie Maker Tasks pane and click the Import audio or music link.

5. Navigate to the Chapter 2 Exercise folder and import the NiteLife.mp3 file. When you click the Import button, a progress bar will appear, showing you the progress of your import. After it finishes, the file will appear in the central pane.

Working with clips

You never get exactly the shot you need. Usually it is a little way into the clip, or there is a section of the clip that should be used. Movie Maker lets you split and combine clips. Here's how:

1. Select a clip and move the playback head in the preview pane to the point where you want to split the clip.

2. Click the Split Clip button on the controller (see Figure 2-5). If you look at your central pane, you will see you now have two clips (see Figure 2-6).

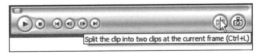

Figure 2-5. Splitting a clip

Figure 2-6. A split clip

But what if you make a mistake and split the clip in the wrong place? No problem.

3. Select both of the clips and right-click to open the context menu.

4. Select Combine (see Figure 2-7), and the clip will be restored. This step really doesn't create a new clip. Although they may look like separate clips in the Collection window, they are more closely related to bookmarks than anything else.

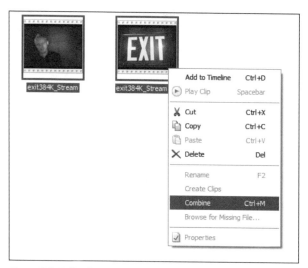

Figure 2-7. Split clips can be combined into a single clip.

Editing in Movie Maker

Editing your movie in this application is as simple as dragging and dropping. You drag a clip from the clip pane and drop it into place when you release the mouse.

The arrangement of the clips on the timeline can be done in one of two ways: using the storyboard or the timeline. Although they are different, they are both extremely useful. You can switch between them at any time by clicking the Show Storyboard or Show Timeline button.

Let's start with Storyboard mode, shown in Figure 2-8.

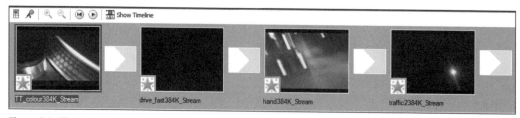

Figure 2-8. The Movie Maker Storyboard mode

Storyboard mode allows you to arrange the clips in the video in chronological order; the movie will run from left to right. The arrows between the clips allow you to add transitions and other special effects between the clips.

This view is great for just getting the clips in some semblance of order. To add them to the timeline, simply drag them from the clip pane and release them into the frames. Once you have done that, click the Play button in the controller and review your work.

Although it is useful, using Storyboard mode is much like fishing with hand grenades. You just don't have the precision in timing and trimming offered by Timeline mode.

Timeline mode is where the "heavy lifting" is done with Movie Maker. When you are looking at this mode (see Figure 2-9), the timeline changes to a number of channels (Video, Transition, Audio, Audio/Music, Title and Overlay), and each clip can be trimmed.

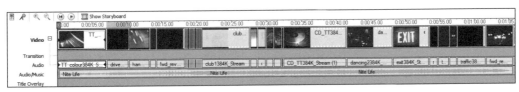

Figure 2-9. Timeline mode is where the "heavy lifting" is done.

As you can see, the clips are arranged on the timeline. The neat thing about adding clips here is they are "butted" right up against the end of the preceding clip. You can then fine-tune them by dragging them to different positions on the timeline. If you want precision, click the zoom buttons (magnifying glasses with a + or – symbol) to get a closer look at your editing decisions and transitions.

Instead of getting into an overly long "how-to" regarding the video to be created, let's just hone our basic skills. Once you have them in place, you can open the Chapter 2 Movie Maker exercise file—Clubbing.MSWMM—and build your own version using the clips and audio in the folder.

1. With your Movie Maker file open, drag the audio file from the clip pane onto the audio track in the timeline.

2. With the collection open, click the TT_colour384_Stream file and drag the clip onto the video channel.

3. Click once on the drive_fast384_Stream file and drag it from the clip pane onto the timeline (see Figure 2-10).

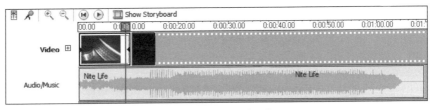

Figure 2-10. Two clips and the audio track are on the timeline.

4. So what does it look like? Click the Rewind button above the timeline and then click the Play button.

The Turntable clip and the Drive Fast clip are a bit long, which gives us a good excuse to show you two ways of shortening a clip. The process of shortening a clip is called **trimming**.

5. Click the Zoom tool and click the Turntable clip on the timeline.

6. Switch to Timeline mode and click the Turntable clip in the timeline. When you select it, you will notice that a small tool tip appears that gives you the clip's duration. Two small arrows, pointing inward, appear on the right and left edges of the clip. These arrows are the **trim handles**. Place the cursor over the handle on the right edge of the clip, and the cursor changes to a red double arrow. Click and drag that edge toward the left edge of the clip (see Figure 2-11). As you drag, the time inside the tool tip will change. When the time reaches 0:07:00—7.0 seconds—release the mouse. You have just trimmed 3.5 seconds off of the end of the clip and reduced its duration to 7 seconds.

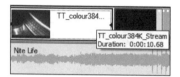

Figure 2-11. Trim a clip by dragging a handle.

Clicking and dragging is a rather inexact science, but it does work. Another way of trimming a clip is to use the preview as your guide. In this next example, you will remove the bit of black at the start of the Drive Fast clip and change its duration to 3.2 seconds.

7. Drag the playback head to the start of the Drive Fast clip on the timeline. Click the Next Frame button on the controller in the preview area. Keep clicking it until you are beyond the black area of the clip and can see the street. This should be at about the 7:40 mark in the controller. Click once on the clip and select Clip ➤ Set Start Trim Point. Now that you have trimmed off the start of the clip, you can now concentrate on setting the duration of the clip.

Remember, the clip is to last for 3.2 seconds. The one in front of it is 7 seconds, so all you need to do is trim off the end of the clip.

8. Using the Next Frame button, keep clicking until the duration reaches 10.20 seconds in the preview window (see Figure 2-12). Select the clip and select Clip ➤ Set End Trim Point. The clip shortens to 3.2 seconds.

Figure 2-12. Use the time code on the controller to precisely set when a trim occurs.

Exporting

Once everything is in place and working to your satisfaction, you can export the movie.

1. Select File ➤ Save Movie File to open the Save Movie Wizard.

2. In the first screen, select My Computer as the location for the file and click Next.

3. When the next screen appears, name the file and save it to a folder on your computer. Click Next to open the Movie Setting dialog box (see Figure 2-13). The Setting details are important. You need to make sure that you are exporting a file that is 320 x 240 pixels with a 30 fps frame rate. Click Next, and the movie will be converted to a WMV file.

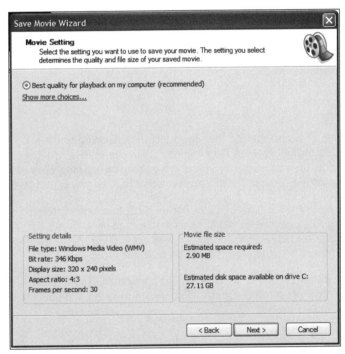

Figure 2-13. The format for the video is determined in this screen.

> *You aren't limited to one format for output. In the* Movie Setting *dialog box, click* Show more choices. *Click the* Other settings *drop-down menu (see Figure 2-14) and you can output the video to everything from a Pocket PC to your television.*

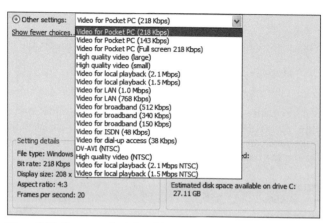

Figure 2-14. You can output the video to a number of formats and uses.

Apple iMovie

Since the introduction of QuickTime and then the addition of FireWire to the Mac, Apple has been at the vanguard of video technologies on the computer. With the release of iMovie a few years back, Apple re-established its predominance as a producer of easy-to-use (and even easier-to-learn) software. Along the way, iMovie rekindled the video revolution that led you to this section of the book.

The current iteration of iMovie is iMovie '08, or iMovie 7.1.1. In an effort to remain current—at least until Apple releases a new version—we will be using that version here. Finally, the creative process and the decisions you make are the same, regardless of whether you use Movie Maker, iMovie, or another video application. This exercise, therefore, should be regarded more as a "how to" than anything else.

Getting started with iMovie is not terribly difficult. The application can be found in the MacintoshHD/ Applications/Apple Application folder. Double-click the iMovie icon and you will be presented with the interface shown in Figure 2-15.

The neat thing about video applications is that if you have used one, you can pretty well use them all. For example, this interface and that of Movie Maker aren't terribly different from each other when you look at their fundamentals. Both have a Timeline and a Storyboard view. Both contain an area in which clips are stored and dragged onto the timeline. Both contain a controller and zoom-in and zoom-out controls for precise clip positioning.

Although you can capture video directly to iMovie, we will concentrate on using a series of clips that are brought into iMovie and assembled to construct the same movie as in the previous exercise. We have also included the completed project files in the Chapter 2/Complete/iMovie folder. Feel free to open it up and examine how we created the "Clubbing" video.

Figure 2-15. The iMovie interface

To get started, you need to create a project and import the clips you will be using.

1. Select File ➤ New Project to open the Create Project dialog box. Enter a name in the Project box. Now click the Video format drop-down arrow, which will open a list of video formats used by iMovie. Select Standard (4:3), as shown in Figure 2-16, and click the Create button.

Figure 2-16. All iMovie videos start as a project.

2. When you are returned to the interface, select File ➤ Import Movies. When the Import window opens, navigate to the Videos folder located in the exercise folder. Select all the movies and click the Import button. You will be shown the progress of the import process as the videos are copied into the Source Video area; when it is finished, the clips will all appear in the clip window (see Figure 2-17).

Figure 2-17. The clips are imported and ready to be added to the video.

Editing in iMovie

Movies can be edited in two ways. The first is to simply rearrange the clips in the Project panel. To do this, just click and drag them to their new position. The other way is to edit the clip itself in the Project panel.

As you drag clips from the clip pane to the Project panel, they will all be placed against each other in the order in which they are placed. If you want to rearrange the order, simply move the clip to the new position; the clips in the Project panel will adjust to accommodate the change (see Figure 2-18).

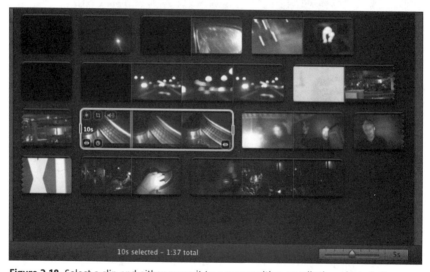

Figure 2-18. Select a clip and either move it to a new position or edit the selected clip.

The Project panel is the workhorse of the application. Here you can trim clips, add transitions between clips, and even adjust the volume of a section of the audio track associated with the clip (see Figure 2-19).

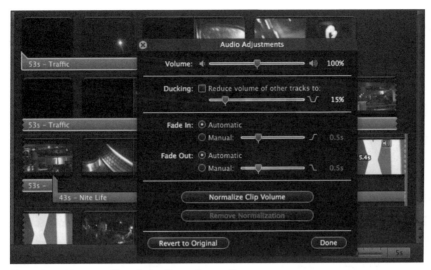

Figure 2-19. You can adjust the audio track as well.

Working with iMovie clips

Now that you are familiar with the interface and know how to add your content, let's turn our attention to adding the content to a video.

1. Click on the first clip in the Project panel to select it. When you do this, the clip will contain a yellow bounding box and appear in the preview window. If you roll your mouse across the clip, you will see that you are, in fact, scrubbing across the video.

This is the place where the true power of iMovie comes to the surface. In this pane you can do the following:

- Preview a clip or scrub it by dragging the mouse to the right or the left.
- Play the clip in the window or even full-screen.
- Trim the clip.

It is this last technique that is of most concern to us because clips are edited and the extraneous pieces in the clip are removed.

2. Drag the Magnification slider in the bottom-right corner of the Project panel all the way to the left to change the view to frame-by-frame. Note the black frame right at the start of the clip. Select Edit ➤ Trim to open the Trim panel.

3. Click and drag the Trim handle on the left edge of the clip to the left edge of the next frame. Do this at the end of the clip as well. If your selection resembles Figure 2-20, click the Done button to return to the Project panel.

> *You can also trim clips right in the* Project *panel. Select the clip and move the Trim handles to their new positions. You can then either select* Edit ➤ Trim to Selection *or press* Cmd+B.

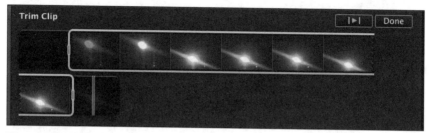

Figure 2-20. Video can be cropped.

A less invasive way of trimming out unwanted content is to split the clip. Here's how:

3. Select a clip in the Project panel and use the Trim handles to set the in and out points for the clip.

4. With the clip selected, select Edit ➤ Split Clip. The clip will be split on the timeline into two or three clips depending on the position of the Trim handles (see Figure 2-21).

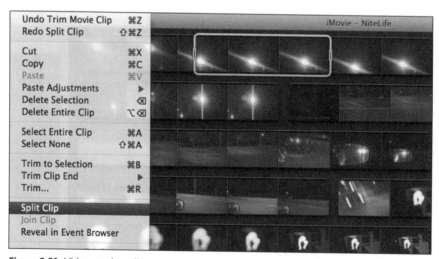

Figure 2-21. Video can be split.

Adding and adjusting audio

Audio can be added to a movie in two ways: it can be added to the Project panel or to a specific clip. Let's look at both methods.

Before you start, you need to understand that iMovie will look in only three places for an audio file: the iTunes Library, the iMovie Sound Effects folder, or Garage Band. To get started, do the following:

1. Minimize iMovie and open the iMovie Sound Effects folder: MacintoshHD\Library\Audio\AppleLoops\Apple\iLifeSound Effects.

2. Add a new folder named Nite Life. Drag the NiteLife.mp3 file from the exercise folder to the one just created. Maximize iMovie.

3. Drag the Magnification slider all the way to the right to reduce the view to individual clips.

4. Click the Show/Hide Audio button (it looks like a music note under the preview panel). Click the drop-down menu that appears and select iLife Sound Effects ➤ Nite Life. The audio file, shown in Figure 2-22, will appear in the Music and Sound Effects panel.

5. Drag the audio clip onto the first clip in the middle row. When you release the mouse, the audio file will appear under the clips.

Figure 2-22. Drag video onto a clip to have it play when that clip appears.

6. The movie starts with a car driving to the club. Let's add a traffic sound to the start of the video. Select iLife Sound Effects ➤ Ambience. Drag the Traffic.aiff file onto the first clip in the Project panel.

7. You will immediately notice a couple of problems: the Nite Life audio file ends before the last clip in the Project panel, and the Traffic audio file is a bit long. To fix the first issue, click the Nite Life audio file and drag it to the end of the last clip. The start point will also shift, which is no problem.

8. Roll over the end of the Traffic clip and when the cursor changes to the Trim cursor (it looks like two arrows) at the end point of the clip, click and drag to the start point of the Nite Life clip, as shown in Figure 2-23.

9. Click the Play button or press the spacebar to preview your video.

Figure 2-23. Click and drag to move audio files or to adjust their start and end points.

> *The other method of adding audio is to simply drag the audio file onto the* Project *panel. This is great for background tracks, but it is really difficult to manage if you need to adjust the audio file's duration.*
>
> *If you need to adjust the audio, select the file in the* Project *panel and click the* Adjust Audio *button, choose the speaker in the button group under the Magnification slider, or simply press* A *to open the* Audio Adjustments *panel (which you saw in Figure 2-19).*

Exporting your movie

After you have a video that meets your objectives, you can export it so that it can be placed into Flash by using the Flash Video Encoder.

1. Select Share ➤ Export Using QuickTime. Name the file NiteLife and navigate to the folder in which the video will be saved.

2. Select Movie to QuickTime Movie in the Export drop-down menu. Click the Options button to open the Movie Settings dialog box.

3. Click the Settings button to open the Standard Video Compression Settings dialog box. Select the Animation codec from the Compression Type drop-down menu and select Millions of Colors from the Compressor: Depth drop-down menu, as shown in Figure 2-24. Click OK. When you return to the Movie Settings dialog box, click OK to close it as well.

4. Click OK when you return to the Save Exported File as dialog box to create the video. When the video is created, quit iMovie '08.

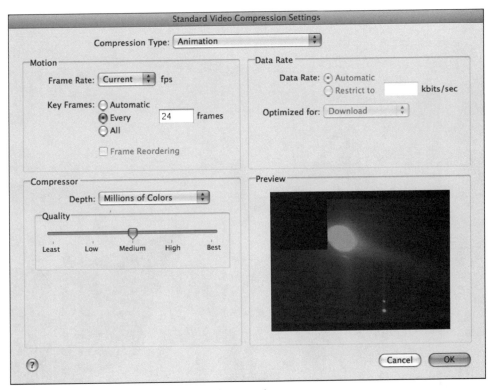

Figure 2-24. The QuickTime movie is about to be created.

What you've learned

This has been a chapter designed to make you aware of how the files you will work with are created. You have discovered the following:

- How to use video and audio clips in a Windows Movie Maker project
- How to use audio and video clips in an iMovie '08 project
- How to prepare video projects for Flash video

Now that you have had a chance to use the editing features of Movie Maker and iMovieHD, start playing with them to create your own videos. See what ideas you can bring to life and what you can do with these applications. You will soon discover that the amount of fun you can have with them should be illegal, and your only constraint will be that which you place on your creativity. In the next chapter, we'll look at a couple of products that don't use the FLV Encoder or Flash to create the FLV file.

Chapter 3

ALTERNATIVE FLV-CREATION TOOLS

Up to this point you have been creating video, encoding it, and playing it through Flash. If the previous two chapters have whetted your appetite to really get into using Flash video, you will eventually encounter the products offered by On2 and Sorenson Media. Although their codecs are integral features of the Flash CS3 Video Encoder, they also offer commercial FLV-creation tools—On2 Flix and Sorenson Squeeze—which offer even more features and control than the Flash Video Encoder.

An obvious question is this: *"Why should I purchase these applications if I already have them in Flash?"* First off, we are not here to sell their products but, if you will be creating and using a lot of Flash video, these applications will make your life easier. For example, both offer 2-pass variable bit rate encoding options. We'll get deeper into what that means later on in this chapter, but for now understand that the advantage is usually a smaller FLV file with no loss of quality. Another feature offered by both applications is batch processing. Instead of encoding videos individually, both allow you to encode an entire folder of videos at once using a single setting.

What we'll cover in this chapter:

- Using Flix Pro
- Using Sorenson Squeeze 4.5

Files used in this chapter:

- tortoise.mov (Chapter03\ExerciseFiles_Ch03\Exercise\tortoise.mov)

Before we dig into these tools, it is a good time to take a small break and explain data rate. You will be asked to set this value in both applications, and a bad choice can have a profound impact—both upon the quality of the FLV file and the user's experience.

Data rate

One of the fundamental maxims of working with digital video is this: Data rate controls quality; bandwidth controls the user experience.

Regardless of which computer platform is used, bandwidth (or "the pipe") is your prime consideration. When it comes to creating and playing Flash video, always keep an eye on the pipe.

The pipe can make or break the user experience. If you have a lot of bandwidth, such as a T1 line at work or high-speed Internet at home, you can view full-length movies with little or no disruption. If you are in a remote or rural situation, the odds are very good that you have a dial-up modem, meaning that your bandwidth is limited. To wrap your mind around the differences, think of a highway tunnel that goes under a lake. If the tunnel is part of an eight-lane highway, thousands of cars simply approach the tunnel and zip through it at the posted speed because the tunnel's entrance is the same width as the highway.

Now abruptly reduce the diameter of the tunnel from four lanes to one lane each way. We have all experienced how infuriating the delay can be as thousands of cars squeeze into one lane of traffic and reduce their speed to a crawl as they approach the tunnel's entrance and proceed into the tunnel. The cars in this example represent data, and the car speed is the data rate. Think of a T1 line as the tunnel for the four-lane expressway, the single-lane tunnel as a dial-up service, the highway as the server, and the user as the poor guy behind the steering wheel in the car.

It goes without saying that when you plan to deliver video you need to have a solid bandwidth strategy in place for the user, the server, and the video. The server bandwidth strategy must take into account the maximum number of users who can access the video at any one time. The last thing you need is for your user to get into the middle of a traffic jam waiting to download and view the video.

When it comes to the user, you need to be aware of the width of the tunnel up ahead. You need to leave enough room for the data stream and also other Internet activities. Not doing this is quite similar to having a transport truck sitting at the side of the road and jutting out into traffic. Things will stop or seriously slow down as the cars reduce their speed to avoid driving into the back of the truck. In a dial-up situation, a user with a 56.6KB connection can drive along the highway at 56.6kbps. When it comes to video, a target data rate of 40kbps is normal, which leaves room for other activities.

So what is data rate? It is simply the amount of data (cars on a highway) transferred per second (emerging from the tunnel) to the user's computer. This, in turn, determines the bandwidth required to play the video. The data rate calculation is as follows:

- Data rate = (w✕h✕color depth✕frames per second)/compression.

Let's do the data rate calculation for the Tortoise video used in this chapter. The video's values are the following:

- Width = 320
- Height = 240
- Color depth = 24
- Frames per second (fps) = 15
- Compression = 60. The benchmark compression ratio for both On2 and Squeeze is 30:1.
- Data rate = (320 x 240 x 24 x 15)/60
- Data rate = (27,648,000)/60
- Data rate = 460,800

The data rate for the video at 15 fps is 460,800 bits per second or 461kbps. I have included the second line of the calculation there for a deliberate reason. You can see from that line that if you were to apply no compression to the video, you would use a data rate of about 27.6 million bits per second. To deliver that video, you would need an Internet connection the size of a tunnel between Britain and France. Toss in the compression, and the video can safely be delivered to most users.

> Flash Player supports a maximum data rate of 4,096kbps.

Other factors that can affect the user experience are frame rate and key frame placement.

Frame rate is the speed at which a video plays. One of the more common frame rates for digital video is 29 fps or 30 fps, which fall into line with the North American NTSC video standard of 29.97 fps. Another common frame rate is 25 fps, which matches the European and Asian PAL standard. Regardless of which one you have been handed, sometimes you might want to reduce the rate—such as in low-bandwidth situations. If you want to lower the frame rate, you should use equal divisions of the source frame rate. For 30 fps, use 15 fps, 10 fps, 7.5 fps, and so on. For 25 fps, use 12 fps, 8 fps, 6 fps, and so on.

Chapter 1 explained how key frames work. By spreading out the key frames you can have quite a positive impact upon the final size of the FLV file. Don't think that all video is created equal. If there is a lot of motion—a Formula One race—you need more key frames. If it is a tree in a field, you can get away with fewer key frames. The bottom line is that this decision is up to you, but it is the prudent developer who reviews the entire video prior to converting the file to an FLV file.

One final consideration regarding data rate is that the number shown in the compression applications is a bit disingenuous. In Chapter 1, you set the data rate of a video to 300kbps. This is not the final data rate. Remember that video is composed of both an audio track and a video track. The number you set affected just the video track. The data rate for the audio track was set to 96kbps. This means that the data rate for the video is 396kbps. If you use the default values shown in Figure 3-1, the number is even higher.

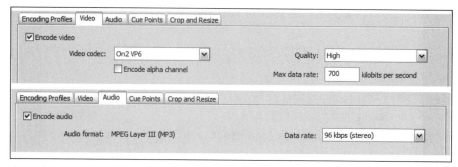

Figure 3-1. Add the data rate values for both the audio and video tracks to determine the total data rate for the FLV file.

Regardless of whether you use Flash Professional 8, Flix Pro, or Sorenson Squeeze 4.5 to create the video, each asks you the following questions:

- What bit rate will be used to stream the video?
- What frame size will be used to present the video?
- What frame interval should be used for the key frames?

To help you answer those questions, Tables 3-1 and 3-2 give you some suggested values.

Table 3-1. High-motion video (e.g., a Formula One race)

Type	Video Bit Rate	Audio Bit Rate	Frame Size	Frame Rate	Key Frames
Modem: Progressive	64KB	16KB mono	160 x 120	8 fps	8 sec
Modem: FlashComm	24KB	16KB mono	160 x 120	8 fps	8 sec
Small	188K	32KB mono	240 x 180	15 or 12 fps	8 sec
Medium	336K	64KB mono	320 x 240	30 or 24 fps	8 sec
Large	850K	96KB stereo	480 x 360	30 or 24 fps	8 sec
Full screen	1304K	96KB stereo	640 x 480	30 or 24 fps	8 sec

If you are targeting a 56KB modem, you must keep the rate under 40KB. Don't use less than 16KB for the audio.

The key frame number is an approximation. Start there and work backward.

Table 3-2. Low-motion video (e.g., a tree in a field)

Type	Video Bit Rate	Audio Bit Rate	Frame Size	Frame Rate	Key Frames
Modem: Progressive	34K	16KB mono	160 x 120	8 fps	8 sec
Modem: FlashComm	24K	16KB mono	160 x 120	8 fps	8 sec
Small	68K	32KB mono	240 x 180	15 or 12 fps	8 sec
Medium	132K	48KB mono	320 x 240	30 or 24 fps	8 sec
Large	286K	64KB stereo	480 x 360	30 or 24 fps	8 sec
Full screen	504K	96KB stereo	640 x 480	30 or 24 fps	8 sec

Using Flix Pro

Flix Pro for Macromedia Flash (the current version is 8, which is available for both the Macintosh and the PC) from On2 Technologies is a standalone application that encodes high-quality video for Flash CS3 Professional. Although it uses the same FLV compressor as that in Flash (VP6) it also offers a wide feature set not available in Flash. In this section, you will import the Tortoise video into Flix and compress it. After the FLV file is created, it can be used by the FLVPlayback component in Flash. You can download a trial version of the application at www.on2.com/downloads/flix-demo-software/.

With Flix Pro open, let's discuss what can be seen in Figure 3-2.

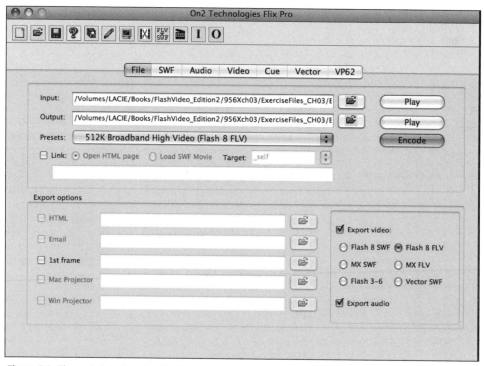

Figure 3-2. The main interface for Flix Pro

The menus contain all the features in the interface, and the Button bar gives you one-click access to a number of encoding and playback tasks.

> *Be careful with the Button bar because the icons perform tasks that aren't commonly associated with the icons.*

The buttons, from left to right, are the following:

- **Clear Settings**: Click this button to clear all the settings and fields in the file.
- **Open Settings**: Click this button to navigate to an FLX file that contains the settings for the encoded video.
- **Save Settings**: Click this button to create an FLX file.
- **Help**: Click this button to launch the Help menu.
- **Batch**: Click this button to open the Batch Processing window.

- **Overlay**: Click this button to add a watermark to the video.
- **Player Maker**: Click this button to launch the Create Player window. This allows you to create standalone EXE files.
- **Media Editor**: Click this button to open the Editor window (which does exactly what the button says).
- **FLV to SWF Converter**: Click this button to embed the FLV file into a SWF file using the FLV to SWF Converter window that opens.
- **Encode**: Clicking this button has the same effect as clicking the Encode button on the interface.
- **Play Input**: Click this button to play the video in the Player window.
- **Play Output**: Click this button to play the encoded file in the Player window.

Now that you have had a short walk through the main screen, let's encode a video using Flix Pro.

1. Open Flix Pro and navigate to the Chapter 3 Exercise folder and double-click the tortoise.mov file. The path to the file will appear in the Input area, and the same path will be used in the Output area. This means that the FLV file you create will be placed in the same folder as the source video.

2. Select the Flash 8 FLV option in the Export video area and click the Video tab.

A video encoding settings window will open (see Figure 3-3). Although it might appear to be a bit overwhelming at first glance, it is actually set up in much the same manner as the Flash 8 Video Encoder and asks you essentially the same questions. Let's go through each section of this window.

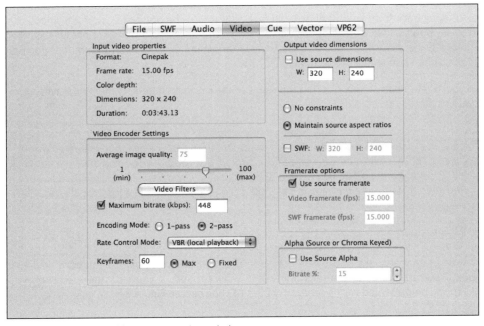

Figure 3-3. The Flix Pro video output settings window

Input video properties simply gives you the properties of the Tortoise video. The values shown are those used in calculating the data rate.

3. Select Maintain source aspect ratios in the Output video dimensions area.

This selection ensures that if you resize the video, the 4:3 aspect ratio of the video will be maintained, and no distortion will occur. For example, if you change the width of the video to 300 pixels, the height value will automatically change to 255 pixels to maintain the aspect ratio.

4. Set the Video framerate (fps) value to 15.000 in the Framerate options area.

This value matches that of the video. If the video is being placed into a Flash movie that has a different frame rate, such as 12 fps or 24 fps, change the frame rate of the FLV file to match that of the FLA file.

5. In the Video Encoder Settings area, select 2-pass from the Encoding Mode drop-down menu and VBR (local playback) from the Rate Control Mode drop-down menu. Set the Maximum bitrate (kbps) to 448.

The 2-pass setting produces higher-quality video while requiring additional processing time, which makes sense because Flix takes two looks at the video during the encoding process. During the first look, or pass, Flix will try to figure out the best way to compress the video based upon your maximum bit rate. During its second pass through the video, Flix looks at the motion in the video and allocates more bandwidth to high-motion sections and lower bandwidth to areas where nothing is really happening.

The second setting is VBR (or Variable Bit Rate). On2 tells you that you would choose VBR only if the video is playing back from your hard drive. In fact, VBR is also the option to use if the video is being progressively downloaded from your web server. You would choose CBR (or Constant Bit Rate) only if the video is being streamed through a Flash video streaming service, Flash Communication Server (FlashComm), or Flash Media Server (FMS).

A Maximum bitrate (kbps) setting of 448 is the result of the calculation done earlier and leaves room for the audio stream.

> *If you are really concerned about the final file size of the FLV file, change the audio from stereo to mono, which cuts the size of the audio track by about 50 percent. If the audio track is already mono, you can't "super size" it by selecting stereo. All this will do is to put the mono track into separate channels and increase the file size by 50 percent.*

6. Click the File tab to return to the File window.

If you would rather stay out of the Video or Audio areas because they can be rather intimidating or confusing, you can always let the software do the work for you. If you click the Preset drop-down menu you will be presented with a serious number of choices (see Figure 3-4).

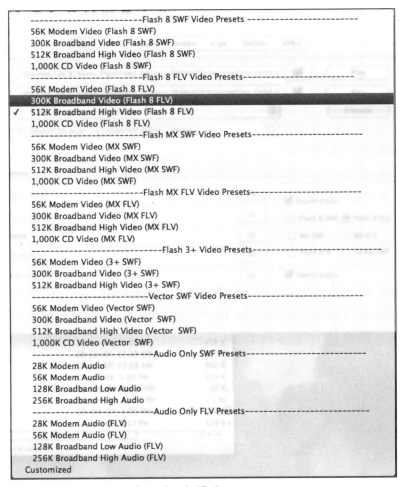

```
----------------------Flash 8 SWF Video Presets ----------------------
  56K Modem Video (Flash 8 SWF)
  300K Broadband Video (Flash 8 SWF)
  512K Broadband High Video (Flash 8 SWF)
  1,000K CD Video (Flash 8 SWF)
-----------------------Flash 8 FLV Video Presets---------------------
  56K Modem Video (Flash 8 FLV)
  300K Broadband Video (Flash 8 FLV)
✓ 512K Broadband High Video (Flash 8 FLV)
  1,000K CD Video (Flash 8 FLV)
-----------------------Flash MX SWF Video Presets--------------------
  56K Modem Video (MX SWF)
  300K Broadband Video (MX SWF)
  512K Broadband High Video (MX SWF)
  1,000K CD Video (MX SWF)
-----------------------Flash MX FLV Video Presets--------------------
  56K Modem Video (MX FLV)
  300K Broadband Video (MX FLV)
  512K Broadband High Video (MX FLV)
  1,000K CD Video (MX FLV)
-----------------------Flash 3+ Video Presets-----------------------
  56K Modem Video (3+ SWF)
  300K Broadband Video (3+ SWF)
  512K Broadband High Video (3+ SWF)
-----------------------Vector SWF Video Presets---------------------
  56K Modem Video (Vector SWF)
  300K Broadband Video (Vector SWF)
  512K Broadband High Video (Vector SWF)
  1,000K CD Video (Vector SWF)
-----------------------Audio Only SWF Presets-----------------------
  28K Modem Audio
  56K Modem Audio
  128K Broadband Low Audio
  256K Broadband High Audio
-----------------------Audio Only FLV Presets-----------------------
  28K Modem Audio (FLV)
  56K Modem Audio (FLV)
  128K Broadband Low Audio (FLV)
  256K Broadband High Audio (FLV)
Customized
```

Figure 3-4. The preset encoding values in Flix Pro

Although the choices are quite extensive, only the Flash 8 FLV video presets are necessary for our purposes. They anticipate a number of bandwidth situations ranging from dial-up to playback from a CD. For example, if you select the 300K Broadband Video (Flash 8 FLV), you are selecting one of the most common choices available. This is the one appropriate for home use. If you then select the Audio tab, you will also see that the Maximum bitrate (kbps) setting has been reduced to 280, which is right in the ball park if you include the Audio Output Settings Bitrate of 40 kBit/s.

7. Click the Encoding button to open the Encoding window (see Figure 3-5).

You will be shown the progress of the encoding process and you can determine what happens when the encoding is completed by selecting one or all of the options in the When finished area.

53

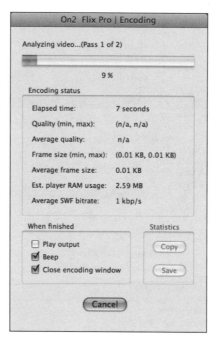

Figure 3-5. The Flix Pro Encoding window

8. After you preview the video in the Flix Player (see Figure 3-6), close the Player window and quit Flix Pro by selecting File ➤ Exit.

Figure 3-6. The FLV file is playing in the Flix Player.

Now that you have created the FLV file you can open Flash and link the FLV file to the FLVPlayback component added to the Flash stage.

If you want to see the difference between 2-pass encoding and 1-pass encoding in the Flash 8 Video Encoder, select the FLV file you just created and note the file size. In this case, the video dropped in size from 41.3MB to 12.6MB. The same file encoded in Chapter 1 is 13MB or 14MB when encoded using CBR in the Flash Video Encoder. When it comes to the Web, every little bit helps.

Using Sorenson Squeeze 4.5

If any one company can claim to have sparked the streaming media boom with video, it is Sorenson Media. When it released the Sorenson video codec a few years ago, bloated streaming video files became a thing of the past. It was no surprise, then, to see Sorenson Spark appear as the video encoder in Flash.

Like the On2 VP6 codec introduced in Flash Professional 8, Sorenson Spark is good, but (as the authors wrote in this volume's predecessor, *Flash MX Video*) "there is something even better. It is called Sorenson Squeeze."

Sorenson Squeeze 4.5 is a standalone product available in both PC and Macintosh versions. You can download a trial copy at www.sorensonmedia.com/misc/free_trial.php.

When you first open Squeeze, you will discover that everything you need to do is contained in the main screen, as shown in Figure 3-7.

The Format & Compression Settings presets are just as extensive as those in Flix, and when a video is imported, you can use the preview window to play the video and set the in and out points if you want to shorten the video or use a specific clip in the video. When a video is ready to be squeezed, the file is shown; then the audio and video codecs are applied to the video. When you are ready to create the FLV file, simply click the Squeeze It! button, and the progress of the compression and conversion process will be shown in the output files window.

A really neat feature of Squeeze is its capability to capture video directly from a video camera. The only downside to this is if you want to add a soundtrack to the video that will have to be done in an audio or a video editor such as Adobe Premiere Pro.

The batch processing feature of Squeeze is found in the Watch Folder item of the INPUT area of the interface. Once a folder is identified as a watch folder, all you have to do is to drop a video into the folder, and Squeeze will automatically create the FLV file.

Figure 3-7. The Squeeze interface

Now that you have been introduced to the interface, let's "squeeze" a video.

1. Click the Import File button and navigate to the tortoise.mov file in the Chapter 3 example folder. The file will appear in the preview window and the output files window.

> *Feeling lazy? Drag a video directly from a folder onto the preview window—it will appear in Squeeze.*

2. You now need to choose an encoding format. Click the + sign beside the Macromedia Flash Video (.flv) area in the presets area to open the preset choices shown in Figure 3-8, available to you. Click once on the VP6_384K_Stream selection and click the Apply button. The selection will appear in the output window.

Do not double-click a preset value in the Format & Compression Settings *area. Doing so opens the preset's values in the audio/video settings window. Any change you make here becomes the new preset value. We'll show you how to change these values in the next step.*

Still feeling lazy? Drag a preset value to the output window and it will appear in the window (see Figure 3-9).

Figure 3-8. The FLV presets in Squeeze

Figure 3-9. The preset is applied to the video in the output window.

3. In the output area, click the + sign beside the preset, and the Spark Pro and MP3 encoders that are contained in the preset will appear. Double-click either one to open the Audio/Video Compression Settings dialog box (see Figure 3-10).

This dialog box allows you to customize the settings without changing the preset. As you can see, the dialog box is divided in two. The left side is for the Audio settings, and the right side contains the Video settings. The key value to notice in this dialog box is the Total Data Rate value in the upper-right corner. It is the sum of the audio data rate and the video data rate.

The dialog box you are looking at is the advanced options dialog box. If you click the Simple button in the lower-left corner, all the video-encoding options below the frame rate will be hidden (see Figure 3-11).

In order to do a fair comparison between Flix and Squeeze, this total is going to have to be increased to about 460 kilobits per second.

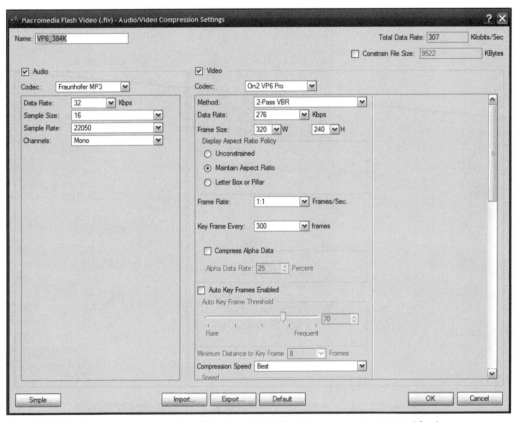

Figure 3-10. The Squeeze advanced settings dialog box is ideal for the power user or control freak.

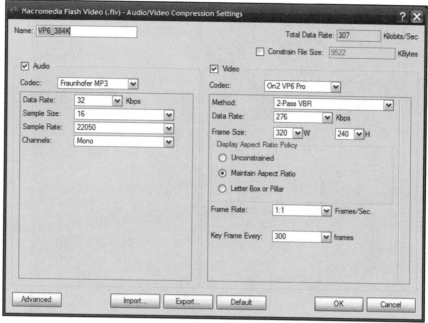

Figure 3-11. The "simple" audio/video compression settings

4. Where Squeeze moves apart from Spark—the Flash Professional 8 codec—is that (as in Flix) it also offers a 2-pass variable bit rate encoding option. In the Method drop-down menu, select 2-Pass VBR.

5. Select the value in the Date Rate input box and change it to 420 kbps. You can also choose from a number of other values in the drop-down menu.

6. Select the Data Rate value in the Audio section and change it to 40 by selecting the value from the drop-down menu. Notice that the Total Data Rate value changes.

7. Select the file name in the Name text input box and change it to SqueezeTest. Click the OK button to close the dialog box and return to the Squeeze interface.

8. Click the Squeeze It! button to start the encoding process. The progress bar will appear in the output window, and the Squeeze It! button will change its name to Stop It! (see Figure 3-12).

9. When you finish the process, select File ➤ Save Project (Ctrl+S on a PC or Cmd+S on a Mac). What you won't be saving is the FLV file. You will instead be saving an SQZ file. This format is used by Squeeze to remember the settings used for this compression and is quite similar to the FLX file you can save in Flix Pro. This is a really handy feature if you need to change a setting or can't remember the values used to squeeze the video. Double-clicking the SQZ file will open Squeeze and present you with the video and compression setting in the output window.

If you are at all curious, the final file size of the FLV file you created in Squeeze is 12.6MB, which is the same as the value for the FLV created in Flix.

Figure 3-12. The video is being "squeezed."

Previewing your work

Prior to the release of Flash Professional CS3, being able to preview a freshly created FLV file was problematic at best. Your choices were limited to hunting the Internet for a third-party FLV Player or creating the Flash movie and previewing the video at that time. A funny thing happened on the way to this book: Adobe released a new product—Adobe Media Player (AMP)—which gives you this ability by simply double-clicking your freshly-minted FLV file. To use AMP strictly for this purpose would be quite similar to using Photoshop CS3 extended as an image viewer. AMP is a very powerful product designed to deliver video streams from a variety of providers directly to your desktop. The full use of this software is out of the scope of this book, and we will be concentrating only on its preview capabilities.

There is another solution as well, and we are feeling a bit chagrined in not having mentioned it in the previous edition of this book: *Foundation Flash 8 Video*. The solution is Adobe Bridge CS3, which is installed on your computer when you install any of the web, video, or print CS3 bundles offered by Adobe.

The following sections show you how to use each one.

Adobe Media Player

If you have installed AMP, follow these steps:

1. Navigate to the folder containing the FLV file you just created. You will notice that the icon for the FLV file has changed to an AMP icon (see Figure 3-13).

2. Double-click the file to launch AMP.

3. When the interface shown in Figure 3-14 opens, the video will be shown on the right side of the interface and will start to play. It will also be added to the My Saved Videos list on the left side of the interface.

Figure 3-13. The Adobe Media Player icon is used for FLV files.

Figure 3-14. Previewing an FLV file using AMP

4. Click the play/pause button to pause and play the video. Click the rewind button to return to the start of the video or click the audio icon to mute the audio.

> Don't click the Watch Full Screen *button because it will scale your FLV file up to the full dimensions of your computer screen and introduce all the nastiness—chunk pixels—associated with it.*

5. After you finish, click the close button to close AMP.

> *Although the controls might seem rather basic, don't forget that the key word in the product's name is* Player.

Previewing an FLV file can prevent a lot of grief. A few months back, one of the authors created a QuickTime movie and previewed it in the QuickTime player. Satisfied that everything was working, he simply encoded the FLV file and posted it. Almost immediately after posting, he received e-mail complaining about the fact that the video's audio track stopped about 1.5 minutes into the FLV file. When he opened the FLV file just posted, sure enough the sound kicked out after 1.5 minutes in AMP. Had he previewed the video prior to posting, he would have seen this problem and not had to waste a lot of time dealing with "nasty" e-mail and re-encoding and reposting the video.

Adobe Bridge CS3

Although used primarily as a content management system on your computer, Bridge also allows you to preview a variety of media, including FLV files. Here's how:

1. If you have a PC, select Start ➤ Adobe Bridge CS3, or select C:\Program Files\Adobe\Adobe Bridge CS3 and double-click the Bridge application icon. If you have a Mac, select Macintosh HD\Applications\Adobe Bridge CS3 and double-click the Bridge application icon to launch Bridge.

2. Navigate to the folder containing the FLV file you want to preview and select it in the Bridge interface.

3. The FLV file will appear in the preview area of Bridge, as shown in Figure 3-15. Again you can play the video and turn the audio on and off.

> *Be careful with Bridge. If you double-click the FLV file, you will launch Flash CS3 and be asked if you want to embed the video in the Flash timeline.*

Figure 3-15. Previewing an FLV file using Bridge CS3

What you've learned

As you may have guessed, you have a few more encoding tools at your disposal than the Flash CS3 Video Encoder. This chapter looked at the two major tools available to you. You learned the following:

- How to create an FLV file using Flix Pro
- How to create an FLV file using Sorenson Squeeze 4.5
- How to preview an FLV file

So there you have it: Flix and Sorenson went head to head, and the result is a draw. Their file sizes matched each other. Mind you, if we wanted to we could have brought the file sizes down even further by reducing the visual or sound quality.

If the comparison resulted in a draw, which one should you choose? We aren't going to endorse one product over the other because they both do an admirable job of creating an FLV file that can be used in Flash Professional CS3.

Based on the chatter and "buzz" around the inclusion of the On2 VP6 codec in Flash Professional CS3, the consensus is that you get better image quality on playback with Flix. Although the arguments are both complex and technical, the bottom line is that the recommendation to go with Flix is more subjective than objective because no two video producers can ever agree on a common definition of quality.

Instead, approach these applications as tools. If your reference Flash Player is Flash Player 7, Squeeze is the tool of choice. If it is Flash Player 8 or higher and/or the video to be encoded contains an Alpha mask, the On2 codec is the tool you should use.

Instead of getting technical, maybe you should take the advice we offered at the start of this chapter and simply "keep an eye on the pipe." It is the user who matters most, so it is important, regardless of the tool, to keep an eye on the hardware, the bandwidth, and where the video will be viewed. To achieve this, you will have to simply experiment and learn which compromises best fit which situation: high-quality audio and video vs. small, quickly loading video files.

One of the authors refers to The First Rule of FLV Creation, which states: "For every action there is an equally ugly and opposite implication." Too many developers forget this rule in their rush to be a "cool kid" and get into the "Flash video game." The results are big ponderous videos that take forever to download or play.

Now that you know how to create a video, turn the page, and let's start seeing how much fun you can have with Flash video.

Chapter 4

CREATING A CUSTOM PLAYER

The past three chapters have covered the creation of the raw material—the video and the FLV file—and also what you need to do before you "fire up" Flash. In this chapter, and for the remainder of the book, we start dealing with many of the creative things you can do with video in Flash.

This chapter is the start of that process.

In Chapter 1, you created a simple FLV file that used the FLVPlayback component. This chapter expands on it and shows you how to use many of the video tools in the application, including some interesting uses of the FLVPlayback component, creating a set of custom controls using the FLVPlayback custom user interface (UI) components, and streaming and controlling an FLV file using a Video object from the library. Each of these approaches allows you to get your video on the Web and leaves you the flexibility to decide which approach to use.

What we'll cover in this chapter:

- Buffering a video
- Using the FLVPlayback custom UI components
- Using a Video object in Flash
- Using ActionScript to control a video
- Using ActionScript to add components at runtime

- Creating a Progress bar and using a Timer object
- Using Fireworks CS3 to create a custom video interface for Flash CS3
- Controlling video volume using ActionScript 3.0
- Creating a Scrubber bar using ActionScript 3.0

Files used in this chapter:

- `tortoise.flv` (Chapter04\ExerciseFiles_Ch04\Exercise\tortoise.flv)
- `Cigars.flv` (Chapter04\ExerciseFiles_Ch04\Exercise\Cigars.flv)
- `video_player.fla` (Chapter04\ExerciseFiles_Ch04\Exercise\CustomVideoPlayer_01\ video_player.fla)
- `tortoise.flv` (Chapter04\ExerciseFiles_Ch04\Exercise\CustomVideoPlayer_01\ tortoise.flv)
- `Cigars.flv` (Chapter04\ExerciseFiles_Ch04\Exercise\CustomVideoPlayer_01\Cigars.flv)
- `JoseDesign_flat.png` (Chapter04\ExerciseFiles_Ch04\Exercise\CustomVideoPlayer_02\ JoseDesign_flat.png)
- `Button.png` (Chapter04\ExerciseFiles_Ch04\Exercise\Button.png)
- `CustomPlayer02.fla` (Chapter04\ExerciseFiles_Ch04\Exercise\CustomVideoPlayer_02\ CustomPlayer02.fla)
- `Through_A_Door.flv` (Chapter04\ExerciseFiles_Ch04\Exercise\CustomVideoPlayer_02\ Through_A_Door.flv)

The FLVPlayback component and buffering

Chapter 1 covered how to attach a video to this component and get it playing. Instead of revisiting what has already been done, we'll dig a little deeper into the use of this component and examine it from the perspective of optimizing it for a streaming video. What you learn here can be applied elsewhere.

No matter how you approach the subject, Flash video streams into a browser. This happens either through the use of the default Progressive Download method, in which the video streams from your web server, or through the use of a streaming server such as the Flash Media Server (FMS).

The Progressive Download method is one of the most common because it is the easiest to accomplish. This is what happens: The video data loads into the Flash Player, and the video starts playing when enough of it has been downloaded to smoothly play the video. That's the good news. The bad news is that the FLV file that has been downloaded sits in the browser's cache. This means the FLV file is in the cache and can be accessed just like a JPG or GIF image on a web page if the user chooses.

The other issue is file size. If you are using the Progressive Download method to play an FLV file that is 25MB in size, you are assuming that users have that kind of room on their hard disk. If your client is concerned about file security, the Progressive Download method is actually the worst choice.

Streaming an FLV file through the use of an FMS is a totally different process. The video is streamed into the Flash Player and starts playing when the first bit of the FLV file hits the Flash Player. As well, nothing hits the browser's cache—meaning that there is no way a viewer can reuse the video for other purposes. Naturally there are a couple of downsides to this process. First, the FMS is not cheap. Second, you will need to learn quite a bit of ActionScript to take advantage of the FMS's power. Finally, files are handled in a completely different method than simply uploading the SWF and FLV files to an HTTP server. FMS uses the proprietary Real Time Media Protocol (RTMP) method to call the files into the SWF file.

Still, no matter how you approach delivery of the FLV file, you will be working with a data stream.

There are a couple of terms that have sprung up around the subject of streaming, and this is as good a place as any to introduce them. A movie that creates a stream in a network connection is said to be **publishing**, whereas the movie that receives the stream is said to be a **subscriber**. Just be aware, as you move through this chapter, that a stream can contain only one video or one audio file at any one time. This means if your boss hands you a dozen videos you can't simply toss them up to a server and expect each one to use the same stream. In this case, either the video that is currently playing has to be removed from the stream before the next video is added, or a new stream must be created and the video attached to that new stream.

Streaming in Flash is a little bit different from traditional approaches to the subject. Think of a video stream this way: little packets of information are handed to the Flash Player when it needs them. Depending on the streaming choice, your video will either wait a second or two for enough packets to get going (if you're using Progressive Download), or the first packet will kick off the movie (if you're using FMS). If it is done well in either scenario, the user won't have to sit around, drumming fingers on the desk, waiting for the video to load and play. The key to successful playback is the data rate—the speed at which the packets are flowing into the Flash Player (as discussed in the previous chapter). The second factor is storing enough of these packets before the video starts playing. This process is called **buffering**.

Although we could go "techie" on this, the best way to think of buffering is to imagine a dam on a river. The purpose of this dam is to help the farmers downstream to keep their crops irrigated because the river has a bad habit of either flooding or drying up, depending on the rainfall pattern in their little patch of the countryside.

When the dam is built, the river flows to the dam, and the water starts to back up and form a lake. There is an opening in the dam to allow the water to pour out in a controlled manner that keeps the river flowing at a constant rate. This allows the farmers downstream to have a constant, controlled source of water for their crops.

So what do dams and farmers have to do with video buffering? Think of the farmers' experience with the rainfall pattern and relate it to video playback. We have all had the bad experience of choppy video or video that starts and stops, which is due to running out of video packets. When that happens, the computer stops the process, and we start drumming our fingers on the desk waiting for enough packets to load so we can continue with the video. Buffering stores those packets and releases them when there are enough in the computer to smoothly play the video.

When one packet leaves the dam, another is added to the lake to replace the packet just used. In this example, the raindrops are the data packets, the river into the lake is the data stream, the lake behind the dam is the buffer, the opening in the dam allows the packets to stream into the Flash Player, the river to the farmers' fields is the stream to the Flash Player, and the field being irrigated is the video playing in the Flash Player.

The FLVPlayback component makes this possible. Let's get started.

1. Open Flash, drag a copy of the FLVPlayback component to the stage, and link the component to the Tortoise.flv file created in the last chapter.

> *In Flash 8, if you click the* Parameters *tab, you will see that the item named* bufferTime *from previous versions of this component is missing in action (see Figure 4-1) because this reworked version of the component is smart enough to handle the buffering duties.*

You can use ActionScript to manage this task. The property used is bufferTime; and if you use it, the code line would look something like this:

```
myFLVPlaybackComponent.bufferTime = 0.1;
```

The value you enter as the property, measured in seconds and tenths of seconds, determines the size of the lake behind the dam. The default is one-tenth of a second. This means that if the video is playing back at 24 frames per second (fps), three frames of the video, representing one-tenth of a second of playback, will always be in the buffer. When a frame is released from the buffer during playback, the next one in line behind the buffer replaces it in the buffer.

There are no hard and fast rules regarding bufferTime. What works for you might not work for your competitor across town. Just be aware that there is little or no advantage to changing the default value if your video is playing back from your web server and using Progressive Download. In this situation, the Flash Player will take on the buffering duties and essentially ignore any value you might set in this parameter. If you are using a Flash Communication Server (FlashComm) or an FMS, values between one-tenth (0.1) second to one-half (0.5) second are common buffer values.

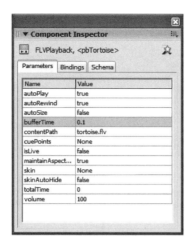

Flash Professional 8

Flash CS3 Professional

Figure 4-1. The bufferTime parameter is no longer a parameter used by the FLVPlayback component.

Creating a custom video controller

Sometimes you don't want to give the user a full set of controls or, let's admit it, you are just fed up with the skins offered by the FLVPlayback component. An example is a situation in which all the user needs to do is to click a start button to watch the video and click a pause button to stop it. Including volume controls, jog controls, and so on would be overkill in this case. This is where the FLVPlayback custom UI components, shown in Figure 4-2, become invaluable.

This collection of 12 components lets you customize the video controls. And best of all, they operate in what we call a "code-free zone."

1. Open a new Flash document and drag a copy of the FLVPlayback component to the stage. Click once on the Parameters tab and use these values:

   - autoPlay: False
   - source: Tortoise.flv (be sure to click the Match source FLV dimensions check box)
   - Skin: None

2. Select the component on the stage and give it the instance name of pbTortoise in the Property Inspector, as shown in Figure 4-3. Now add two more layers to the timeline and name them Controls and Actions. While you are at it, change the name of the layer containing the component to Video.

> You don't necessarily have to add an instance name for the component. If you are simply adding the various bits and pieces from the video components, they work in a code-free zone. We added an instance name simply to get you into the habit of doing it, even when you don't need ActionScript.

Figure 4-2. The FLVPlayback custom UI components

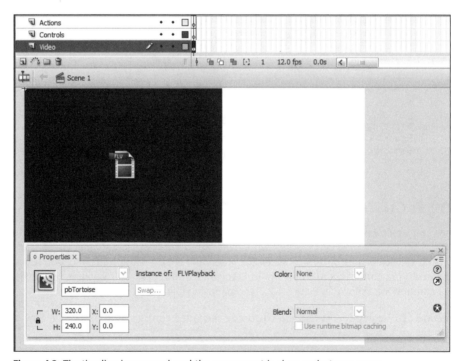

Figure 4-3. The timeline is prepared, and the component is given an instance name.

3. Select the Controls layer and drag a copy of the play and pause buttons from the Components panel to the stage. Place them under the Playback component. Select each button on the stage and give the play button the instance name of mcPlay and the pause button the instance name of mcPause.

> When you drag these components to the stage, they are added to the library (as shown in Figure 4-4), and a copy of the component is added to the FLVPlayback Skins folder in the library. This means that the controls can be customized. If you don't like the color of the gradient used in the play button or you want to change the play button's icon color to yellow, you can open the button's movieclip in the FLVPlayback Skins folder and make the change. Best of all, this change won't affect the original component in the Components panel.
>
> You would be amazed at how many users still can't figure out which is a play button and which is a pause button. If you are at all nervous about this, add a text layer and enter the names of the controls, using the Text tool.

Figure 4-4. UI components appear in the library, and their skins are added to the FLV Playback Skins folder.

With the assets assembled and on the stage, all you need to do is to simply test the video. You no longer need to write ActionScript to enable these components.

4. Save the video and test it. Notice that the pause button is grayed out because the video is paused: autoPlay = False. Click the play button, and the video will start to play. When you do that, the pause button will "light up," and the play button will be grayed out (see Figure 4-5). Click the pause button, and the video will stop.

Now that you understand how to add the video control components to a movie and control the video playback, feel free to add the rest of the controls in the Components panel.

Figure 4-5. The video is under the control of the two buttons.

Adding the components at runtime

In this exercise, you'll learn how to add the FLVPlayback controller and a skin at runtime. By that we mean that the Flash stage has a hole in it where the FLVPLayback and the skin will be located. They will appear on the stage when the movie starts. Here's how:

1. Open a new Flash File ActionScript 3.0 document, add an instance of the FLVPlayback component to the stage, and delete it. If you open the library, you will see that the component is there, which is exactly what you need.

2. Add an Actions layer. Select the first frame in the Actions layer and open the Actions panel.

3. Click once in the Script pane and enter the following code:

```
import fl.video.*;
var my_FLVPlybk = new FLVPlayback();
my_FLVPlybk.x = 0;
my_FLVPlybk.y = 0;
my_FLVPlybk.width = 320;
my_FLVPlybk.height = 240;
addChild(my_FLVPlybk);
my_FLVPlybk.skin = "file:///C:/Program Files/Adobe/Adobe FlashCS3 ➡
/en/Configuration/FLVPlayback Skins/ActionScript 3.0/ ➡
SkinOverPlaySeekMute.swf";
my_FLVPlybk.source = "Cigars.flv";
```

The first line of code imports all the classes of the `fl.video` package into the SWF file. You need to do this to make everything work. The next five lines give the component in the library an instance name—`my_FLVPlybk`—place it on the stage, and change the component's dimension to those of the video. The next line—`addChild(my_FLVPlybk);`—determines how the component is placed on the timeline.

The next line adds the skin. In this code we are grabbing the skin from the Flash Configuration folder on your computer. If you are a Mac user, the path is HD/Applications/Adobe FlashCS3/ Configuration/FLVPlaybackSkins/ActionScript 3.0/SkinOverPlaySeekMute.swf.

If this project is destined for web playback, it would pose a serious problem because you are assuming that the user has the Flash authoring environment installed. In this case, you would copy and paste the skin to the same folder as the SWF file and use a relative link instead: `my_FLVPlybk.skin = "SkinOverPlaySeekMute.swf";`. If you'll be using the same skin in a variety of locations, you could also add the skin to a folder on your web site and point the SWF file to it: `my_FLVPlybk.skin = "http://www.mySite.com/FLVSkins/SkinOverPlaySeekMute.swf";`.

The final line identifies the FLV file that will play in the FLVPlayback component.

4. Save the movie and test it.

Be careful with these components. No matter how you slice it, they will add "weight" to the SWF file. For example, this movie uses only one component, yet the SWF file weighs in at a hefty 52KB. This might not be an issue if you are running the video from your personal site, but commercial applications of Flash video technology will regard 52KB as simply being in the realm of unacceptable because in the Flash world, small is king. How would you like to play the same video in a space smaller than 5KB? Read on.

A word about skinning the components

In the previous edition of this book we didn't discuss "reskinning" the components and we immediately started receiving e-mail that asked why we overlooked this aspect of the component. If this is the first time you have encountered this term, **reskinning** is the process of changing the color and the look and feel of the components. We did this deliberately because this process is dangerous if you don't know what you are doing. In fact, Adobe is quite clear that if you feel the urge to reskin a component, work on a copy of the component, not the original.

To reskin the FLVPlayback component, follow these steps:

1. Navigate to `C:\ProgramFiles\Adobe\AdobeFlashCS3\en\Configuration\FLVPlaybackSkins\ FLA\ActionScript3.0` on your PC or to `HardDrive\Applications\AdobeFlashCS3\en\ Configuration\FLVPlaybackSkins\FLA\ActionScript3.0` on a Mac.

2. Double-click the FLA file you want to change to open it in Flash and immediately save it to the same directory using a different name. When the file opens, all the bits and pieces that make up the component, as shown in Figure 4-6, are laid out on the page and they are also symbols in the library.

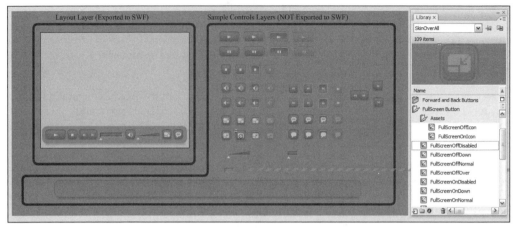

Figure 4-6. You can reskin a component.

3. Open the library and double-click the symbol you want to change.

4. When the symbol opens, make the change and save the file.

Creating a custom video player

So far, we have spent a lot of time singing the praises of the FLVPlayback component and the video components. They are great tools and are marvelous for getting the job done. Still, many Flash developers tend to shy away from a reliance on components, claiming they "add weight to the SWF file." For example, the Tortoise video, using only the FLVPlayback component and no controls, weighs in at 50KB. For serious Flash developers, to whom obtaining the smallest SWF file with the highest quality is the Holy Grail, 50KB is seen as being somewhat ponderous . . . an elephant sitting on the stream.

There is a way of bringing the SWF file down in size to around 1KB with no loss of quality or sacrifice of playback accuracy, however. The technique involves the pairing of ActionScript with a Video object.

The Video object can be found in the library. After it is on the stage and given an instance name, you can use ActionScript to feed the stream into the Video object and manage the stream. To do this, you will need to use two classes of ActionScript. The first class, the NetConnection class, is the one the Flash SWF file uses to communicate—connect—to your server. Flash doesn't care whether the server is your web server or an FMS; all it does is to connect the stream from the server to your browser. The second class is composed of the NetStream class in ActionScript, which does nothing more than display the video and play the sound in the SWF file.

When it comes to using ActionScript to play video, it is easy to explain it in technical terms and dazzle you with our coding prowess, but drill down and you will see it is really not that difficult to understand. There are only three steps in the process:

1. Connect to the server.

2. Create the stream for the video.

3. Play the video.

In fact, using these three steps, here is the minimum ActionScript required to play the Tortoise.flv file from your web server:

```
var nc:NetConnection = new NetConnection();
nc.connect(null);
var ns:NetStream = new NetStream(nc);
myVideo.attachNetStream(ns);
var listener:Object = new Object();
listener.onMetaData = function(md:Object):void {};
ns.client = listener;
ns.play("tortoise.flv");
```

In the code, the first two lines create the connection to the server and keep it open. The next line tells Flash that the connection we have made with the server is to be used for the stream and that the stream is to be fed through a Video object on the stage with the instance name of myVideo. The listener object tells Flash to pay attention to and then ignore the metadata in the FLV file, and the final line tells Flash which video to shoot down the stream. This code will be used quite a bit through-out this chapter (and in the rest of this book).

Now that you understand how it is done, let's actually build a player using a Video object and ActionScript.

1. Open Flash and create a new Flash document.

2. Open the library by pressing Ctrl+L (PC) or Cmd+L (Mac) and then click and hold the library's drop-down menu. Select New Video, as shown in Figure 4-7.

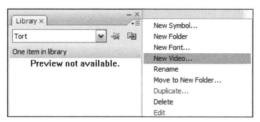

Figure 4-7. Video objects are available through the library's drop-down menu.

3. When the Video Properties dialog box shown in Figure 4-8 opens, name the Symbol as Tortoise, select Video (ActionScript-controlled) from the Type choices, and click OK.

> *The* Embedded (synchronized with Timeline) *option is rather dangerous. If you select it, the entire video will be placed on the timeline. There are uses for it—special effects such as rotoscoped video—but the practice of placing a video on the timeline started to disappear when video could be streamed through Flash. If you must place video on the timeline, use it for short videos lasting maybe 1 to 10 seconds.*

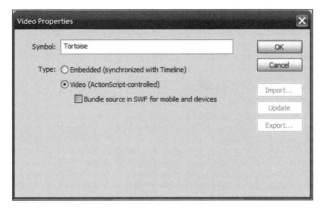

Figure 4-8. Video Properties dialog box

When you click OK, the dialog box closes and, if you look at your library, you will see a small video camera with the name you entered in the Properties. This is the Video object.

4. Drag the Video object from the library to the stage, as shown in Figure 4-9.

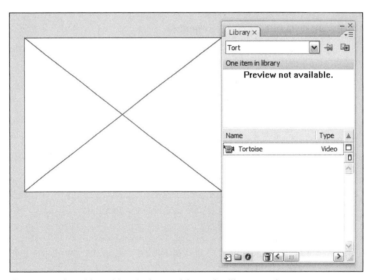

Figure 4-9. The Video object is dragged from the library to the stage.

When you drag the Video object from the library to the stage, you will see just how different this object is from anything else you add to the stage.

It is nothing more than a box with a big X through it. That box is where the video will appear; it will remain invisible at runtime until a video is fed into it. This object is quite unique in that it really is nothing more than a placeholder instead of a real "thing" like the FLVPlayback component. It can only use features of the Video class. The Video class has methods and properties, but there are no events associated with it. Sure, it inherits some functionality from the EventDispatcher and DisplayObject classes, which include events, but those events aren't video-related. On the whole, it doesn't "do" anything other than display a video. You can move the object, resize it, rotate it, mask it, and even stick it in a movieclip. What you can't do is use it to control a video.

The best way of understanding the Video object is to look at your TV screen: the Video object is the display. The knobs or buttons that turn the TV on and off or change the channel are not part of the display.

5. Select the Video object on the stage and click the Properties tab of the Property Inspector. Enter the following values:

- W = 320
- H = 240
- X = 0
- Y = 0
- Instance name = myVideo

Now that the properties have been set and the object given a name, you can now turn your attention to using ActionScript to "wire it up." Before you move on, it might be a good idea to save the file to the same folder used for the FLV file.

Connecting the Video object to a web server

As we said earlier, the process involves three steps: connect, stream, and play.

The first step—connect—is managed by the NetConnection class in ActionScript. This class manages the communication between the server and the user's computer. The NetConnection class has only four native methods, two of which are available only if you are using an FMS or a Flash video streaming service. The three most commonly used methods are the following:

- NetConnection.connect(): This method does exactly what it says—it makes the connection request with the server where the FLV file is located.
- NetConnection.close(): This method, used only by streaming servers, turns off the connection with the server.
- NetConnection.call(): This method, used only by streaming servers, calls remote methods from the Flash Player.

From there, you simply establish the video stream using the NetStream class and attach the Video object to the stream:

1. Open the file you have been working on and add a new layer named Actions.

2. Select the first frame in the Actions layer and press F9 (PC) or Option+F9 (Mac) to open the ActionScript panel. Click once in the Script pane and add the following code:

```
var nc:NetConnection = new NetConnection();
nc.connect(null);
```

The first line of code declares and instantiates a NetConnection object and gives it the instance name nc. We could have named the connection bigHonkingVideoStream, but we prefer to use names that tell us exactly what the variable does. The second line uses the connect method to establish the connection. The null parameter is there because it establishes the connection between a local web server—IIS or Apache—or your computer's hard drive.

3. Press Return/Enter and add the following line of code:

```
var ns:NetStream = new NetStream(nc);
myVideo.attachNetStream(ns);
```

You have just created and instantiated (a fancy name for creating an instance of something) a NetStream object passing in the NetConnection object, used in the first line of the code, as a parameter. If you will be loading a video from an HTTP server or an FMS video, you need to use both a NetConnection and a NetStream.

With the connection made and the stream established, all you now need to do is to feed the stream into the Video object named myVideo on the stage.

4. Press Return/Enter and add the following two lines of code:

```
var listener:Object = new Object();
listener.onMetaData = function(md:Object):void {};
ns.client = listener;
```

The listener object and the onMetaData handler function team up to "chill out" ActionScript because you don't need to actually "do" anything with the event handler. You can if you want, but all you have to do to avoid errors is handle the event.

By setting the client property of the NetStream instance to the listener object, you have effectively told Flash Player to ignore the metadata in the FLV file. This is the purpose of the last line.

> *If you don't add the listeners you will inevitably wind up with a series of really curious errors in the* Output *panel such as the following:*
>
> Error #2044: Unhandled AsyncErrorEvent:. text=Error #2095: flash.net.NetStream was unable to invoke callback onMetaData. error=ReferenceError: Error #1069: Property onMetaData not found on flash.net.NetStream and there is no default value. at TortoiseCodeNoListener_fla::MainTimeline/TortoiseCodeNoListener_fla::frame1()
>
> *When translated into English, it says, "Dude, where's my metadata?"*

5. Press Return/Enter and add the following line of code:

```
ns.play("tortoise.flv");
```

Having established the connection to the server and created a stream, you attached the Video object on the stage to the NetStream. Now that the Video object is attached to the stream, this line of code essentially uses the play() method to load the "tortoise.flv" file to the stream and play it through the Video object on the stage.

If you have a lot of video that is being reused on your site, it doesn't make sense to be using the same FLV file in multiple locations or folders. If this is the case, you can create an absolute link (as opposed to a relative link) to the video. The code would be ns.play("http;//www.mySite.com/FLVfolder/Tortoise.flv").

6. Save the movie and test it. First, the video plays, as shown in Figure 4-10. More importantly is the size of the SWF file. The SWF file for this video, which does exactly what the FLVPlayback component does, is 1KB in size. That is a serious reduction in file size and explains why developers tend to use a code-based approach to projects instead of using the components.

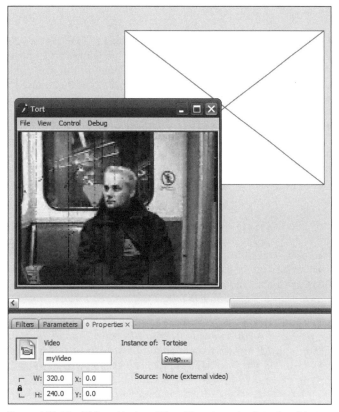

Figure 4-10. The Video object and the video streaming into the object through the Flash Player

Don't panic. If you are just getting going with ActionScript and/or video, we aren't going to suddenly start using ActionScript from this point onward. There will be quite a few projects coming up in this book that are completed in a "code-free zone."

Adding playback controls to a streaming video

Now that you have the video streaming through a Video object, it would be nice if the user could control the playback of the video. In this exercise, you'll do just that. You'll learn the following:

- How to pause a video before it starts playing
- How to pause a video through a pause button
- How to play a paused video using a play button

1. Open the file you just created and click once on the stage. Open the Property Inspector and click the Size button to open the Document Properties dialog box. Set the width of the stage to 320 pixels and the stage height to 275 pixels. Click OK. Add a new layer above the Video layer and name it Controls.

Reducing the size of the stage is a great habit to develop. Having a video that is 320 x 240 sitting on a blank stage that is 600 x 500 leaves a lot of unused space. In the Flash world, unused space can mean an extra bandwidth requirement. Considering that the whole point of this exercise is to get a video to play in the most efficient manner possible in the smallest space possible, unused stage areas defeat the purpose of the exercise.

Now that the housekeeping chores have been addressed, you can turn your attention to the controls.

Depending on personal preference, you can use either button symbols or movieclips in Flash as navigation or media controls. In this case, you'll use a couple of buttons that were installed in a button library when you installed Flash CS3 Professional.

> *If there was one common complaint among Flash developers and designers, it was that the buttons packaged with the application were rather "lame." We won't argue with this observation except to add that they were useful in situations in which the client was given an idea of how controls would work. The guys at Adobe seem to have finally gotten the message because there is a button library that is both extensive and useful starting with Flash Professional 8.*
>
> *Yes, you can "roll your own" buttons and add them to Flash. Adobe Fireworks CS3 is a great tool for this, and if you really want to go to town, Adobe Photoshop CS3 is another excellent tool. Just be aware that you should have at least two button states— Up and Down—meaning that you will need two copies of each button created.*

2. Select Window ➤ Common Libraries ➤ Buttons to open the Buttons panel.
3. Scroll down to the playback rounded folder in the Buttons panel and open it.
4. Select the Controls layer and drag a copy of each of the rounded grey pause and rounded grey play buttons to the stage.
5. Select the pause button and, in the Property Inspector, give the instance name of btnPause. Select the play button and give it the instance name of btnPlay, as shown in Figure 4-11. Save the movie.

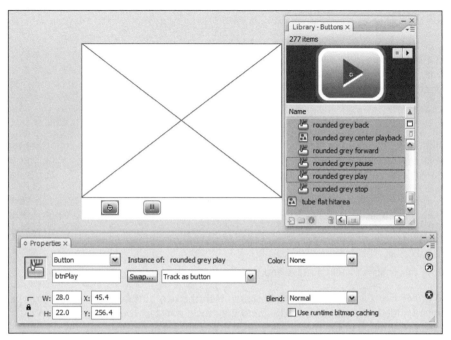

Figure 4-11. The buttons are dragged from the library to the stage, where they are given instance names in the Property Inspector.

6. Select frame 1 in the Actions layer and press F9 (PC) or Option+F9 (Mac) to open the ActionScript editor.

7. Press Return/Enter after the last line of code and enter the following:

```
ns.pause();
```

This single line of code deals with the first objective. All it does is pause the stream into the Video object. This means the video screen will be blank and require the user to click the play button to get it playing.

> We started off this chapter by talking about buffering video. To do this, enter the following line of code before pausing the video:
>
> ```
> ns.bufferTime = 1;
> ```
>
> This code places one second of video in the buffer. Mind you, this becomes a moot point if the video fails to load for some reason.

8. Press Return/Enter and add the following code:

```
// Pause Button code
btnPause.addEventListener(MouseEvent.CLICK, btnPauseClickHandler);
function btnPauseClickHandler(evt:MouseEvent):void {
```

```
    ns.pause();
};

// Play Button code
btnPlay.addEventListener(MouseEvent.CLICK, btnPlayClickHandler);
function btnPlayClickHandler(evt:MouseEvent):void {
  ns.resume();
};
```

The two little functions Play and Pause actually play and pause the movie. The important aspect of this code is your discovery that the video can be turned on or off simply by adding the pause() method to get a button to stop the video.

The other important aspect of all three pieces of code is that they affect the NetStream and don't turn the video on and off, as you might assume. When you think about it, this makes a whole lot of sense. The video is attached to the NetStream, so to pause a movie, you pause the flow or stream of information into the browser.

9. Close the Actions panel and save and test the movie.

When the movie starts, you will see a blank screen with the two buttons, thanks to the ns.pause(); statement you added. Click the play button, and the movie will start to play, as shown in Figure 4-12. Click the pause button, and the movie will pause. If you check the final size of the SWF file, you will see that the size, thanks to the buttons, has doubled from 1KB to 2KB.

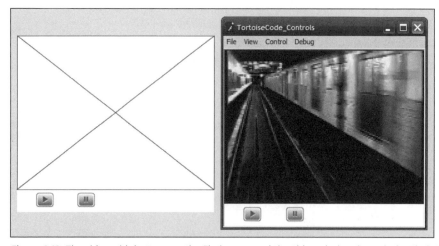

Figure 4-12. The video with buttons on the Flash stage and the video playing through the Flash Player

Adding a Playing Progress bar and a timer to a streaming video

This exercise takes the next step in the construction of a custom video player. You'll learn the following:

- How to add a virtual Video object to the stage
- How to choose a video to play

- How to create a Playing Progress bar indicator
- How to show the current and remaining time in the video that is playing

If you can master these four skills, you are on your way to creating a totally custom player. (You'll also be doing it in the final exercise of this chapter.)

Before you start, let's talk about how you can show the playing progress of a video and display the current and remaining time of the video that is playing. When you encode an FLV file, you actually create quite a bit of metadata: duration, width, height, and frame rate. As you can see, one of the bits of metadata embedded into the FLV file is the duration of the video, which is measured in hours, minutes, seconds, and milliseconds. The duration metadata parameter is accessible through ActionScript.

> *The metadata information that is added to your FLV file depends on the software you use to encode your FLV file or the software you use to add metadata information.*

Now that you have an idea of what you'll be doing, let's get started:

1. Open the Custom Video Player_01 folder found in your Chapter 4 exercise folder and double-click the video_player.fla file to open the file in Flash.

When the file opens, you'll see that the buttons and text boxes have already been added to the stage and the library, and that there is no Video object on the stage or in the library (see Figure 4-13). We know that the design is rudimentary. The reason we went this route—sometimes referred to as "programmer art"—is that the focus is the code that makes everything work, not the design.

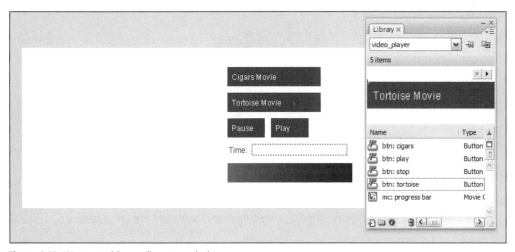

Figure 4-13. We start with a rudimentary design.

2. Select the first frame of the Actions layer and press F9 (PC) or Option+F9 (Mac) to open the Actions panel.

3. Click once inside the Script pane and add the following code:

```
var videoDuration:Number = new Number();
var client:Object = new Object();
client.onMetaData = metadataHandler;
function metadataHandler(metadataObj:Object):void {
  videoDuration = metadataObj.duration;
}
```

You start by identifying the metadata you want to obtain. The first line makes sure that the metadata is only a Number and gives it the variable name of videoDuration. Having done that, you have to next create an Object named client for the metadata. If we don't add the Object named client, the metadaData has nowhere to go, and the Output panel will tell you so with this "clear as mud" error message:

Error #2044: Unhandled AsyncErrorEvent:. text=Error #2095: flash.net.NetStream was unable to invoke callback onMetaData. error=ReferenceError: Error #1069: Property onMetaData not found on flash.net.NetStream and there is no default value. at TortoiseCodeNoListener_fla::MainTimeline/ TortoiseCodeNoListener_fla::frame1()

The next line tells Flash what to do with that information: execute the metadaHandler() function.

Flash, being stone-cold stupid, doesn't have a clue what you are talking about, which is why the metadataHandler() function is written. This function accepts a parameter by the arbitrary name metadataObj, which is brought to this function when the onMetaData event is dispatched. The onMetaData event carries with it, among other things, a duration property, whose value is given to the previously declared videoDuration variable for later use.

4. Press Return/Enter twice and enter the following code:

```
var nc:NetConnection = new NetConnection();
nc.connect(null);
var ns:NetStream = new NetStream(nc);
ns.client = client;
ns.play("Cigars.flv");

var myVideo:Video = new Video();
myVideo.attachNetStream(ns);
addChild(myVideo);
```

Not a lot new here other than ns.client = client and addChild(myVideo).

The ns.client property identifies the metadata object created earlier as the object that will be called by ActionScript. You need to add this when you start digging into an FLV file's metadata.

The line var myVideo:Video = new Video(); is used to create the virtual Video object. The NetStream is fed into the Video object, and the last line—addChild(myVideo)—is how the object is placed on the stage when you use ActionScript 3.0. The other thing you should know is that the default placement for that object is exactly where we want the video to appear: 0,0 on the X and Y coordinates of the stage.

If you want to change the dimensions of the object from the default value of 320 x 240, you can add them to the constructor as properties (var myVideo:Video = new Video (640,480);) or through the actual properties of the object. In this case, the code would be the following:

```
var myVideo:Video = new Video();
myVideo.width = 640;
myVideo.height = 320;
```

5. Having created an object for the metadata and added a Video object to the movie, we can now turn our attention to "wiring up" the Progress bar and getting the text into the text box. Press Return/Enter a couple of times and enter the following:

```
var myTimer:Timer = new Timer(100,0);
myTimer.addEventListener(TimerEvent.TIMER, onTick);
function onTick(event:TimerEvent):void {
   timeTB.text = ns.time.toFixed(1) + " of " + ➡
videoDuration.toFixed(1) + " seconds";
   progressMC.width = 200 * (ns.time / videoDuration);
}
myTimer.start();
```

This code block solves a potential issue: you simply can't grab the time information you need without telling Flash how often to grab it. When you think about that statement, it makes a lot of sense. The video plays back at a rate of 15 fps, which means that the duration number will constantly change as the video plays.

The first line of the code creates a new Timer object that fires every 100 milliseconds and the second parameter (0) means that the Timer will repeat indefinitely. The next line tells Flash what to do every time that event occurs: execute a function named onTick.

The onTick function does two things. The first thing it does is to fill the text box (timeTB.text) with the current point of time in the video and the duration (videoDuration) of the video. It uses the toFixed() method of the Number class to trim off the decimal point to one instead of three places. This is the purpose of the number 1 as the parameter in the toFixed(1) method.

The second thing we can do with the metadata number (videoDuration) is to use it to scale the ProgressMC movieclip on the stage. You simply divide the current time of the video by the duration of the video to obtain a decimal value. Where does that 200 number come from? It is the width of the movieclip on the stage.

> *Just because you are dealing with the duration of the video using a variable named videoDuration, it doesn't mean that value can't be used for other purposes. A wise Flash coder once gave us a stellar piece of advice: "It is just a number. Use it." It is a piece of advice that we have never forgotten, and one of the authors has it tattooed to the inside of his left eyelid. In this case, the same number is being displayed in a text box and is used to determine the width of a movieclip on the stage.*

6. It is now time to wire up the buttons and test the movie to see if it works. Press Return/Enter a couple of times and enter the following:

```
cigarsBTN.addEventListener(MouseEvent.CLICK, cigarsBTNClickHandler);
function cigarsBTNClickHandler(evt:MouseEvent):void {
  ns.play("Cigars.flv");
};

tortoiseBTN.addEventListener(MouseEvent.CLICK, tripodBTNClickHandler);
function tripodBTNClickHandler(evt:MouseEvent):void {
  ns.play("tortoise.flv");
};

pauseBTN.addEventListener(MouseEvent.CLICK, pauseBTNClickHandler);
function pauseBTNClickHandler(evt:MouseEvent):void {
  ns.pause();
};

playBTN.addEventListener(MouseEvent.CLICK, playBTNClickHandler);
function playBTNClickHandler(evt:MouseEvent):void {
  ns.resume();
};
```

The important aspect of this code is how the videos are played when their respective buttons are clicked. What is not obvious here is a fundamental rule of Flash video: only one video per stream is allowed. This is why there are separate ns.play() methods. When a button is clicked, the video that is currently being played is bumped off of the stream, and the one called in the new ns.play() method is added to the stream.

The ns.resume() method is normally used after an ns.pause() is called. What happens is the stream is "paused" at the point where the button is clicked. The resume() method simply restarts the stream from that point.

7. Save and test the movie. As you can see in Figure 4-14, the metadata object does double duty, regardless of which video is chosen. Best of all, is that you get all of that functionality through a SWF file that is only 3KB in size.

Figure 4-14. Swapping videos, showing the time and even the playback progress

Your turn: Creating your own custom player

There will come a time when you will need to create your own player from scratch. This could be due to clients requesting something that is unique to their brand, or you might find yourself bored with the sameness of the Flash video players you have been using. Regardless of how you reach that point, you still have to make some fundamental decisions. The two most important are the following:

- What software will be used to create the player?
- What features will need to be incorporated into the player?

In this exercise, you'll construct a full-featured custom player. Instead of using Photoshop CS3, you'll use Fireworks CS3 for the construction of the player.

For those of you who are "hard-core" Photoshop users, this might appear to be a bit of heresy but, in actual fact, Fireworks CS3 (which is included in the Adobe Creative Suite 3 Web Premium bundle or in the Master Collection) has been repositioned as a prototyping tool. In fact, you can still create the interface in Photoshop CS3 and then pass it over to Fireworks CS3 to prepare the pieces for Flash CS3.

> You can also create an entire player using the tools in Flash CS3. If you check out the Chapter 4 extras folder in the chapter download, you'll see we have included two extra custom players. One is based on a YouTube design and the other, `CustomPlayer_Flash.zip`, has been totally constructed in Flash CS3.

The process started by opening up Fireworks CS3 and "sketching out" what we needed.

When it came to specific controls, the decision was to include the following functionality:

- A play/pause button
- A rewind button
- A download progress indicator bar
- A jog controller to scrub through the video
- A volume controller
- A button that enlarges the video without going full screen
- A button that returns the video to its original dimensions

This is a fairly tall order and can be a rather daunting task to the average Flash designer. At this point of the process, though, it was more important to map out where everything would go before worrying about how the Flash Player would look and how each piece would function. We opened up Fireworks CS3 and, as shown in Figure 4-15, created a mockup of the player.

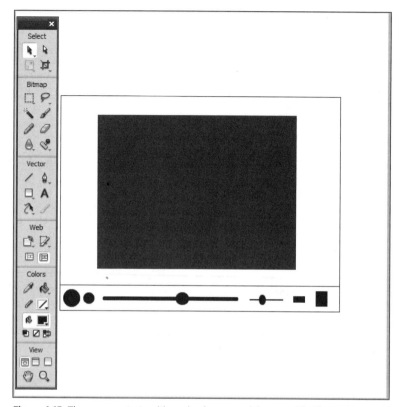

Figure 4-15. The process starts with a wire frame model, created in Fireworks CS3, that outlines the interface elements and their placement.

Knowing what we wanted and where we wanted it is nice, but the big question was: "How will it look?" This resulted in a trip to Mexico.

If you have ever poked through the pages of the Fireworks CS3 Developer Center at www.adobe.com/ devnet/fireworks or watched a demonstration of this software, the odds are really good that you have either been exposed to or are familiar with the work of José Angel Rivera Dominguez, located in Mexico City, Mexico. José's design sense and a passion for detail are the hallmarks of his work. Who better to bring the wire frame to life than José?

The primary considerations were that the video had to fit into an area that was 450 pixels wide and 300 pixels deep. The controller area was to also match the rough size of the skins used in Flash CS3, which meant the controller could not exceed a height of 45 pixels.

The wire frame and the specs were shipped off to Mexico City, and a few days later José sent us the design shown in Figure 4-16.

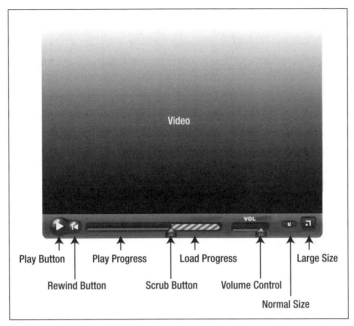

Figure 4-16. The wire frame is translated into a full-blown design.

Preparing to move from Fireworks to Flash

Designing a Flash interface in Fireworks is always a two-step process:

1. Build the pieces.
2. Move the pieces from Fireworks to Flash.

Naturally it isn't as simple as that, but that is the process. The key is realizing that even though Fireworks has a lot of power under the hood, many of the meticulous gradients and so on created in Fireworks simply won't move, intact, into Flash. We'll get into how to deal with that in a moment.

The process started with José drawing the various interface elements using the Rectangle and Ellipse tools on the Flash toolbar. These shapes were then filled with gradients, set to varying opacities, to provide the illusion of depth. The file José sent to us was in a rather raw state (see Figure 4-17), which is quite normal.

The file contained a series of layers that we then grouped into their respective elements (see Figure 4-18) prior to moving them. The other thing we did was to name each layer, select each layer, and flatten the layer to create the bitmap because moving vector gradients from Fireworks CS3 to Flash CS3 is still a bit problematic. We have included this file (JoséDesign_flat.png) in the Custom Video Player 02 folder in the chapter exercise file.

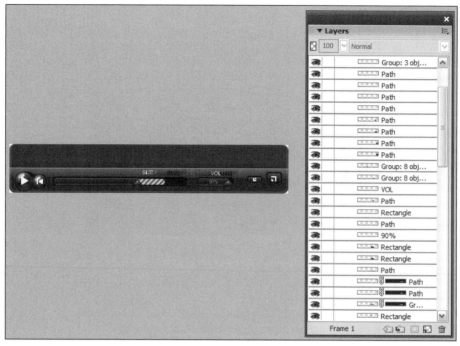

Figure 4-17. A Fireworks CS3 drawing is a collection of layers.

The purpose of flattening was to preserve the gradients in the interface. You flatten a layer in Fireworks by selecting the layer and choosing Flatten Selection from the Layers menu or by right-clicking (PC) or Ctrl+clicking (Mac) on the object on the Fireworks canvas and selecting Flatten Selection from the resulting context menu.

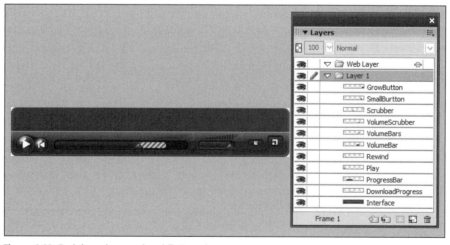

Figure 4-18. Each layer is named and flattened.

Fireworks symbols and Flash symbols

The intersection of Flash and Fireworks is one of those areas that very few Fireworks and Flash artists have explored. It is too bad because Fireworks symbols do move very smoothly into Flash. Here's how:

1. Open the Button.png file in Fireworks CS3. You will see we have created a simple graphic that contains a beveled edge and is filled with the Flames pattern found in the Fill drop-down menu in the Fireworks CS3 Property Inspector. The image was converted to a symbol by selecting it on the canvas and selecting Modify ➤ Symbol ➤ Convert to symbol (or in Flash by simply pressing F8).

2. Double-click the button to open the Fireworks CS3 Symbol editor shown in Figure 4-19. The Fireworks Symbol editor that opens is remarkably similar to Flash's Symbol editor, including the use of 9-slice scaling. Click Done to close the Symbol editor.

> The three Fireworks symbol types are Graphic, Button, and Animation. Although Fireworks only creates GIF animations, they can be placed into Flash as movieclips.

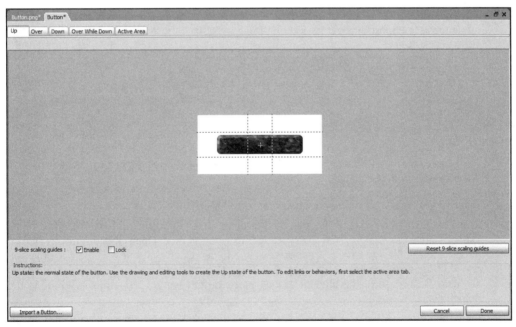

Figure 4-19. The Flash and Fireworks Symbol editors are remarkably similar.

3. Open the Layers panel and click once on the Web Layer visibility icon. The symbol will be covered with a green overlay indicating a slice. Open the Assets panel and click once on the Library tab. Note the Button symbol icon. Save the file.

4. Open a new Flash CS3 ActionScript 3.0 document and when the document opens, select File ➤ Import ➤ Import to Library. When you release the mouse, the Import Fireworks Document dialog box opens (see Figure 4-20).

The dialog box is not complicated. Here's what each area means:

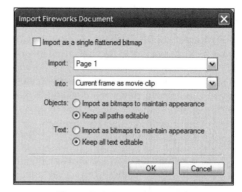

- Import as a single flattened bitmap: Selecting this option is your call, but in the case of José's design, this choice is fatal. Everything in the file will be flattened into one layer, instead of many layers.

Figure 4-20. Importing a Fireworks PNG document into Flash

- Import: Fireworks documents are composed of layers on separate pages. This drop-down menu allows you to choose which page to import into Flash.

- Into: You have two choices with this drop-down menu. The document can be imported into the library as a movieclip or into a separate layer on the Flash timeline.

- Objects: You can either choose to flatten everything or, because Fireworks is a vector tool, you can choose to import the vectors and edit them in Flash.

Be careful with this selection. Textures, gradients, and bitmap fills won't import into Flash if Keep all paths editable *is selected. If you choose the first item, each of the symbol states will be converted to a bitmap—a very small one—and the fills will move, intact, into Flash.*

- Text: Select Import as bitmaps to maintain appearance if you don't expect to change the text. Otherwise go with the default.

5. Select Import as bitmaps to maintain appearance and click OK.

6. Open the Flash library. You will notice the button has been imported as a graphic, and a folder named Fireworks Objects has been added to your library. Open the Fireworks Objects folder and the file you have just imported is in a folder. Open that one and the page the button is sitting on in the Fireworks document (Page 1) has its own folder. Open it and, as shown in Figure 4-21, each of the bitmaps as well as the button symbol and a movieclip are in this folder.

7. Drag the Button symbol to the stage. The movieclip is nothing more than a placeholder, so feel free to delete it from the library if you won't be using it.

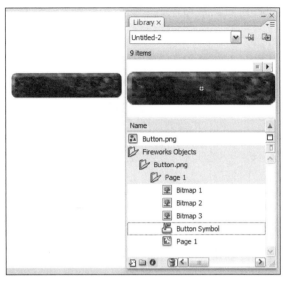

Figure 4-21. The Fireworks symbol and accompanying bitmaps are placed in the Flash library.

If you are really lazy, simply drag and drop the button from the Fireworks canvas onto the Flash stage. You will still get the PNG Import *dialog box, but when you click* OK, *the button that is sitting on the Flash stage is the movieclip symbol, not the button.*

Now that you know how to move stuff from Fireworks to Flash, let's concentrate on getting José's custom player "wired up" and working.

Wiring up the custom player with ActionScript 3.0

Before we started writing up the ActionScript, we first brought all the bits and pieces into the Flash library, converted them to movieclips, and then placed them in layers and folders (refer to Figure 4-21) on the main timeline. We decided to go with movieclips instead of Fireworks buttons because we can show you not only how to treat a Flash movieclip as a button but also how to apply a blend effect, programmatically, to a movieclip.

There is one addition we made to the interface. If you look closely at Figure 4-22 you will see that we have added a white box over the volume bars. This box will actually be used as a mask and will move when the volume slider is moved. What it will do is to reveal the white bars that indicate increasing volume in José's interface. By doing this in Flash and not Fireworks, we are actually following one the fundamentals of this business: *let the software do the work.* In this case, it is easier to add the element and treat it as a mask in Flash than to do the same thing through Fireworks. The same thing goes for the text used to indicate the total and current times of the video and the volume level. These will be "dynamic" text instances; this means that it is better to add them in Flash instead of Fireworks.

Now that everything is in place, let's get to work.

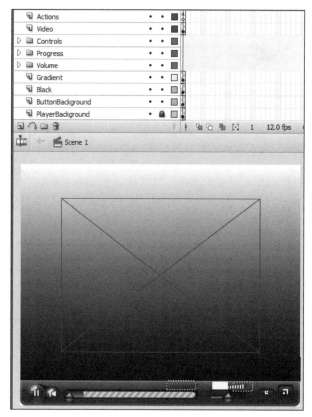

Figure 4-22. The The assets are in place and ready to come to life through ActionScript.

1. Open the CustomPlayer02.fla file. When it opens, select the first frame in the Actions layer and press F9 (PC) or Option+F9 (Mac) to open the Actions panel.

2. When the panel opens, open the Actions panel drop-down menu and select Line Numbers. Numbering your code lines makes it much easier to isolate any syntax errors that might appear in the Output panel when you test the movie.

3. Click once on the first line of the Script pane and enter the following:

```
var videoDuration:Number;
var client:Object = new Object();
client.onMetaData = metaDataHandler;
function metaDataHandler(metaDataObj:Object):void{
  videoDuration = metaDataObj.duration;
}
```

One of the keys to this project is the slider that will allow you to scrub through the video as it is playing. The Progress bar will also "grow" as more and more of the video plays. Both of them are tied into the duration of the video, and this value is found in the FLV file's metadata.

The first line of code gives that value a variable name, and the second line creates a new `Object()` named `client` to hold the metadata contained in the FLV file.

The function is also critical because Flash will generate an error if you do not specify an `onMetaData` event handler. Earlier, we added a "dummy" stand-in event handler simply to avoid an error message. Here, the handler actually gets used.

4. Press Return/Enter twice to make some space, and enter the following code:

```
var nc:NetConnection = new NetConnection();
nc.connect(null);
var ns:NetStream = new NetStream(nc);
ns.client = client;
videoVO.attachNetStream(ns);
my_ns.play("Through_A_Door.flv");
```

Nothing new here. The connection is made to the HTTP server, a stream is added to the NetConnection, and the stream is fed into the Video object named `videoVO` on the stage. The code finishes by adding the video to the stream.

With the housekeeping chores out of the way, it is time to start adding the functionality to the various controls on the interface.

5. Press Return/Enter twice and enter the following:

```
playMC.buttonMode = true;
playMC.visible = false;

playMC.addEventListener(MouseEvent.MOUSE_DOWN, playMCMouseDownHandler);
function playMCMouseDownHandler(event:MouseEvent):void {
  playMC.blendMode = BlendMode.ADD;
  stage.addEventListener(MouseEvent.MOUSE_UP,➡
 playMCReleaseOutsideHandler);
}

playMC.addEventListener(MouseEvent.MOUSE_UP, playMCMouseUpHandler);
function playMCMouseUpHandler(event:MouseEvent):void {
  playMC.visible = false;
  pauseMC.visible = true;
  my_ns.resume();
  playMC.blendMode = BlendMode.NORMAL;
}
function playMCReleaseOutsideHandler(event:Object):void {
  playMC.blendMode = BlendMode.NORMAL;
  stage.removeEventListener(MouseEvent.MOUSE_UP,➡
 playMCReleaseOutsideHandler);
}
```

The first part of the functionality is concerned with what the user sees. When the movie starts, the video is playing, so it makes sense to change the icon in the play button to the two bars indicating pause. This explains the second line of the code (playMC.visible = false;), which turns off the arrow used to indicate play.

The next three functions treat the movieclip as a button and tell ActionScript what to do based on the user's input. This process actually starts with the first line of the code you entered (playMC.buttonMode = true;), which is new to ActionScript 3.0. This line is what turns the arrow cursor into the pointing finger cursor when the mouse is over the movieclip.

The first handler deals with what happens when the mouse is pressed. As you can see, the Add blend mode is applied to the button to let the user know that the movieclip is interactive. The next function uses the MOUSE_UP state to turn off the play icon, turn on the pause icon, start the video playing, and return the button to its normal look through the use of playMC.blendMode = BlendMode.NORMAL;.

The final function deals with what happens if the mouse is pressed and then released somewhere else in the interface. With ActionScript 3.0, there is no onReleaseOutside event as there was in ActionScript 2.0, so after a button is pressed, we add a MOUSE_UP listener to the stage to detect a ReleaseOutside. After the MOUSE_UP event occurs, we remove the listener form the stage. This process is used for every button in this exercise.

6. The next button to deal with is the pause button. Press Return/Enter twice and enter the following:

```
pauseMC.buttonMode = true;

pauseMC.addEventListener(MouseEvent.MOUSE_DOWN,➥
pauseMCMouseDownHandler);➥
function pauseMCMouseDownHandler(event:MouseEvent):void {
  pauseMC.blendMode = BlendMode.ADD;
  stage.addEventListener(MouseEvent.MOUSE_UP,➥
pauseMCReleaseOutsideHandler);➥
}

pauseMC.addEventListener(MouseEvent.MOUSE_UP, pauseMCMouseUpHandler);
function pauseMCMouseUpHandler(event:MouseEvent):void {
  playMC.visible = true;
  pauseMC.visible = false;
  my_ns.pause();
  pauseMC.blendMode = BlendMode.NORMAL;
}

function pauseMCReleaseOutsideHandler(event:MouseEvent):void {
  pauseMC.blendMode = BlendMode.NORMAL;
  stage.removeEventListener(MouseEvent.MOUSE_UP, ➥
pauseMCReleaseOutsideHandler);
}
```

7. The next button to deal with is the rewind button. Press Return/Enter twice, and let's deal with it:

```
rewindMC.buttonMode = true;

rewindMC.addEventListener(MouseEvent.MOUSE_DOWN, ➡
rewindMCMouseDownHandler);
function rewindMCMouseDownHandler(event:MouseEvent):void {
  rewindMC.blendMode = BlendMode.ADD;
  stage.addEventListener(MouseEvent.MOUSE_UP, ➡
rewindMCReleaseOutsideHandler);
}

rewindMC.addEventListener(MouseEvent.MOUSE_UP, rewindMCMouseUpHandler);
function rewindMCMouseUpHandler(event:MouseEvent):void {
  my_ns.seek(0);
  rewindMC.blendMode = BlendMode.NORMAL;
}

function rewindMCReleaseOutsideHandler(event:MouseEvent):void {
  rewindMC.blendMode = BlendMode.NORMAL;
  stage.removeEventListener(MouseEvent.MOUSE_UP,➡
 rewindMCReleaseOutsideHandler);
}
```

The "new" aspect of this code is the use of the seek() method in the rewindMCMouseUpHandler function. What this method does is to go to a specific point in time (in this case, the start of the video) in the FLV file. When using the seek() method, it is important to understand that the seek() method is applied to the stream, not to the FLV file.

8. Over on the right side of the interface are two buttons that expand and contract the video. Press Return/Enter twice, and let's wire them up:

```
normalMC.buttonMode = true;

normalMC.addEventListener(MouseEvent.MOUSE_DOWN, ➡
 normalMCMouseDownHandler);
function normalMCMouseDownHandler(event:MouseEvent):void {
  normalMC.blendMode = BlendMode.ADD;
  stage.addEventListener(MouseEvent.MOUSE_UP, ➡
normalMCReleaseOutsideHandler);
}

normalMC.addEventListener(MouseEvent.MOUSE_UP, normalMCMouseUpHandler);
function normalMCMouseUpHandler(event:MouseEvent):void {
  videoVO.width = 320;
  videoVO.height = 240;
  videoVO.x = 65;
  videoVO.y = 53;
```

```
    normalMC.blendMode = BlendMode.NORMAL;
  }

  function normalMCReleaseOutsideHandler(event:MouseEvent):void {
    normalMC.blendMode = BlendMode.NORMAL;
    stage.removeEventListener(MouseEvent.MOUSE_UP,➡
normalMCReleaseOutsideHandler);
  }


  fullscreenMC.buttonMode = true;

  fullscreenMC.addEventListener(MouseEvent.MOUSE_DOWN, ➡
  fullscreenMCMouseDownHandler);
  function fullscreenMCMouseDownHandler(event:MouseEvent):void {
    fullscreenMC.blendMode = BlendMode.ADD;
    stage.addEventListener(MouseEvent.MOUSE_UP, ➡
  fullscreenMCReleaseOutsideHandler);
  }

  fullscreenMC.addEventListener(MouseEvent.MOUSE_UP,➡
   fullscreenMCMouseUpHandler);
  function fullscreenMCMouseUpHandler(event:MouseEvent):void {
    videoVO.width = 450;
    videoVO.height = 338;
    videoVO.x = 0;
    videoVO.y = 0;
    fullscreenMC.blendMode = BlendMode.NORMAL;
  }

  function fullscreenMCReleaseOutsideHandler(event:MouseEvent):void {
    fullscreenMC.blendMode = BlendMode.NORMAL;
    stage.removeEventListener(MouseEvent.MOUSE_UP, ➡
    fullscreenMCReleaseOutsideHandler);
  }
```

There isn't anything new here. All this does is to resize the Video object and place it where it belongs in the interface when the object is resized.

Controlling the volume level of a video

A video is composed of two tracks: an audio track and a video track. The audio track is not under the control of the Video class. Audio falls squarely in the realm of the Sound class and other related classes, which is why, when managing audio volume in a video, you will need to put the video track under the control of the new ActionScript 3.0 SoundTransform class. Here's how:

1. Press Return/Enter in the Script pane a couple of times and enter the following code:

```
var videoSound:SoundTransform = new SoundTransform();
videoSound.volume = .5;
ns.soundTransform = videoSound;
```

A SoundTransform object that will hold the sound is created, the volume level is set to 50 percent (videoSound.volvume = .5), and the sound is pulled from the video on the stream and added to the soundTransform object.

With the SoundTransform object created, we can turn our attention to the slider, which increases and decreases the volume.

2. Press Return/Enter twice and enter the following code:

```
var volumeBounds:Rectangle = new Rectangle(300,355,50,0);
volumeMC.buttonMode = true;
volumeMC.addEventListener(MouseEvent.MOUSE_DOWN, ➡
volumeMCMouseDownHandler);
```

As you might have guessed, you don't simply "wire up" the slider. You first need to make sure that it remains within a defined area on the screen. This is the purpose of the Rectangle object, which will determine the boundaries (volumeBounds) of the slider. The numbers for the rectangle use the following parameters: newRectangle(x,y,width,height).

> *You can obtain these numbers by simply drawing a rectangle on the screen and noting the values shown in the* Property Inspector. *When you have noted the values, delete the rectangle. Setting the height of the Rectangle object to* 0 *ensures that the slider can't be moved up or down.*

3. Now that you have done the housekeeping, let's turn our attention to making the slider fully functional. Press Return/Enter twice and enter the following three functions:

```
function volumeMCMouseDownHandler(event:MouseEvent):void {
  volumeMC.startDrag(false,volumeBounds);
  volumeMC.blendMode = BlendMode.ADD;
  stage.addEventListener(MouseEvent.MOUSE_UP, volumeMCMouseUpHandler);
  stage.addEventListener(MouseEvent.MOUSE_MOVE, ➡
volumeMCMouseMoveHandler);
}

function volumeMCMouseUpHandler(event:MouseEvent):void {
  volumeMC.stopDrag();
  volumeMC.blendMode = BlendMode.NORMAL;
  stage.removeEventListener(MouseEvent.MOUSE_UP, ➡
volumeMCMouseUpHandler);
  stage.removeEventListener(MouseEvent.MOUSE_MOVE, ➡
volumeMCMouseMoveHandler);
}
```

```
function volumeMCMouseMoveHandler(event:MouseEvent):void {
    videoSound.volume = (volumeMC.x - 300) / 50;
    volumeTB.text = String(Math.round(videoSound.volume * 100));
    my_ns.soundTransform = videoSound;
    volumeBarsMaskMC.width = (volumeMC.x - 300);
    volumeBarMC.width = 7 + (volumeMC.x - 300);
}
```

The first two functions simply make the button draggable when the mouse is pressed and change its color using the Add blend mode to let the user know it is a button. The second simply puts everything back when the mouse is released. The third function is where the magic happens.

The function starts by setting the volume level. The volume calculation, (volumeMC.x-300) / 50, is fairly simple. The position of the slider on the x-axis is noted; 300, the width of the bounding box, is subtracted from that number. The result is divided by 50, and the volume level is set to that result. For example, let's assume that the slider is located at 326 pixels along the x-axis. The calculation would be the following:

- (326-300)/50
- 26/50

The volumeSound value would then be .52 or just about 50 percent of full volume. To give the user a visual indication of this level, the result is added to the dynamic text box on the stage—volumeTB— and the result is multiplied by 100 (which means that the user will see the number 52 in the text box). This result is then reapplied to the soundTransform property of the NetStream class to set the volume of the audio.

The final two lines of the code reveal the volume bars by setting the width of the mask (volumeBarsMaskMC) and the volumeBarMC movieclip to the location of the slider (volumeMC) on the x-axis.

> *When using the x- or y-axis of one object to determine the size or location of another object, the result uses the registration point of the movable object. In this case, it would be the registration point of the slider.*

Showing the loading and playing progress of an FLV file

The final bit of "wiring" that needs to be done is to show the loading progress of an FLV file. Before you start, there are a few things you need to know:

- The value used is the amount of data from the FLV file (measured in bytes) that has loaded into the Flash Player.
- You need to tell Flash how often to check this value. It is not an automatic function of the application.

- A scrubber that allows the user to move through the video only works based on the amount of the video that has downloaded into the Flash Player at any point in time. You can't, for example, drag a scrubber to the end of the video if only 50 percent of it has downloaded. The only time you can do this is if the video is being delivered through an FMS.

- When you scrub a video, you are moving between the key frames of the video. This means that when the mouse is released, the video will start at the nearest key frame to the point of release. If you are an absolute nut for precision, the best solution for "scrub accuracy" is to set the FLV key frames to 1 key frame every second instead of the default value of every 300 frames when you create the FLV file in the Encoder. This will increase the FLV file's size considerably.

Armed with this knowledge, let's create the Progress bar and the Scrubber bar.

1. In the Script pane, press Return/Enter key and enter the following code:

```
var progressBounds:Rectangle = new Rectangle(65,355,➡
loadProgressMC.width - 7,0);
var progressDragStatus:Boolean = new Boolean(false);
```

Nothing new here, although you might be wondering about the new Rectangle() parameters. The reason we "trimmed" off 7 pixels from the width of the loadProgressMC movieclip is to ensure that we don't completely cover the area for the load progress and to show a little bit of the striped bar—the ProgressIndicator movieclip in the library. Note that parameters can be entered as numbers by hand or entered as values of properties, such as width and height. Again, they're just numbers. Use them.

The second line acknowledges the fact there will be two sets of code that move the progress slider:

- When the user is dragging the slider
- When the movie is playing

The variable progressDragStatus ensures that only one of these events is moving the slider at any given time.

2. Press Return/Enter twice and enter the code that creates the load progress indicator:

```
var playProgressTM:Timer = new Timer(100,0);

playProgressTM.addEventListener(TimerEvent.TIMER, ➡
playProgressTMTimerHandler);
function playProgressTMTimerHandler(event:TimerEvent):void {
  loadProgressMC.width = (207 * my_ns.bytesLoaded / ➡
my_ns.bytesTotal) + 7;
  if(progressDragStatus == false){
    progressTB.text = Math.round(my_ns.time) + '/' + ➡
Math.round(videoDuration);
    progressMC.x = 70 + 207 * (my_ns.time / videoDuration);
    playProgressMC.width = (207 * my_ns.time / videoDuration) + 7;
  }
}
playProgressTM.start();
```

The process starts by telling Flash how often to check the load progress by setting the Timer to "fire" every 100 milliseconds, or 10 times per second. The best way of envisioning a Timer is to think of a clock on the wall. If you watch the second hand, it will move from second to second on the clock face. We call this movement a **tick**. In Flash we can be even more precise. Flash "ticks" every millisecond, so we can use this value to set how often the timer fires—in this case, it is every 100 ticks.

The rest of the code tells Flash what to do when the Timer fires.

First the width of the gray bar (loadProgressMC) is set. We then check to see whether the bar is draggable. If it isn't (if(progressDragStatus == false), it shows the user how much of the FLV file has loaded by putting that value in the dynamic text box named progressTB. At the same time, the x location of the indicator (progressMC) and the width of the playProgressMC movieclip under the indicator are set.

The final bit of wiring that has to be done is to add the scrubbing functionality to the ProgressMC movieclip.

3. Press Return/Enter twice and enter the following code:

```
progressMC.buttonMode = true;

progressMC.addEventListener(MouseEvent.MOUSE_DOWN, ➡
progressMCMouseDownHandler);

function progressMCMouseDownHandler(event:MouseEvent):void {
  progressDragStatus = true;
  progressBounds = new Rectangle(65,355,loadProgressMC.width - 7,0);
  progressMC.startDrag(false,progressBounds);
  progressMC.blendMode = BlendMode.ADD;
  stage.addEventListener(MouseEvent.MOUSE_UP, ➡
progressMCMouseUpHandler);
  stage.addEventListener(MouseEvent.MOUSE_MOVE, ➡
progressMCMouseMoveHandle);
}
```

We start by switching the movieclip over to buttonMode, which means that it can now react to mouse events. The first event we will deal with is what happens when the mouse is down: MOUSE_DOWN.

The ProgressMC movieclip becomes draggable by changing its progressDragStatus value to true. We then set the constraints for the drag and turn off the drag value when the movieclip is at the edges of the rectangle. The next bit of functionality gives the user a visual indication that the movieclip is being dragged by changing its Blend mode to Add. The last two lines of the function deal with what happens if the mouse is not over the movieclip when it is pressed.

4. Let's finish the project by writing two final functions that deal with what happens when the user releases the mouse and moves the mouse to drag the movieclip right or left. Press Return/Enter twice and add the following:

```
function progressMCMouseUpHandler(event:MouseEvent):void {
  progressDragStatus = false;
  progressMC.stopDrag();
  progressMC.blendMode = BlendMode.NORMAL;
```

```
    stage.removeEventListener(MouseEvent.MOUSE_UP, ➥
progressMCMouseUpHandler);
    stage.removeEventListener(MouseEvent.MOUSE_MOVE, ➥
progressMCMouseMoveHandle);
}

function progressMCMouseMoveHandle(event:MouseEvent):void {
  my_ns.seek(videoDuration * (progressMC.x - 65) / 207);
  playProgressMC.width = (progressMC.x - 70 + 9);
}
```

5. Check your code. If there are no problems, save and test the movie. Try out the controls as shown in Figure 4-23. If you check the size of your SWF file, you are in for a rather pleasant surprise. You have packed all the functionality of the FLVPlayback component into a SWF file that weighs in at 13KB.

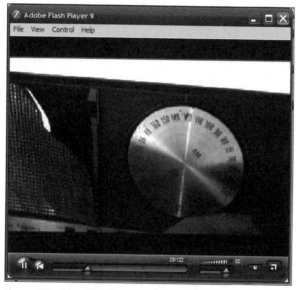

Figure 4-23. Congratulations. You have created a fully functioning video player.

What you've learned

This marks the end of the chapter and of this section of the book. We covered a lot of ground, and in many respects, this is one of the more important chapters in the book. It is all well and good to be able to create a video and convert it to an FLV file, but if you don't know how to play it using the tools available to you in Flash CS3 Professional, why bother?

In this chapter, you've learned how to do the following:

- Buffer a video
- Use the FLVPlayback custom UI components
- Use a Video object in Flash
- Use ActionScript to control a video
- Use ActionScript 3.0 to add components at runtime
- Create a Progress bar and use a Timer object
- Use Fireworks CS3 to create a custom video interface for Flash CS3
- Control video volume using ActionScript 3.0
- Create a Scrubber bar using ActionScript 3.0

We started off by reviewing the concept of streaming and buffering video by using the analogy of a dam upstream from a farming community. You learned the difference between publish and subscribe, how buffering a video works, and how to set the buffer time using ActionScript 3.0.

You then discovered how to build your own custom video controller using the FLVPlayback video control components and how to add them at runtime to the FLVPlayback component through ActionScript.

The last part of the chapter showed you how to connect and play a video through a Video object on the stage and stream it using ActionScript. As you saw, there was a major size reduction in the SWF file because the FLVPlayback component wasn't used. You also learned that streaming a video is a simple three-step process of connect, stream, and play.

The chapter ended by you creating a fully loaded custom video player from scratch. It also marks the end of this section of the book. If you were to stop here and go no further, you would have the basic skills necessary to create, encode, and deploy Flash video on your sites.

Now that you have the basics under control, turn the page and let's start seeing what we can do with your new skills. More importantly, let's spend the rest of the book having fun and getting very creative with video.

Chapter 5

"TALKING HEAD" VIDEO AND ALPHA CHANNELS

You have seen this technique used on your local television station's weather broadcast. The weatherman will stand in front of a radar image and start pointing out the features in the image that are important. If you were in the studio while all this is going on, it would be rather disconcerting. The weather broadcaster would be standing in front of a green or blue wall and pointing to it while delivering the broadcast. What happens is that he or she is looking at a monitor in which they are standing in front of the radar image "behind" them. The green (see Figure 5-1) or blue color is being "keyed out" of the signal and replaced with the radar image.

Figure 5-1. The "Talking Head" video. Note the green screen in the background.

What we'll cover in this chapter:

- Creating a video containing an Alpha channel in Premiere CS3, After Effects CS3, and Final Cut Pro
- Outputting an FLV file from After Effects CS3
- Trimming an FLV file
- Playing video-on-video
- Adding Alpha channel FLV files to a Text Box component
- Creating a video reflection
- Using Alpha video with HTML

Files used in this chapter:

- GSFOE.mov (Chapter05\ExerciseFiles_Ch05\Exercise\GSFOE.mov)
- Trim.fla (Chapter05\ExerciseFiles_Ch05\Exercise\Trim.fla)
- VidonVid.fla (Chapter05\ExerciseFiles_Ch05\Exercise\VideoOnVideo\VidonVid.fla)
- Trail2-Video1.fla (Chapter05\ExerciseFiles_Ch05\Exercise\VideoOnVideo\ Trail2-Video1.fla)
- TextVid.fla (Chapter05\ExerciseFiles_Ch05\ Exercise\VideoOverText\TextVid.fla)
- reflect.fla (Chapter05\ExerciseFiles_Ch05\ Exercise\Reflections\reflect.fla)
- video.html (Chapter05\ExerciseFiles_Ch05\ Exercise\VidOnHTML\video.html)

If you are familiar with creating masks in Photoshop or Fireworks you are quite familiar with "keying" video. You essentially target the color to be removed and then manipulate the edges and add a bit of feathering, which smooths out the transition between the subject and the background. Premiere, Final Cut Pro, and After Effects use plug-ins for this task.

In Figure 5-2, which is taken from Premiere, you can see the actual mask that is applied to the video. Anything within the black area will be masked. If you are a Photoshop CS3 user, you should be quite familiar with the look of a mask. Where this type of mask differs from that in an imaging application is that it moves. For example, if the subject were to lean to the right, the white area would change shape to accommodate the movement.

This is an important concept to grasp, especially in Flash CS3 Professional. If you place the video in a movieclip, you can attach a drop shadow, or any other Flash filter for

Figure 5-2. The mask that will be used to remove the green background

that matter, to the mask. The shadow will move and change shape in conjunction with the change in shape of the video mask.

This chapter lets you explore the topic of Alpha channels in Flash CS3 Professional. It is essentially divided into three distinct sections. The first section shows you how to add an Alpha channel to a green screen video using Adobe Premiere Pro CS3, Adobe After Effects CS3 on the Mac and PC, and Final Cut Pro on the Mac. The next section shows you how to encode it and use the video in a Flash movie, and the final section answers this question: "Yeah, that's interesting, but what can I really do with it?"

> *When Final Cut Pro started muscling out Adobe Premiere as the video editor of choice in the Macintosh universe, Adobe quietly retreated and offered only a PC version of Premiere. The release of the CS3 Studio marks the re-entry of Premiere onto the Macintosh platform.*

Creating an Alpha channel video with Adobe Premiere Pro CS3

The first thing you need to do is find out what you are working with. When creating video, it is important that the project settings match those in the source file, or else you will be setting yourself up for problems at a later date.

> *We want you to understand that this section falls into the category of "Beginner Tutorial." The process of keying video can be quite complex. In fact, entire chapters are devoted to this task in many of the video books on the market. Having said that, if you are familiar with the process, your first reaction will most likely be the following: "That ain't the way I would do it." It probably isn't, and in many respects it ain't the way we would do it, either. Still, our response will be, "We have to start somewhere," and this tutorial reviews the basic workflow involved.*

1. Open the GSFOE.mov file in QuickTime and select Window ➤ Show Movie Info.

The Info dialog box provides you with the information you will need to create the project file in Premiere. Notice that the movie is 320 x 240, which is a standard size for web video, and the frame rate is 24 frames per second (fps). The other bit of information you will need is the audio information. In this project, the audio is 16 bit at 44.1kHz.

2. Open Premiere and select New Project on the splash screen. Projects are wonderful documents because they "keep" your work (and any effects you might have applied to the project) intact. This is very handy when the client starts asking for changes.

3. When the New Project dialog box opens (see Figure 5-3), click the Custom Settings tab and use the following values:

- Editing Mode: Desktop
- Timeline: 24.00 frames/second
- Frame Size: 320 horizontal **and** 240 vertical
- Pixel Aspect Ratio: Square pixels (1.0)
- Sample Rate: 44100 Hz

In the Location area, target the folder you will be using to hold the project and the files used in the project and give the project a name. When finished, click OK.

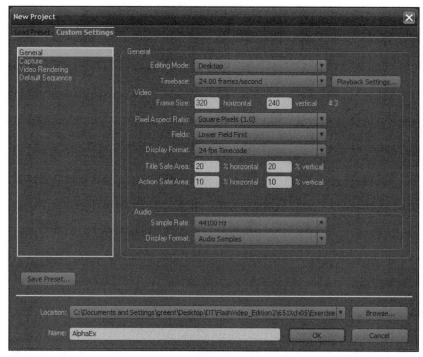

Figure 5-3. The project's preset format, location, and name are created.

Feel free to use the folder containing the files for this tutorial as your project folder. Regardless of what you do, don't change the folder's name or location after you create the project. Premiere stores a lot of the files associated with a project in this folder, and changing the name or the folder's location will break all the links to the files used in the project. If you must change the location, select Edit ➤ Preferences ➤ Scratch Disks (PC) or Premiere Pro ➤ Preferences ➤ Scratch Disks and navigate to the folder to be used.

4. When the Premiere workspace opens, select File ➤ Import and import the GSFOE.mov file into your project. When the file appears in the Project panel, select it and click the Play button to preview the video.

5. Drag the video from the Project panel to the Video 1 layer in the timeline. The video, shown in Figure 5-4, is now composed of an audio and a video layer, and the Monitor window opens.

Figure 5-4. Everything is ready to work on in the Premiere workspace.

With the video on the stage, take a close look at the green background in the Monitor window. You will notice that it really isn't a solid green. There are gradations of the color here and there in the background. The time you take to study the background is time well spent because it will determine which keying effect will be used. The filter used in this situation is the Color Key filter.

> Even though the clip was shot in a studio and lit properly to eliminate shadows, there are still variations in the lighting on the green background. This is quite common and you will see how the Color Key filter deals with it.

6. To start the process of keying out the green background, select Window ➤ Effects to open the Effects panel. As you will see, there are a lot of effects that come bundled with Premiere. Alternatively, if it is already visible, select the Effects tab.

7. Select Video Effects ➤ Keying ➤ Color Key in the Effects panel. With the plug-in selected, drag it from the Effects panel and drop it on top of the thumbnail in the Video 1 channel.

8. To open the Color Key Plug In settings, select Window ➤ Effect Controls or click the Effect Controls tab, as shown in Figure 5-5. As you make changes to the settings, they will be reflected in the image in the Monitor window. The window that opens contains four settings that you can adjust:

   ■ Key Color: You can choose a color to remove by selecting a color from the Color Picker or using the eyedropper to sample the color to be removed.

   ■ Color Tolerance: If you are familiar with the Magic Wand tool in Fireworks CS3 or Photoshop CS3, the tolerance chooses how wide a range of the selected color to remove.

- Edge Thin: This control expands or contracts the mask.
- Edge Feather: Does exactly what it says. The transition between the edge of the mask and the subject can be rather abrupt. This control adds a small amount of feathering to the edges of the mask to smooth things out.

Figure 5-5. Selecting the color to remove and using the Tolerance slider allows you to control the masked area.

9. Click and drag the eyedropper in the Key Color setting onto the green area of the clip in the Monitor window. You will notice that as you drag the eyedropper, some of the green area turns black, which indicates the color to be masked. Release the mouse to sample the color.

10. Drag the Color Tolerance slider to the right. As you drag, the black area expands. As you drag, pay particular attention to the hair and shoulders of the Talking Head. Try to remove as much green as possible. We found a value of 69 to be just about right.

11. Drag the Edge Thin slider to the right to "choke" the mask in order to remove the green edge. A value of about 3 seems to work because you run the risk of having a green fringe around the subject. This is called **spill** and is the reflection of the green background on the subject.

12. Drag the Feather slider to a value of about 1.1 to 1.5. When you remove the green, the edges of the Talking Head become pixelated. This slider adds a bit of feather to smooth out the edge.

> You don't have to use the sliders. Click and drag the values, the blue numbers, in the percentage area to change them. This is a neat trick, called **scrubbing**, but we suggest using the sliders until you are more comfortable with the application. You can also double-click the values and enter them directly.

Now that you have keyed out the green screen, you need to create the QuickTime file that will be used by the Flash Video 8 Encoder. Here's how:

1. Select File ➤ Export ➤ Movie. When the Export dialog box opens, navigate to the folder in which you will be saving the video, and, name the video TalkingHead (see Figure 5-6). Click the Settings button to open the Export Movie Settings dialog box, which is the key to successful completion of this exercise. This dialog box is where you choose the file type for the video and select the appropriate codec that will render the Alpha channel.

Figure 5-6. Name the movie, but don't click Save; click the Settings button instead.

2. Click the General category and select QuickTime from the list in the File Type drop-down menu. Also be sure to select the Export Video and Export Audio radio buttons. Clicking the Add to Project When Finished radio button ensures that you can return to these settings if changes are required after the video file is created. Select None in Embedding Options. Embedding a project in the file does nothing more than add to the metadata by letting QuickTime know that the video is part of a Premiere project.

3. Click the Video category. Select Animation as the codec and select Millions + of colors from the choices in the Color Depth drop-down menu (see Figure 5-7).

These two choices are the keys to creating a video with an Alpha channel. By selecting Millions + of colors from the Color Depth drop-down menu, you have included the Alpha channel created by the Green Screen Key filter in the video. Selecting Millions + of colors will create a video with a lot of color, but will result in the loss of the Alpha channel.

You can ignore the Audio portion of the Export Movie Settings dialog box because even though the audio file will be exported out of Premiere as a 44kHz 16-bit stereo audio track, it will be knocked back to mono when this video is eventually encoded.

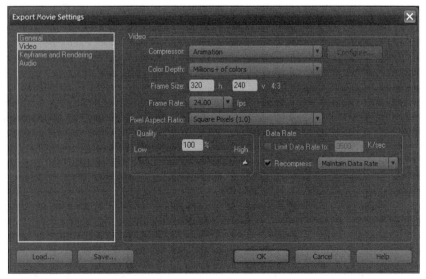

Figure 5-7. The key to retaining the Alpha channel is to select Millions + of colors from the Color Depth drop-down menu.

4. Click OK to close the Export Movie Settings dialog box. When you return to the Export Movie Settings dialog box, click Save. This will open a small dialog box showing you the progress of the compression. It will close when the compression is finished.

5. Select File ➤ Save to save the Premiere project file and quit Premiere.

If you open the video file in the QuickTime player, you are in for a bit of a surprise. The green screen is still there. Don't worry; the Alpha channel is there, too. This technique is most commonly used when "compositing" video. For example, you could overlay the Talking Head video over a video of a busy street and, if you were to play that video, you would see the subject talking and cars zooming by in the background. In the case of this video, the Alpha channel is definitely there, you just aren't using it. Yet.

Creating an Alpha channel video with Adobe After Effects CS3

After Effects is one serious video-editing application, and the things it can do with video are simply amazing. With the advent of Flash video, this application will become more and more important to our workflow, and giving you a full overview of what it can do for you is well out of the scope of this book. In fact, if you get so excited about how it can be used to key video, and you use it strictly for that purpose, you have made a mistake. It would be similar to using a Formula 1 race car to drive up to the corner store for milk or a lottery ticket.

Still, a lot of Flash developers use this application, and a lot of you are getting into working with video and are soon to be introduced to it. There are quite a few keying tools in After Effects; one of the most popular, for our purposes, is the Keylight filter. Talk to any video guy who uses After Effects—inevitably he or she will swing a keying conversation around to Keylight.

A custom version of the Keylight filter was introduced into version 6 of After Effects and is bundled with After Effects CS3. Just be aware that we won't be delving deeply into this filter's capabilities. In fact, we will only be scratching the surface of what it can do. Even so, you will be amazed at its power and ease of use.

Follow these steps to create an Alpha channel video using the Keylight filter:

1. Open After Effects and select Composition ➤ New Composition; or press Ctrl+N (PC) or Cmd+N (Mac). When the Composition Settings dialog box, shown in Figure 5-8, opens, enter these values:

   - Composition Name: FlashVidAlpha. This is a name for the composition.
   - Preset: Custom. We'll change a few things that aren't a part of the preset values.
   - Width: 320.
   - Height: 240.
   - Frame Rate: 24 Frames per second. This matches the frame rate of the clip we will be using.
   - Duration: 0:00:13:08. This is the duration of the clip being used.

2. Click OK and the After Effects workspace will open. Select File ➤ Import ➤ File and navigate to the GSFOE.mov file. Select it and click Open. When you do this, the clip is placed in the Project window (see Figure 5-9). Drag the video clip onto the timeline.

Figure 5-8. The composition settings used in this project

Figure 5-9. The Talking Head is on the timeline, and we can go to work.

3. Click once on the Composition window—it has the preview of the video—and select Effects Keying ➤ Keylight (1.2). This will open the Effect Controls window and show you the controls for the Keylight filter. Although there are a lot of items contained in this dialog box, we'll only concern ourselves with the Screen Colour control.

> What's with the spelling of the word "color" and "colour"? Keylight is produced by a British company, so the spelling of the word colour—using the Queen's English—is correct.

4. Click the eyedropper and move it over the green background behind the Talking Head. Click once; not only does all the green disappear but the color just sampled also appears in the Screen Colour color chip, as shown in Figure 5-10.

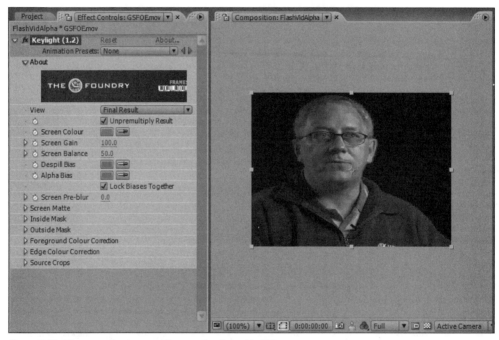

Figure 5-10. The green background is gone thanks to Keylight.

As it now stands, you can proceed to creating the MOV file with the mask. Still there are those of you who fall into the realm of "control freak," so before proceeding, let's satisfy the cravings of the control freaks and make things even better.

The control freak will look at the image and think, "Gee, I wonder if the mask is a good as we can get it?" Looking at the preview, you can easily answer, "Well, looks fine to me." Let's find out if the control freaks have a point.

5. In the View drop-down menu, select Status. The preview will change to show us the mask and it looks like the control freaks might have a point. The background should be a solid black, not the gray seen in the preview (see Figure 5-11). That gray indicates semitransparent pixels.

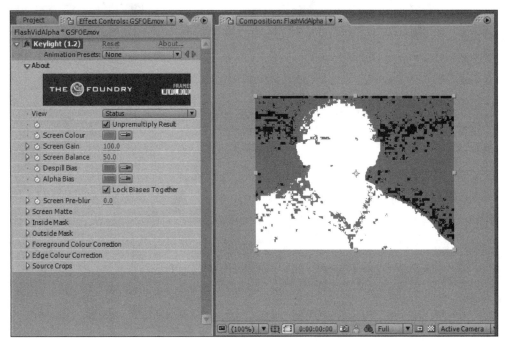

Figure 5-11. Score one for the control freaks: we didn't get all the green.

6. Click once on the arrow beside the Screen Gain setting. When the slider appears, drag it to the right. Keep an eye on the background. When it is completely black (at a value of about 118), release the mouse.

> *There is an After Effects gotcha here and it is a doozy. If you leave the view at* Status, *the video you see in Figure 5-12 is exactly what will be output. Be sure to change the View to* Final Result *before you create the QuickTime file.*
>
> *Don't just worry about the first frame of the video when adjusting the matte. Scrub through the timeline and you will discover areas of the matte that might actually require an increase in the value of the* Screen Gain *and other settings.*

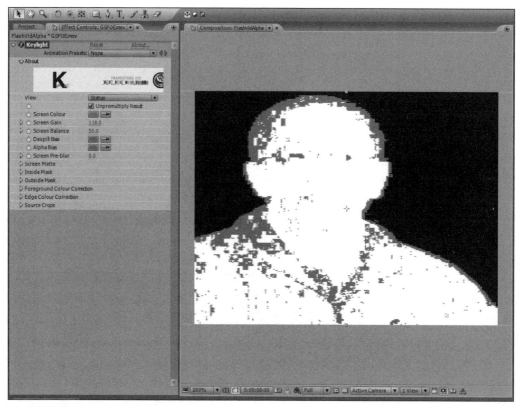

Figure 5-12. That's much better.

The control freaks will most likely ask, "Isn't a mask supposed to be black outside and white inside?" They have a point.

7. Click the Screen Matte twirly to open the Screen Matte properties. Click once on the Clip White value and drag the mouse to the left until a value of about 29 is showing. What clipping does is essentially change any pixel in the mask with a value higher than 0 to a value of 29.

Twirly? If you have lived in the Flash universe, there is some new terminology you have to learn. The drop-down menu triangles used to open properties in a panel or palette in some Adobe products has been given the name of **twirly** *by the users. When asked to open one of these menus, the process of clicking the twirly is actually called* **twirl down**. *Thus, if you are speaking to an Adobe user, you now know what the heck they are talking about when you are asked to twirl down the Screen Matte properties.*

If you see black pixels inside the matte, use the Clip Black slider to remove them.

---

8. Select the Combined Matte view and you will see that things have vastly improved. Still, a little attention should be paid to the edge of the mask. Select the Final Result view and you will notice that the subject is a bit pixilated on the edges. The first thing to do is to set the Clip Rollback value to about 0.7, which essentially tightens the mask and makes the edges crisper.

9. Set the Screen Softness to a value of about 1 and return to the Final Result view.

10. The mask is fine, but let's remove some of the green from the background that has "spilled" onto the subject's skin tones. Click the Despill Bias eyedropper and click a darker color on the subject's forehead. Notice that both the Alpha Bias and Despill Bias color chips pick up the color. If the effect is a bit strong, scrub the Screen Balance value to make things a bit more natural, as shown in Figure 5-13.

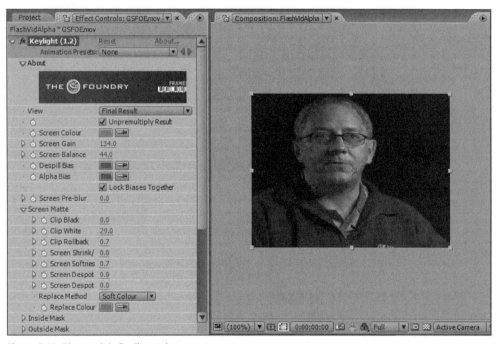

Figure 5-13. The mask is finally ready to go.

Now that the mask is vastly improved over the first effort, let's get this video created before the control freaks start looking for more improvements.

Creating the video is quite similar to what you did in the previous exercise. You'll still need to create a QuickTime video using the Animation codec that uses the Millions + of colors setting to save the Alpha channel. In After Effects, you don't merrily save the file. All that does is to create an AEP file that contains all the project settings. You have to render the composition by adding the project to the Render Queue. Here's how:

1. Click once on the Composition window and select Composition ➤ Add to Render Queue. The Render Queue dialog box opens (see Figure 5-14). If you are new to After Effects, this can be one scary and terribly confusing place. In actual fact, it is not all that difficult to master. All you need to do is to click the blue links.

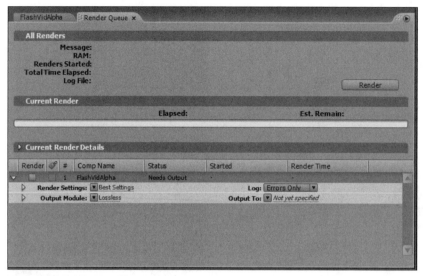

Figure 5-14. The Render Queue panel

2. Click the Best Settings link to open the Render Settings panel, which allows you to manually override the composition settings. We have no intention of doing that, so click OK to close this dialog box.

3. Click the Lossless link to open the Output Module Settings dialog box, which is where the real heavy lifting will be done. This dialog box is where you choose the final output and compression settings for the video.

> Another way of opening the Output Module Settings *dialog box is to click the twirly beside the* Lossless *link and select* Lossless with Alpha *from the drop-down menu.*

4. Click the Format drop-down menu and select QuickTime Movie. Now that we know what type of file we are outputting to, we can turn our attention to the Compression settings. They are found by clicking the Format Options button in the Video Output area or by selecting RGB+Alpha in the Channels drop-down menu. If you don't see the Animation codec under the Format Options button, click the Format Options button. This opens the Compression Settings dialog box shown in Figure 5-15. The key here is to choose the Animation codec with a color depth of Millions of Colors +. The plus sign indicates the Alpha channel.

Before you apply the Alpha mask, check with your video guys as to how they want the color handled. The Color *drop-down menu contains two settings:* Straight (Unmatted) *and* Premultiplied (Matted). *More often than not, the choice will be* Straight *even though the default is* Premultiplied.

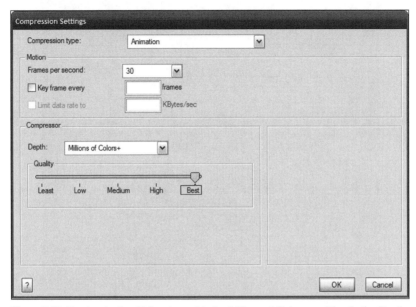

Figure 5-15. The key to the Alpha channel is the Millions of Colors + setting in the Depth drop-down menu.

5. When you click the Format Options button, the Compression Settings dialog box will open. Select Animation from the drop-down menu list at the top of the dialog box and select Millions of Colors + from the Color Depth drop-down menu. Leave the Quality slider at Best and don't change the frame rate. Click OK to close the Compression Settings dialog box and to return to the Output Module Settings dialog box. This will change to reflect the compression choices you just made.

6. Finally click the Audio Output check box (see Figure 5-16). If you don't select it, the audio won't be added to the video. Click OK to close the dialog box.

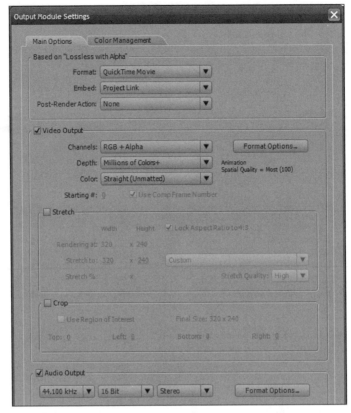

Figure 5-16. The output settings are good to go.

7. Now all you need to do is to create the MOV file. Click the Not yet specified link in the Output To area. This will open the Output to dialog box. Navigate to the folder where you want the video to be saved, name the file FlashVidAlpha.mov and click Save. Check your final render settings and, if everything is correct, click the Render button.

When the movie renders, you will be shown the progress of the process (see Figure 5-17). When it finishes, you will hear a chime. Close the Render dialog box and quit After Effects.

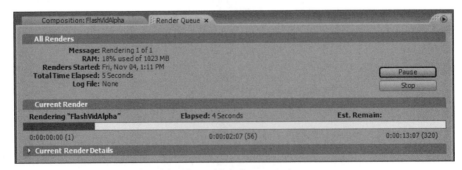

Figure 5-17. The video with the Alpha channel is being created.

Creating an FLV file directly out of After Effects CS3

New to After Effects CS3 is the capability to create the FLV file directly out of the Render Queue. This raises an obvious question: "Why bother going the QuickTime route if this puppy is destined for Flash?" Sometimes these things are edited yet again. For example, the video might be put over another video, or the background in Flash simply isn't working and it is decided that a return trip to After Effects is called for. The other reason lies squarely in the realm of Chapter 3. You might want to apply 2-pass VBR compression to the FLV file in Squeeze or Flix Pro. In this case, you need to output the QuickTime video.

Follow these steps to output an FLV file from After Effects:

1. In the Render Queue, select Adobe Flash Video in the Format drop-down menu of the Output Module dialog box. This will open the Adobe Flash Video dialog box shown in Figure 5-18.

Figure 5-18. The Adobe Flash Video dialog box in After Effects

In many respects, this dialog box is nothing more than an elongated version of the Flash CS3 Video Encoder.

2. Select Encode Alpha Channel in the Basic Video Settings area and set the Frame Rate [fps] to 24 frames per second.

125

3. Double-click the value in the Bitrate Settings and enter 300 to set the video's bitrate.

4. Click the Audio tab, select Mono in Basic Audio Settings and select 48 from the Bitrate [kbps] drop-down menu, as shown in Figure 5-19. Click OK to close the dialog box, to accept the changes, and to be returned to the Output Module Settings dialog box. Click OK once more to close the dialog box and return to the Render Queue.

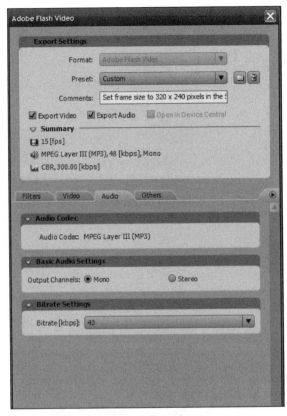

Figure 5-19. The Flash video audio settings

5. Now all you need to do is to create the FLV file. Click the Not yet specified link in the Output To area. This will open the Output to dialog box. Navigate to the folder where you want the video to be saved, name the file TalkingHead.flv and click Save. Check your final render settings and, if everything is correct, click the Render button.

Creating an Alpha channel video in Final Cut Pro

A few years back, Macromedia owned a video-editing product that just didn't seem to fit its product mix and corporate direction. Macromedia decided to sell it, and Apple bought the application. The application became Final Cut Pro. Since then, it has become a de factor video-editing standard among Macintosh users and video producers. It is also a feature-rich application and, like many Apple products, has a very shallow learning curve.

If you have a Mac, here's how to create an Alpha channel video using Final Cut Pro:

1. Open Final Cut Pro, create a New Project (select Cmd+Shift+N) and import the GSFOE.mov file into the project. Place the video on the timeline and drag the MOV file to the Viewer window.

2. Click the Effects tab in the Browser panel, select the Key folder to open it and drag a copy of the Color Key filter (shown in Figure 5-20) from the panel and drop it on the video on the timeline.

Figure 5-20. We are ready to get rid of the green.

3. Click the Filters tab in the Viewer window, and the Color Key settings will be available. This filter works very much like its counterpart in Premiere. Click the eyedropper in the Color area, roll the cursor over to the video in the Sequence panel, and click the mouse to sample the color to be removed.

When the color is selected, pay close attention to the green background. You might see nothing more than a faint black "smudge" when you make your selection. This means you have only grabbed a few pixels. Use the Tolerance, Edge Thin, and Edge Feather sliders to adjust the selection. We found that these settings, shown in Figure 5-21, worked for us:

- Tolerance = 33
- Edge Thin = 48
- Edge Feather = 4

127

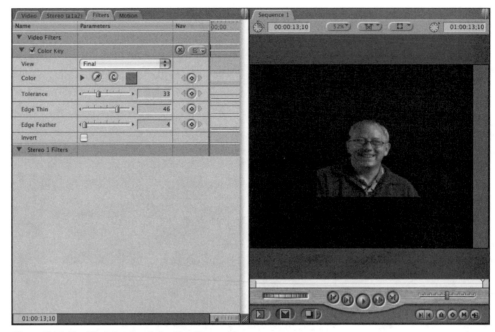

Figure 5-21. The Final Cut Pro Color Key filter settings

Just to be sure that you have everything, select Matte from the View drop-down menu. The screen will change to show you the mask, as shown in Figure 5-22. If there are any gray pixels in the background, adjust the sliders to remove them. When they vanish, return to the Final view.

Figure 5-22. The mask is looking good.

To export the movie and the Alpha channel, set the In and Out points to the start and end points of the video, respectively. Select File ➤ Export ➤ Using QuickTime Conversion. When the Save dialog box opens, give it a name and choose the location where the movie will be saved. Follow these steps to add the Alpha channel:

1. In the Save dialog box, click the Options button to open the Movie Settings dialog box. The Animation codec is found in the Settings area, so click the Settings button.

2. When the Standard Video Compression Settings dialog box opens (see Figure 5-23), select Animation from the Compression Type drop-down menu, select 24 from the Frame Rate drop-down menu, and select Automatic in the Key Frames section in the Motion area. The Alpha channel is found by opening the Depth drop-down menu in the Compressor section and selecting Millions of Colors +. While you are at it, drag the Quality slider to the Best setting. Click OK to close the dialog box.

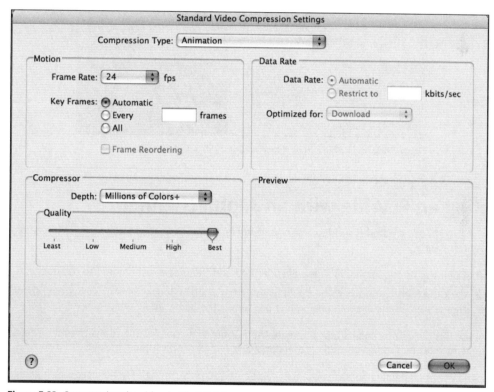

Figure 5-23. Compressing the video in Final Cut Pro

3. When you return to the Movie Settings dialog box, deselect Prepare for Internet Streaming. Flash will handle the duties here, so this selection is a bit redundant.

4. Click OK to return to the Save dialog box. Click the Save button to create the MOV file.

Here's something you might not have noticed when using After Effects or Final Cut Pro. In Final Cut Pro, Macromedia Flash Video (FLV), *as shown in Figure 5-24, is one of the options in the* Format *drop-down menu found in the* Save *dialog box. Unfortunately you can't export any footage to which you have attached an Alpha channel.*

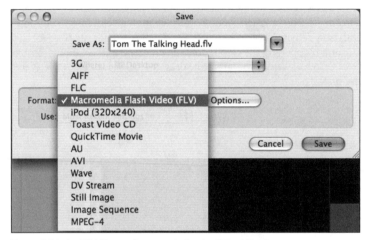

Figure 5-24. An FLV file can be exported out of Final Cut Pro.

Creating an FLV file with an Alpha channel

Now that you have created the video to be used in Flash, you have to create the FLV file containing the Alpha channel:

1. Open the Adobe Flash CS3 Video Encoder and add the movie just created to the queue.
2. Click the Settings button to be taken to the Flash Video Encoding Settings dialog box, shown in Figure 5-25. In the Output filename text box, enter the name TalkingHead.

You'll use this dialog box and its tabs to create the FLV file that contains the Alpha channel. There are a couple of rules regarding Flash CS3 Professional and FLV files with Alpha channels:

- FLV files containing an Alpha channel can be played only through Flash Player 8 or higher.
- Alpha channels can be added only to FLV files created using the On2 VP6 codec.
- You must tell Flash CS3 Professional to include the Alpha channel.

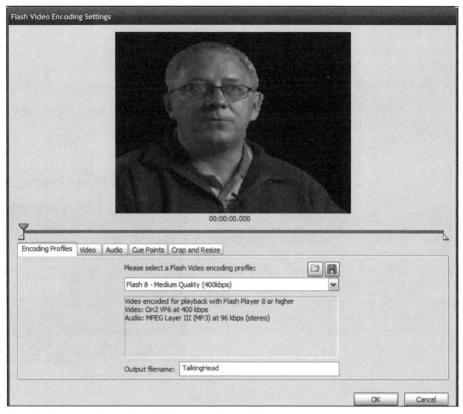

Figure 5-25. You need to select a Flash 8 encoding profile.

3. Click the Video tab to open the Video Encoding settings. When they open, click the Encode alpha channel radio button, shown in Figure 5-26, which is located under the Video codec drop-down menu. Also change the Max data rate to 300 kilobits per second and reduce the Frame rate to 15 fps.

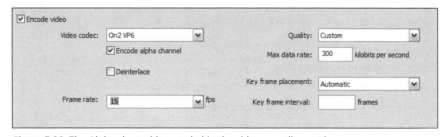

Figure 5-26. The Alpha channel is encoded in the video encoding settings.

4. Click OK to return to the Encoding Queue and click the Start Queue button to start the process. When it finishes, close the Encoder and open a new Flash ActionScript 3.0 document.

> Don't be shocked by the yo-yo file size of the original file. We started with a video that was 8.5 megs and wound up around 47 megs when the Alpha channel was added through the use of the lossless Animation codec. The FLV comes in at a paltry 1 meg because the file is encoded using a lossy codec. When it comes to Flash video encoding, aim for "massive in; small out."

5. Save the file to the same folder as the FLV file you just created. Add a layer to the movie and move it under the Video layer. Import an image into Flash and place it on this new layer.

6. Select the top layer and add a copy of the FLVPlayback component to the layer. In the component Parameters, set the source parameter to your FLV file and set the skin parameter to None.

7. Save the file and press Ctrl+Enter (PC) or Cmd+Return (Mac) to preview your Talking Head video, as shown in Figure 5-27.

Figure 5-27. Tom, the Talking Head

Playing with Alpha channel video in Flash

Okay, the dry stuff is out of the way. Now that you know how to create the channel, compress the video and create an FLV file containing the channel—in three separate video editing applications, we might add—you are probably asking, "That's really great, guys, but what the heck can I do with it?"

Turns out, you can do quite a lot. In order to keep this chapter focused, we won't cover everything you can do. Instead, we'll show you how to do a few things and leave you to look for even more creative ways to use the techniques. What are the techniques? We will be showing you these:

- How to trim a video and use it like a banner ad
- How to play video-on-video
- How to have video and scrollable text in the same SWF file
- How to use cue points in a video to trigger Flash events
- How to have someone "walk" across your web page in a browser

Trimming video

One of the pitfalls of working with video is that sometimes the actual video is either wider or higher than the Flash stage. For Flash control freaks, it can be a rather disconcerting situation. They like neat and tidy, and having a video hanging off the stage is neither neat nor tidy.

If you open `Trim.fla` you will notice that the stage dimensions are 700 pixels wide by 206 pixels high because the photo shows a bunch of "good old boys" hanging out in St. George's Square in Georgetown, Bermuda. The plan is to use some footage in which a young woman walks across the stage and stops to look at the guys on the bench. The problem is that the video's dimensions don't match those of the Flash stage. The video's width is 756 pixels. Here's how to fix that situation:

1. Open the Flash CS3 Video Encoder and add the betina.mov file to the Encoding Queue. When the video is added, click the Settings button, name the file betina.flv, and click the Video tab.

2. Make sure that you select the On2 VP6 codec and that you also click the Encode alpha channel check box. Now click the Crop and Resize tab.

The Crop area contains four sliders that control the cropping from the top, bottom, and two sides of the video. Knowing that the width needed is 700 pixels, you can't simply enter that value. You need to remove 56 pixels from the right edge of the video.

3. Double-click in the Text input box in the Right crop area and enter the value 56. You could use the slider for this, but it is rather imprecise. In fact it will take you longer to use the slider than to simply enter the value.

If you scrub across the timeline of the file, you will notice that Betina is off-screen on the left side of the video, and there is a lot of wasted space at the top of the FLV file. Here's how to fix it:

4. Drag the In point slider toward the right until the time code reads about 1.644 seconds. It is the point just slightly before she enters the stage.

5. Scrub the playback head until Betina is in the middle of the screen. In the Crop area, drag the Top slider down until you see a value of between 63 and 65, as shown in Figure 5-28.

6. Click OK. When you return to the Encoder dialog box, click the Start Queue button to create the FLV file.

> *Don't enter the value and then press* Return/Enter *if you want to make further changes to the file. As soon as a value is entered, it is accepted. Pressing* Return/Enter *is the same as clicking the* OK *button, which returns you to the* Encoding Queue.

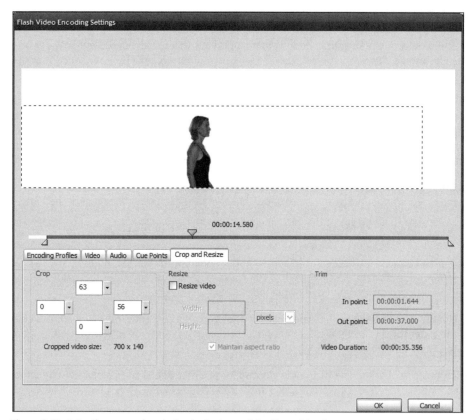

Figure 5-28. Enter the crop values instead of using a slider if precision is paramount.

Now that the FLV file has been cropped, return to Flash and add a new layer. Toss an FLVPlayback component into that layer and link it to the FLV file just created. Select the component on the stage and, in the Property Inspector make sure that the X value = 0 and that the Y value = 65. (Remember, the stage is 65 pixels higher than the video height.) After you have done that, save the movie and test it. As shown in Figure 5-29, Betina will walk across the stage and check out the good old boys.

Figure 5-29. Checking out the good old boys in Bermuda

Video-on-video

Although we have been able to accomplish this "trick" since the advent of Flash MX and the Progressive Download method, it is even simpler to accomplish in Flash CS3 Professional. The inclusion of Alpha channels kicks out the proverbial "creative jams." Need a Talking Head to extol the virtues of a new car model? No problem. Let him talk away while the car is ripping through a race course behind him. Need a Talking Head to discuss the various new features of the product? No problem. You can swap videos depending on what feature is being presented.

The only caution is, don't go crazy. Videos suck up bandwidth and processing on the user's computer. Keep it simple, and the viewer's experience will be positive. Go crazy and toss in a bunch of videos, and the user will not be thanking you for the rather unpleasant experience that awaits.

In this exercise, Betina walks across the stage and then something in the movie trailer playing behind her catches her attention.

1. Open the VidonVid.fla file in your Chapter 5 exercise folder. We have already included a background image and slot for the video. Add two new layers.

2. Select Layer 2 and add an FLVPLayback component to the stage. Click the Parameters tab and link the component to Trail2-Video1.flv. Place the component over the black square in the background image.

3. Select Layer 3 and drag the component from the library to the stage. Link this component of the betina.flv file in your exercise folder. Place the component right at the bottom of the stage, being sure to set its Y value to 160 in the Property Inspector.

4. Test the movie. Betina will walk across the stage, pause to look at the video playing behind her and move off the stage (see Figure 5-30).

Figure 5-30. Video-on-video is now easy to accomplish.

Alpha channel video and scrollable text

Here's a little trick that really works well with Alpha channel video.

1. Open the TextVid.fla file in the Chapter 5 exercise folder. If you test the movie, you will see that we have placed a TextArea component, with some scrollable text, on the stage along with a video of a lady swishing her skirt. You can scroll the text.

2. Drag the video over the text box and test the movie. Notice that the scroll bar isn't accessible to you (see Figure 5-31) because even though the background of the video is keyed out, Flash still regards the video as a solid object.

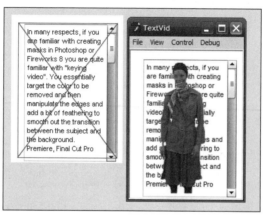

Figure 5-31. The scroll bar is useless when a video is over it.

3. Select the TextArea component on the stage and select the Free Transform tool from the Toolbar. Move the registration point to the middle handle on the left edge of the TextArea component.

4. Drag the right-middle handle of the component to resize the text box. When the scroll bar is just outside the right edge of the component (the scroll bar is to the right of the big x in the Video object), release the mouse.

5. Test the movie. The scroll bar now responds as it should, and the really interesting aspect is that the video, shown in Figure 5-32, appears to be a part of the text box.

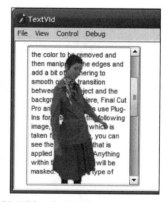

Figure 5-32. Widen the TextBox component, and the text becomes scrollable.

Reflections on an Alpha video theme

This technique was originally presented in the book *From After Effects to Flash: Poetry in Motion Graphics*, published by friends of ED. And whenever one of the authors demonstrates it at workshops and conferences, it never fails to get the audience enthused. We are bringing it back in this section because it has everything to do with the subject of Flash video. More importantly, things changed with the introduction of ActionScript 3.0. Let's create a reflection:

1. Inside the Reflections folder of your Chapter 5 exercise files is a Flash file named reflect.fla. Open it.
2. Open the library and add a new Video object to the library.
3. Create a new movieclip named Video, and when the Symbol editor opens, add a new layer to the timeline. Name the top layer Actions and the bottom layer Video.
4. Select the Video layer and drag the Video object from the library to the stage.
5. With the Video object selected on the stage, enter the following values to the Property Inspector:
   - W: 160
   - H: 210
   - X: 0
   - Y: 0
   - Instance name: myVideo

The object now has the same dimensions as the FLV file that will be used, and the object is tucked up against the upper-left corner of the stage in the movieclip.

6. Select the first frame in the Actions layer, open the Actions panel, and enter the following code:

```
var nc:NetConnection = new NetConnection();
nc.connect(null);
var ns:NetStream = new NetStream(nc);
myVideo.attachNetStream(ns);

var listener:Object = new Object();
listener.onMetaData = function(md:Object):void{};
ns.client = listener;

ns.play("Reflect.flv");
```

Nothing new here. You create the connection and the stream, hook the stream into the video object, tell Flash to ignore the metadata, and add the FLV file to the stream.

Now that you have the video in place, you can turn your attention to creating the reflection.

Even though Flash does not contain this feature, you can still apply a gradient mask to the video. Keep in mind that you can't create a gradient, add it to a masking layer, and use it to mask the movieclip containing the video. Won't work.

For this effect to work, the gradient must be applied using the mask property of the DisplayObject class, and both the gradient movieclip and the movieclip containing the video to be masked must have their cacheAsBitmap properties set to true.

If you add a movieclip to the stage you will see a Use runtime bitmap caching selection item in the Property Inspector. If you select this option, any vectors in the movieclip will be drawn to a bitmap instead of the Flash stage. The upshot is improved performance of the Flash movie. Although used primarily for content that doesn't move around the stage, it is a prerequisite in this case. Both the movieclip being masked and the one containing the mask must use bitmap caching.

Still, don't get hooked on bitmap caching in Flash. If you have movieclips that change between frames or otherwise move, don't use the feature because the time taken to draw the bitmaps in every frame can actually make the SWF file perform more slowly than if it weren't applied.

> *If you do use bitmap caching, be aware that it can be used only in the Flash Player 8 or higher.*

This option can be used in one of two ways: either by selecting the movieclip on the stage and selecting the bitmap caching option in the Property Inspector or through ActionScript.

To start, we are going to create the gradient that will be used as the reflection. Here's how:

1. Create a new movieclip named Gradient.

2. When the Symbol editor opens, select the Rectangle tool and draw a rectangle on the stage.

3. Click once on the rectangle; in the Property Inspector, turn off the stroke.

4. Set the Width property to 160 pixels and the Height to 210 pixels. Finally, set the location of the rectangle to 0,0 in the Property Inspector.

5. Select Window ➤ Color Mixer to open the Color Mixer panel. When it opens, click once on the rectangle on the stage to select it. In the Color Mixer select Linear from the Type drop-down menu. The rectangle will fill with the gradient.

6. Click once on the black crayon in the Color Mixer (the black and white sliders you see above the gradient in the Color Mixer really are called **crayons**) and change the Alpha value to 50%. Do the same thing with the white crayon, but set its Alpha value to 0%. Don't worry about the black crayon turning gray; it represents the Alpha gradation value (see Figure 5-33).

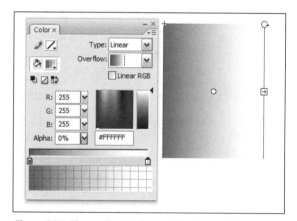

Figure 5-33. The gradient to be used in the mask is created.

7. Switch to the Gradient Transform tool and click once on the rectangle on the stage. Drag the rotate handle in a clockwise direction and release the mouse when the solid area of the gradient is at the top of the object.

8. Click the Scene 1 link to return to the main timeline. Save the file.

What you have done so far is to construct the elements to be used in the movie. The next step is to assemble the elements to create the effect.

1. Create a new movieclip named Reflect. When the Symbol editor opens, add three new layers and name them (from the top down) Actions, Video, Mask, and Reflect.

2. Select the Video layer and drag a copy of the Video movieclip from the library to the stage. In the Property Inspector, set its X and Y position to 0,0. Give it the instance name of mcVideo and lock the layer.

3. Select the Reflect layer and drag a copy of the Video movieclip to the stage. In the Property Inspector, set its X position to 0 and its Y position to 210. Give it the instance name of mcReflect.

4. Select the movieclip in the Reflect layer and select Modify ➤ Transform ➤ Flip Vertical. You won't see anything happen on the stage, but this selection essentially turns the movieclip upside down. Lock the layer.

5. Select the Mask layer and drag a copy of the Gradient movieclip to the stage. Set its position to 0,210 and give it the instance name of mcGradient. If your screen resembles that shown in Figure 5-34, you are ready to "wire it up" with ActionScript.

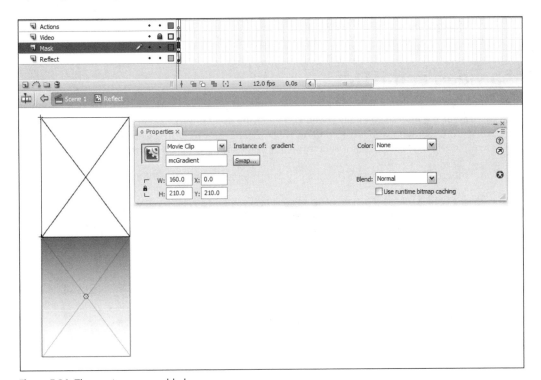

Figure 5-34. The assets are assembled.

Surprisingly, the ActionScript required to make this thing work is not complicated. In fact, it consists of three lines of code. You need two lines of code that set the cacheAsBitmap property for the gradient and the video under the gradient. The third line creates the mask.

6. Click once in the first frame of the Actions layer, open the ActionScript editor, and enter the following code:

```
mcGradient.cacheAsBitmap = true;
mcReflect.cacheAsBitmap = true;
mcReflect.mask = mcGradient;
```

The code is pretty self-explanatory. The last line is where the magic happens. The mask property is applied to the movieclip under the gradient and the calling display object (mcReflect) is masked by the specified mask object mcGradient.

There are a couple of things you need to know about using the mask property. The first thing is that you can't have a movieclip mask itself. The second thing is that if you use this technique in a movieclip that is being used as the mask in a masking layer, the mask property takes priority over the layer mask. Finally, if you want to turn the mask off, the code is mcReflect.mask = null;.

7. Click the Scene 1 link to return to the main timeline and set the stage color to #000000 (Black).

8. Drag the Reflect movieclip to the stage, set the X and Y values to 0,0 and test the movie. The girl fades out, as shown in Figure 5-35.

Figure 5-35. Creating a reflection in Flash

Alpha video and HTML

Although all the hype around Alpha video seems to be centered on Flash, you can also use an Alpha video in a rather creative manner on a web page. Having someone or something walk across a web page, or even interact with web page content, is something sure to grab a viewer's attention. It really isn't as hard as you might think. All it requires is for you to think a bit differently.

When you embed a SWF file in an HTML page, you can expect to see the following:

```
<object classid="clsid:D27CDB6E-AE6D-11cf-96B8-444553540000"➥
codebase="http://download.macromedia.com/pub/shockwave/cabs/➥
flash/swflash.cab#version=7,0,19,0" width="400" height="400">
  <param name="movie" value="file:///C|/Inetpub/wwwroot/➥
tomontheweb4.ca/FLVPlayer_Progressive.swf" />
  <param name="quality" value="high" />
  <embed src="file:///C|/Inetpub/wwwroot/tomontheweb4.ca➥
/FLVPlayer_Progressive.swf" quality="high" pluginspage=➥
"http://www.macromedia.com/go/getflashplayer" type="application➥
/x-shockwave-flash" width="400" height="400"></embed>
</object>
```

The Object and Embed tags simply tell the browser how to handle the SWF file, which SWF file to use, where the SWF file is located, and the dimensions of the SWF file. The important feature of the Object tag is the capability to add parameters or conditions to the content enclosed in the tag. Also, the use of layers in Semantic markup or CSS allows you to place content in a specific location on the web page and to then place that content above the content it covers through the use of an absolutely positioned div.

Instead of getting into a long and involved discussion about how to create CSS web pages or use a visual web page editor such as Dreamweaver CS3, let's dissect an example to see how this can be done.

1. Open the VidonHTML folder.

2. Open the HTML page named video.html in a browser. You will see Betina walk across an image in the page when you click the play button in the SWF file (see Figure 5-36).

Open the code view in your browser or, if you have a visual HTML editor such as Dreamweaver CS3, open the HTML page in the editor and then open Code view.

The first thing you will notice at the top of the code is a div named #videoLayer containing the following code:

```
#videoLayer {
    position:absolute;
    width:700px;
    height:204px;
    z-index:1;
    top: 314px;
    left: 9px;
    }
```

All this code says is to create a div named videoLayer that contains a bunch of attributes. The position attribute ensures that the layer is always in a fixed position on the page. The width and height attributes tell the browser the size of the div (which, incidentally, are the same measurements as the SWF file). The z-index attribute simply tells the browser that this div is sitting above the page and that the top of the div is 314 pixels from the top of the page and the left edge of the div is located 9 pixels from the left edge of the page. Although this might sound complex, all it does is to create an empty box that sits above the page.

If you scroll down the code you will see that the content is placed into the box and the content below it is visible through the SWF file. The code block you are looking for contains the following:

```
<div id="videoLayer">
  <script type="text/javascript"> AC_FL_RunContent('codebase',➡
  'http://download.macromedia.com/pub/shockwave/cabs/flash/➡
  swflash.cab#version=9,0,28,0','width','700','height','203','id',➡
  'FLVPlayer','src','FLVPlayer_Progressive','flashvars','&MM➡
  _ComponentVersion=1&skinName=Clear_Skin_1&streamName=betina&autoPlay=➡
  true&autoRewind=true','quality','high','scale','noscale','name',➡
  'FLVPlayer','salign','lt','pluginspage','http://www.macromedia.com/➡
```

```
go/getflashplayer','wmode','transparent','movie',➡
'FLVPlayer_Progressive'); //end AC code
 </script>
 <noscript>
   <object classid="clsid:D27CDB6E-AE6D-11cf-96B8-444553540000"➡
codebase="http://download.macromedia.com/pub/shockwave/cabs/flash/➡
swflash.cab#version=9,0,28,0" width="700" height="203" id="FLVPlayer">
       <param name="movie" value="FLVPlayer_Progressive.swf" />
       <param name="salign" value="lt" />
       <param name="quality" value="high" />
       <param name="scale" value="noscale" />
       <param name="wmode" value="transparent" />
       <param name="FlashVars"value="&MM_ComponentVersion=1&skinName=➡
Clear_Skin_1&streamName=betina&autoPlay=true&autoRewind=true" />
       <embed src="FLVPlayer_Progressive.swf" flashvars=➡
"&MM_ComponentVersion=1&skinName=Clear_Skin_1&streamName=betina&➡
autoPlay=true&autoRewind=true" quality="high" scale="noscale"➡
width="700" height="203" name="FLVPlayer" salign="LT" type=➡
"application/x-shockwave-flash" pluginspage="http://www.adobe.com/➡
shockwave/download/download.cgi?P1_Prod_Version=ShockwaveFlash"➡
wmode="transparent" />
   </object>
 </noscript>
</div>
```

This is a lot simpler than it first appears.

The code starts by placing the SWF file into the div named videoLayer. When a SWF file gets placed into a web page, it is placed between Object and Embed tags, which the browsers use to read SWF file content.

The key to this exercise can be found in the parameters, which have both a name and a value. So let's start with the parameters between the Object tags. The first one says to use FLVPlayer_Progressive. swf to play the FLV file using the Progressive Download method. The next parameter tells the browser to place the SWF file in the top-left corner of the div.

The next two parameters are not terribly complex. They tell the browser that the FLV file will be played using the high quality setting and that the SWF file can't be scaled if the page is made larger or smaller.

The key to this exercise is the next parameter, wmode, which determines how the window in which the SWF file appears is treated. By setting the wmode to transparent you are essentially making the background that would normally be found in a window invisible. If the value were not set to transparent, the video would appear over the image as a big black box, which defeats the purpose of the exercise. The final cluster of parameters and values tells the SWF file which skin is being used for the controller, the name of the stream, to turn on auto play, and to rewind the video when it finishes. See Figure 5-36.

wmode *set to* transparent *has been widely documented online as buggy. There's a good list of gotchas on Justin Everett-Church's blog at* http://justin.everett-church.com/index.php/2006/02/23/wmode-woes/.

Don't be deathly afraid of wmode, *but know its limitations. Again, for what it's worth, SWF files can be stacked with* wmod *set to* opaque. *Although that would defeat the purpose in this case, it is an option, and* opaque *is generally agreed to be less hazardous than* transparent.

One of the most apparent gotchas about transparent *is that HTML hyperlinks behind the video don't respond while the SWF file is present, even though they can be seen—unless you're in Internet Explorer. But the others in Justin's blog are worth noting.*

Figure 5-36. Alpha channel video can be placed over content on a web page.

What you've learned

The ability to use video containing an Alpha channel is a major new addition to the Flash video lineup, and by now you should have a sense of the possibilities available to you if you use it in your Flash movies. In this chapter you discovered the following:

- How to create an Alpha channel video in a video editor
- The use of the new FLV file output feature of After Effects CS3
- How to trim video
- The nuances of playing video-over-video
- A way of having an Alpha video interact with a Flash component on the stage
- How to create reflected video
- A method for having an FLV file exist in an HTML space

143

Also, you now know a few ways of creating the QuickTime videos that contain the Alpha channels and that the key, regardless of video editing package, is to use the Animation codec with Millions + colors (the + is the Alpha channel). You should also be aware that you won't get the effect if you don't select Encode Alpha Channel in the Advanced Options area of the Flash CS3 Video Encoder. Keep in mind, as well, that the only video that can contain an Alpha channel is one encoded using the On2 VP6 codec, and that Alpha channel video can be played only through the Flash Player 8. If your target is Flash Player 7, you are essentially out of luck.

Although we showed you a number of things you can do with video-on-video—backgrounds and so on—it is just the tip of the iceberg. Why play video-over-video? Why not play video over a Flash animation in a movieclip? Why play a video over an image on a web page? Why not have it play over text or—even better—interact with another SWF file on the page? All we have done is to demonstrate some fundamentals. Your job is to take those fundamentals and drive a truck through them. Your only limit is the limit you place on your creativity.

Speaking of creativity, the amount of fun you can have with Flash filters, blend effects, and video should be illegal. How illegal?

Turn the page to find out.

Chapter 6

ADDING FILTERS AND BLEND EFFECTS TO FLASH VIDEO

In this chapter, we step away from straight video playback and explore the creative side of Flash video. When a video is on the stage, it really is no different from a red box you would draw on the stage, for example. What a video and a box have in common is that they have properties that can be manipulated. They have position, size, color, rotation, and so on that can all be manipulated when a video is in a movieclip.

In Flash CS3, you have access to the filters and the blend effects introduced in Flash 8. Couple them with the things you can already do with movieclips in Flash, and you have a never-ending series of possibilities.

What we'll cover in this chapter:

- Creating simple video effects
- Applying a filter to a video
- Applying a blend mode to a video
- Using ActionScript to add filters and blend modes to a video

Files used in this chapter:

- Effects.fla (Chapter06\ExerciseFiles_Ch06\Exercise\Effects.fla)
- Filters.fla (Chapter06\ExerciseFiles_Ch06\Exercise\Filters.fla)
- Filters2.fla (Chapter06\ExerciseFiles_Ch06\Exercise\Filters2.fla)

- Bikes.flv (Chapter06\ExerciseFiles_Ch06\Exercise\Bikes.flv)
- betina.flv (Chapter06\ExerciseFiles_Ch06\Exercise\betina.flv)
- BlurIt.fla (Chapter06\ExerciseFiles_Ch06\Exercise\BlurIt.fla)
- FilterButtons.fla (Chapter06\ExerciseFiles_Ch06\Exercise\FilterButtons.fla)
- PlasmaTV.flv (Chapter06\ExerciseFiles_Ch06\Exercise\PlasmaTV.flv)
- BlendButtons.fla (Chapter06\ExerciseFiles_Ch06\Exercise\BlendButtons.fla)
- Apple.flv (Chapter06\ExerciseFiles_Ch06\Exercise\Apple.flv)

Video trick #1: The "point-of-light" effect

This one is sort of a throwback to the early days of television. Your parents or grandparents would turn on the television, and the picture would grow out from the center of the screen.

1. Open the Effects.fla file found in your Chapter 6 exercise folder. If you examine the library, you will see that we have placed an FLVPlayback component into a movieclip. The FLVPlayback component is linked to the Bikes.flv file in the Lesson folder.

> The Bikes.flv *file is from a video done by a student of one of the authors, Kyle Crockard. The video is included as a sort of acknowledgment to Hoss Gifford, who wrote the predecessor of this book,* Flash MX Video, *for friends of ED. Besides being one of the most creative and dynamic Flash artists on the planet, Gifford is also a partner in a BMX bike and clothing store in Glasgow, Scotland.*

2. Select frame 36 of the timeline and add a key frame.

3. Select the movieclip in frame 1 and select Modify ➤ Transform ➤ Scale and Rotate. When the Scale and Rotate dialog box opens, set the scale amount to 3%. Click OK.

4. Click once on the timeline between the key frames and, in the Property Inspector, select Motion from the Tween drop-down menu. You could also right-click (PC) or Ctrl+click (Mac) between the two key frames and select Motion Tween from the resulting context menu.

5. Save the file and test the movie. The video, shown in Figure 6-1, seems to grow out of the center of the screen.

Figure 6-1. The video is at the halfway point.

Video trick #2: The "ghost-in-the-machine" effect

Another movieclip property that can be used to great effect is the Alpha property. Set it to a low value; the object inside the movieclip becomes transparent. This means you can use an Alpha tween to actually fade a video in and out. For example, you can use a fade-in as a transition between videos or at the beginning or end of one video. You can also use this effect to give the appearance of a "sputtering" video that seems to flicker. This is quite commonly used in games and so on.

This one is dead simple to do. Simply place the FLVPlayback component in a movieclip and connect it to an FLV file. The movieclip is then placed on the stage, and a key frame is added at frame 36, for example. Select the movieclip on the stage in frame 1 and select Color ➤ Alpha in the Property Inspector. Reduce the Alpha value to 5% when the Alpha dialog box appears. Click anywhere between the two key frames and add a Motion tween. When you test the video, it will appear to fade in.

The "stuttering video" effect is a variation on this theme:

1. Open the video you just worked on and add several key frames, as shown in Figure 6-2.

2. Move the playback head over each key frame, select the video on the stage, and either increase or reduce its Alpha value.

3. Test the movie and it will look like the video is fading in and out (see Figure 6-2).

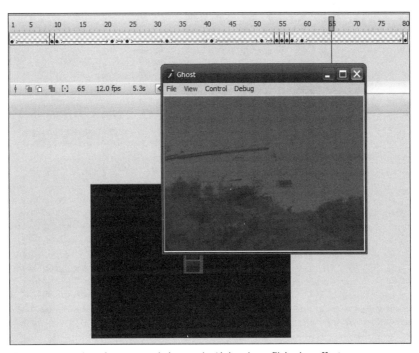

Figure 6-2. A series of tweens and changes in Alpha give a flickering effect.

Video trick #3: Somebody fix the dang color!

This one gives the impression of a color TV that is about to fail. The color keeps changing and finally stabilizes.

1. Open your movie and then remove the tweens and key frames between the first and last frame of the movie. Add key frames at frames 15, 25, 35, 45, and 60.

2. Select the movieclip on the stage in frame 15. In the Color area of the Property Inspector set the Color property to Tint, the color in the Color chip to red, and the percentage value to 65% (see Figure 6-3).

This procedure adds a serious amount of red to the content in the movieclip. The percentage value is critical because at 100%, the movieclip containing the video looks like a red rectangle, which sort of defeats the purpose of the effect. Still, feel free to experiment with various opacity values.

3. Repeat step 2 for each of the key frames at frames 25, 35, and 45. This time choose different colors and opacities. Save and test the movie. The color you apply will affect the entire video, giving the effect of the video changing color.

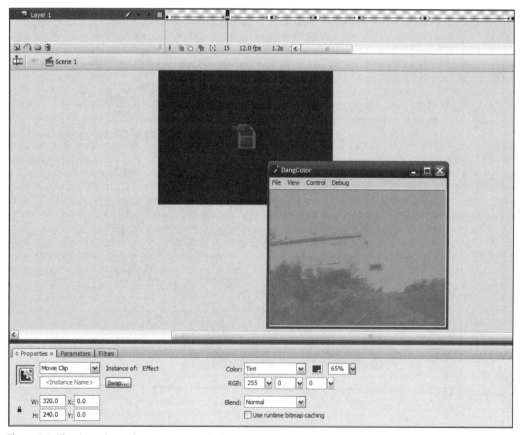

Figure 6-3. The tint color and percentage applied to the movieclip gives the video a rather odd look.

Filters and Flash video

When Flash Professional 8 was still being tested, Chris Georgenes (at Mudbubble) did a small animation of a monkey on a swing to demonstrate how the various filters and blend effects can be applied to movieclips. When we saw it, we thought, "Hmmm, wonder if this works for video as well?"

It does, and the results can be quite spectacular. The filters and blend effects are new to Flash, and if you are familiar with Photoshop or Fireworks, the odds are quite good that you have been exposed to them.

The first thing to understand about the filters in Flash CS3 Professional is they can be applied only to movieclips, buttons, and text. If you select the FLVPlayback component on the stage and then select the Filters tab of the Property Inspector, you will discover that they are unavailable because, technically, the component is not a movieclip.

The easiest way to put the component into a movieclip is to simply drag a copy of the component on the stage, select it, right-click (PC) or Cmd+click (Mac) on the clip, and select Convert to Symbol from the context menu. When the Symbol dialog box opens, name the clip and select the movieclip behavior. After you click OK, the component will be on the stage, but it will be contained in a movieclip in your library.

With the movieclip selected on the stage, you can now click the Filters tab of the Property Inspector, and the + sign won't be grayed-out. Select it, and the drop-down menu shown in Figure 6-4 presents you with a number of choices, ranging from Drop Shadow to Adjust Color.

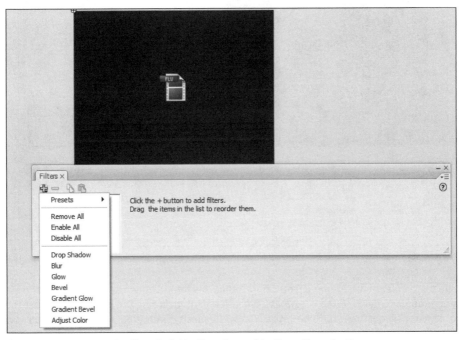

Figure 6-4. You can use the filters individually or in combination with each other.

> *We'll demonstrate several rather interesting effects you can create with filters and blend modes. Just be aware that these effects can be quite processor-intensive for the viewer, so use them judiciously.*

In this first example, we'll go back to the 1940s and convert a video to a black-and-white movie.

1. Open the Filters.fla file from the Chapter 6 exercise folder.

2. Select the FLVPlayback component and set the source in the Parameters to the Bikes.flv file in the exercise folder.

3. With the component selected on the stage, convert it to a movieclip named Video.

4. Select the movieclip and click the Filters tab in the Property Inspector. Click the + sign and select Adjust Color from the drop-down menu.

5. When the Adjust Color menu appears, move the Saturation slider all the way to the left. The value will be –100. When you do this, the red Flash icon in the component will turn gray, as shown in Figure 6-5.

6. Test the movie.

Figure 6-5. The Adjust Color filter has been used to turn a color video into a black-and-white video.

Although this is an extreme example, you can see that this filter can be used to "clean up" a video. If the video is too dark, increase the brightness. If it is too light, decrease the brightness. Adjust the contrast to increase or decrease the contrast of adjacent pixels. Saturation increases or decreases the color intensity of the pixels in the video, and the Hue slider can be used to change the color.

> *Be aware that you are "flying blind" when you use this filter. You can't see the effect of the selection until you test the movie.*

Alpha channel video is where the effects really offer some potential. Filters are applied to the content in the movieclip; with an Alpha channel video, that content is the image inside the mask, so filters can be applied to the mask shape surrounding the content.

1. Open the Filters2.fla file. When the movie opens, notice that the FLVPlayback component has been placed above the screen shot of the FlashinTO web site. The FLV file attached to the component is the Betina video used in the previous chapter. Obviously, Betina is going to take a stroll across the web page.

2. Select the video on the stage and convert it to a movieclip named Video.

3. With the video selected on the stage, open the Filters panel and select the Drop Shadow effect from the drop-down menu. Notice that you have quite a few choices. The second thing to notice is that the movieclip on the stage seems to have developed a drop shadow. Don't pay attention to it.

> *Flash is a panel-based interface. This means the* Property Inspector *is a panel, and clicking a tab in the* Property Inspector *opens a panel, not a tab.*

The Drop Shadow selections are as follows:

- Blur X: This slider determines the horizontal spread of the shadow.
- Blur Y: This slider determines the vertical spread of the shadow.
- Strength: This slider is more of an opacity slider. A value of 100% means that the shadow is full intensity and hides anything behind it.
- Quality: The three choices (Low, Medium, and High) determine the quality of the shadow and the feathering on the edges of the shadow.
- Color: Click this option to choose the color for the shadow.
- Angle: This "knob" lets you determine the source of the lighting that causes the shadow.
- Distance: This slider allows you to determine the offset, in pixels, between the object and the shadow.
- Knockout: Select this option to knock the subject out of the shadow. It is a really neat effect because the subject is gone, resulting in a shadow that can be moved around. Sort of like a ghost.
- Inner shadow: Select this option to apply the shadow inside the subject.
- Hide object: Select this option and only the shadow is visible. If you can visualize the object not obscuring the shadow, you understand what a knockout does.

Now that you know what each of the selections can do, let's have some fun with Betina.

4. With the Drop Shadow menu open, use these settings:

- Bur X: 10
- Blur Y: 10
- Strength: 82%
- Quality: High
- Angle: 45
- Distance: 10

5. Save and play the movie. Notice that as Betina walks across the screen, she has a shadow (see Figure 6-6).

Figure 6-6. A drop shadow can be added to a video containing an Alpha channel.

That is interesting, but what else can you do? How about just the shadow moving across the screen? To do this, open the Filters settings for the movieclip and select Hide object. When you test the movie, only the shadow moves across the screen (see Figure 6-7).

Figure 6-7. Only the shadow knows!

How about a ghost? In this case, open the Filters settings and deselect Hide object. Select Knockout and Inner shadow. Test the movie; the ghost walks across the background, as shown in Figure 6-8.

Figure 6-8. The ghost in the machine

The amount of fun you can have with filters should be illegal. Just keep in mind that they do not need to be overused to be effective.

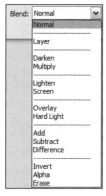

Figure 6-9. Flash CS3 Professional contains 14 blend modes.

The blend modes that ship with Flash CS3 Professional are also quite amazing. Again, if you are familiar with Fireworks or Photoshop, they should be quite familiar tools. Fourteen blend modes are available by selecting the Blend drop-down menu in the Property Inspector (see Figure 6-9).

Without getting overly complex and technical—we do that at the end of this chapter when we discuss how to use ActionScript to apply a blend mode—the blend modes work with the pixels that are over each other. For example, our video has the young lady walking in front of an image. A blend mode would go through each pixel in turn and "grab" the color of the pixel in the subject and the pixel in the image immediately below it. It would then manipulate the color values of the two pixels and change the color of the pixel that is on top.

The Multiply mode is a good example of how this works. Multiply grabs the pixel values of the top source (the video) and the bottom source (the FlashinTO page), multiplies them together, and then divides the result by 256. The result is inevitably a darker pixel. Let's see what this means.

1. Select the movieclip on the stage, remove the Drop Shadow, and select Multiply from the Blend drop-down menu.

2. Test the movie. Notice that as the woman walks across the screen, the darker color results appear on the video subject (see Figure 6-10). Where the color is already dark, the black top, nothing appears because nothing is darker than black.

Figure 6-10. The Multiply blend is applied to the movieclip.

Now that you have applied the Multiply filter, how about having the background look like it is projected onto her? Simply apply the Hard Light filter instead of the Multiply filter (see Figure 6-11).

Figure 6-11. The Hard Light filter applied to a video

You can also mix the filters and the blends to create some rather interesting effects. Apply a combination of the Drop Shadow and Bevel filters with the Multiply filter, and you get a sort of 3-D effect. The key is to apply a small 2-pixel bevel in the Bevel settings, pull the opacity back to about 60–65%, and use the Best quality. The result is shown in Figure 6-12.

Figure 6-12. Filters and blends can be combined.

Applying filters and blends through ActionScript

As you learned in the previous section, filters and blends can be applied without the use of code. They are all available through the Property Inspector and can be applied singly or in combination with each other. The filters and blends can also be applied through the use of ActionScript. In the next two

157

exercises, you will blur a video by dragging your mouse across it. In the next one, you add a screen blend mode that simulates the effect of a video being projected onto an underlying image, but the image shows through.

The final aspect of these two exercises is the absence of the FLVPlayback component. A Video object is used. The great thing about a Video object used in place of the component is a significantly smaller SWF file. The component creates a SWF file that is well above 40KB. Use the Video object to do the same thing with a SWF file that weighs in at 1KB or lower.

In this exercise, you'll blur a video when the mouse rolls across it.

1. Open the BlurIt.fla file. When the file opens, notice that we have already placed a movieclip containing a Video object on the stage and written only the code that plays the video.

The effects and blend modes, regardless of whether they are applied using the Filters panel, Property Inspector or through ActionScript 3.0, can be applied only to movieclips. By putting the Video object into a movieclip, you can select it on the stage and apply a filter. In fact, you can apply any of the effects in the previous section to a Video object in a movieclip. The only difference is that you will need to use ActionScript to connect and stream an FLV file into the object, shown in Figure 6-13, when the video plays.

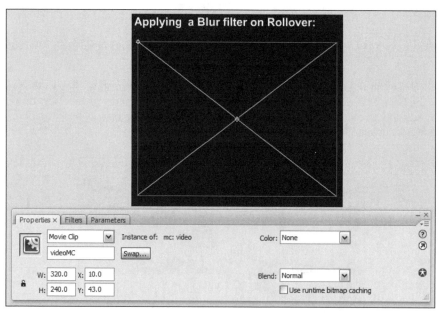

Figure 6-13. The stage is set.

2. Select the first frame in the Actions layer and open the Actions panel. Click once in line 19 and add the following code:

```
var blur:BlurFilter = new BlurFilter();
blur.blurX = 16;
blur.blurY = 16;
blur.quality = BitmapFilterQuality.HIGH;
```

The filter objects you create, however many those may be, will be added to the DisplayObject. filters property of the movieclip that contains the video. Each filter object manages its own various properties.

We start by creating a BlurFilter object named blur. The key is to recognize that the parameters are exactly the same as those you would set if you were to use the Filters tab in the Property Inspector (see Figure 6-14). Note that the word HIGH is uppercase. If you use upper- and lowercase letters, or all lowercase letters, you will get an error.

> *When applying the Blur filter through ActionScript 3.0, apply* Blur X *and* Blur Y *values that are powers of two (2, 4, 8, 16). For example, the values used in the code are more efficient than the following:*
>
> ```
> var blur:BlurFilter = new BlurFilter();
> blur.blurX = 3;
> blur.blurY = 6;
> blur.quality = BitmapFilterQuality.HIGH;
> ```
>
> *Values that are a power of 2 are optimized to render more quickly and the result is a performance boost in the 20–30% range.*

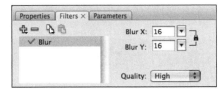

Figure 6-14. The ActionScript parameters match those in the Property Inspector.

3. Let's now turn our attention to having the video blur when the mouse rolls over the video. Press Return (PC) or Enter (Mac) twice and enter the following:

```
videoMC.addEventListener(MouseEvent.MOUSE_OVER,mouseOverHandler);
function mouseOverHandler(event:MouseEvent):void {
   videoMC.filters = [blur];
}
```

The code is not different from what you have done so far. The first line listens for a MOUSE_OVER event; when it detects the event, it executes a custom function named mouseOverHandler. This is the function in the second line that associates your filter objects with the movieclip. Filters are assigned as an array, which explains the square brackets (a shortcut for new Array()). If you had created additional filter objects, they would also appear inside the square brackets separated by commas.)

> *Strictly speaking, the* Video *class also has a* filters *property, which it inherits from* DisplayObject *just as the* MovieClip *class does. What the* Video *class does not have, however, are mouse-related events. That's the secret reason why the* Video *object is wrapped in a movieclip.*

One of the key tenets of this business is this (as one of the authors is fond of saying): "If y'all change, y'all have to put it back." Let's deal with turning off the blur when the mouse rolls off of the video. Here's how:

4. Press Return (PC) or Enter (Mac) twice and enter the following function:

```
videoMC.addEventListener(MouseEvent.MOUSE_OUT,mouseOutHandler);
function mouseOutHandler(event:MouseEvent) :void {
  videoMC.filters = null;
}
```

This function listens for a MOUSE_OUT event. When it detects one, it turns off the filter by giving it a null value.

5. Check your syntax and, if everything is correct, close the Actions panel and test the movie. When you roll the mouse over the video, the video blurs (see Figure 6-15).

Figure 6-15. The blur on the video is a function of the position of the cursor in the SWF file as it plays the video.

Using buttons to turn filters on and off

Now that you know how to apply a filter, let's look at a project that uses buttons to apply the filter effects.

1. Open the `FilterButtons.fla` file and test it. When the SWF file opens, you'll see that the filters are controlled by a series of five buttons. There are four filters (see Figure 6-16) that can be applied to the video, as well as a Reset button that returns the video to its normal state. You can remove an effect by clicking a check box or totally clear the effects by clicking the Reset button. Close the SWF file.

Figure 6-16. Filters can be added singly or in combination with each other.

You might be wondering where the Convolution and ColorMatrix filters are located because they surely are not a part of the Filters list on the Property Inspector. In fact, these two "filters" live exclusively in the realm of ActionScript code. Essentially, what both of these filters do is to use ActionScript to play with the pixels in the movieclip. Although they are more commonly applied to line art and photos in movieclips as well as text and buttons, they can also be applied to video contained in a movieclip.

So what is a **convolution**? It combines pixels in the input image with neighboring pixels to produce an image. By doing this you create quite a few amazing effects such as blurring, edge detection, sharpening, embossing, and beveling. Let's take a look at it.

2. Select frame 1 of the Actions layer and open the ActionScript panel. Scroll down to line 44. You will see the following code:

```
var convolutionArray:Array = [ -2, -1, 0, -1, 1, 1, 0, 1, 2 ];
var convolution:ConvolutionFilter = new ConvolutionFilter();
convolution.matrixX = 3;
convolution.matrixY = 3;
convolution.matrix = convolutionArray;
convolution.divisor = 1;
```

The matrix is the key. In this case, we're building a 3 x 3 grid (`matrixX` and `matrixY`) and filling the grid with the values in the array named `convolutionArray`.

If you could see the matrix, it would look like this:

-2	-1	0
-1	1	1
0	1	2

When Flash Player is applying the Convolution filter to a certain pixel, it will look at the color value of the pixel itself (in this example, the 1 in the middle), as well as the values of the surrounding pixels. However, by setting values in the matrix, you specify how much priority certain pixels have in affecting the resulting image.

For example, this matrix would leave the image, or in this case the video, untouched because the 0s indicate there are no changes made to the pixels surrounding the middle pixel:

0	0	0
0	1	0
0	0	0

If you use this matrix, not only does the intensity of the pixel rise but the intensity of the surrounding pixels also reduces:

0	-1	0
-1	7	-1
0	-1	0

The result, shown in Figure 6-17, is much the same as that obtained by applying too much sharpening to an image.

Convolution Filter

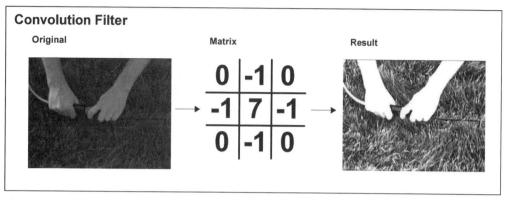

Figure 6-17. The matrix is the key.

3. Close the Actions panel, test the movie, and click only the Convolution Transform check box. The convolution makes the video (shown in Figure 6-18) look like a Photoshop image with embossing applied to it.

Figure 6-18. A Convolution filter can let you do some crazy stuff with video.

4. Deselect the Convolution Transform check box to turn it off and click the Matrix check box. The video, shown in Figure 6-19, turns green. Close the SWF file and let's take a look at how that happened.

Figure 6-19. A Matrix filter is applied to the video.

5. Open the Actions panel and scroll down to line 58 of the code. You will see the following:

```
var colorMatrixArray:Array = [ ➡
    1,0,0,0,0, ➡
    0,2,0,0,0, ➡
    0,0,1,0,0, ➡
    0,0,0,1,0 ];
var colorMatrix:ColorMatrixFilter = new ColorMatrixFilter();
colorMatrix.matrix = colorMatrixArray;
```

The Array is where all of the "action" occurs because you can use a color matrix to change the values of the Red, Blue, Green, and Alpha channels in an image.

The colorMatrix filter lets you apply a 4 x 5 matrix of transformation values to an image (or, in this case, a video inside a movieclip). This explains the 20 numbers that are in the list. If you were to write out the matrix, it would look like this:

```
  R G B A Off
R 1,0,0,0,0
G 0,2,0,0,0
B 0,0,1,0,0
A 0,0,0,1,0
```

If you compare the numbers in the matrix with the numbers in the preceding code, you will see that they match. The 1 in the R column and R row is the red value of the Red channel. The following rows are the Green, Blue, and Alpha channels:

```
   R G B A Off
R 1,0,0,0,0
G 0,2,0,0,0
B 0,0,1,0,0
A 0,0,0,1,0
```

The rows and the columns all represent an R,G,B,A (Alpha) value. The columns have a fifth value of Off. In the preceding array, the number 2 falls in the G value for both the column and the row. This means the green value for each pixel is larger than the others.

If you compare the numbers in the matrix to the numbers in the list, you will see that they match. Row 1 is the Red component of the pixel color; the remaining rows are the Green, Blue, and Alpha components. The numbers used say that there is no change, although later on you will be changing the color using the values in the matrix. When the nonzero numbers are all 1, it is an "identity matrix" that represents the given color values as-is. Here, the 2 calls for a change. Why toss 20 numbers into a list? Because you have to write the values only once.

The really neat thing about the colorMatrix filter is that it allows you to make changes to the hue, saturation, alpha, and other effects while the movie is playing. The numbers used in the last row of the matrix, the Alpha value, can be any number between 0 and 1. For example, if the first number in the Red row is .5, you have just reduced the saturation of the red component of each pixel of the image.

This explains why the video takes on that greenish cast when you clicked the check box. By using a value of 2 in the Green column on the Green channel, you have essentially increased the saturation of the Green component in each pixel of the video.

> *For those of you who are absolute sticklers for detail or have a morbid fascination regarding minutiae, the color model used by this filter is RGBA. When the filter is applied, each pixel is multiplied by the corresponding value in the RGBA matrix. This new value is then applied to each pixel in the original image. For a tremendous overview of this feature, check out this document:* www.adobe.com/devnet/flash/articles/matrix_transformations_04.html.

Although those are the two most important aspects of the code, a couple of methods in the buttons might be new for some of you: push() and splice(). Let's see where they are used.

6. Scroll down to line 67 of the code where the blur is applied. The code block is as follows:

```
blurCB.addEventListener(MouseEvent.CLICK,blurCBClickHandler);
function blurCBClickHandler(event:MouseEvent):void {
if (event.target.selected == true) {
    filtersArray.push(blur);
    videoMC.filters = filtersArray;
  } else {
  for (var filter:String in filtersArray) {
    if (filtersArray[filter].constructor == BlurFilter) {
      filtersArray.splice(filter,1);
```

```
            videoMC.filters = filtersArray;
        }
    }
  }
}
```

The line `filtersArray.push(blur)` adds the values for the Blur filter to an array. The push() method of the Array class simply tacks the values for the Blend filter onto the end of an array and returns the length of the new array. We're not using that return value here, but it's good to know that the information is there.

When you deselect the Blur check box, the Blur filter is removed with the line `filtersArray.splice(filter,1)`. The splice() method of the Array class is used to add or remove items from an array. The first parameter, `filter`, tells ActionScript where to start removing or inserting values; the number 1 tells ActionScript how many objects are to be removed.

The line `videoMC.filters = filtersArray;` simply reapplies any other filters that might be active without the addition of the Blur filter.

Your turn: Using buttons to turn blend modes on and off

The final exercise for this chapter applies a blend mode to a video in a movieclip through the use of ActionScript, not the Property Inspector.

A blend is applied by the Flash Player to each pixel in a movieclip. Remember that each pixel is composed of three colors—Red, Green, Blue—and each color can have hexadecimal values ranging from 0x00 to 0xFF, or RGB values ranging from 0 to 255. When a blend mode is applied to a movieclip, the color values in the overlying pixel are compared with the colors of the pixel in the image directly beneath it.

For example, assume that a video has a dark blue pixel directly above a light blue pixel in the background. If the Lighten blend mode were applied, the dark blue pixel in the video would be replaced with the light blue pixel from the image directly beneath it because that pixel is the lighter pixel (see Figure 6-20).

The blend modes are properties applied to movieclips in ActionScript through the use of `myMovieClip.blendMode.NORMAL;` or `myMovieClip.blendMode = BlendMode.MULTIPLY;`.

The word used (called a **constant** in ActionScript 3.0) determines which of the 14 modes are applied. The modes and their ActionScript values are the following:

■ NORMAL	■ DARKEN	■ ALPHA
■ LAYER	■ DIFFERENCE	■ ERASE
■ MULTIPLY	■ ADD	■ OVERLAY
■ SCREEN	■ SUBTRACT	■ HARDLIGHT
■ LIGHTEN	■ INVERT	

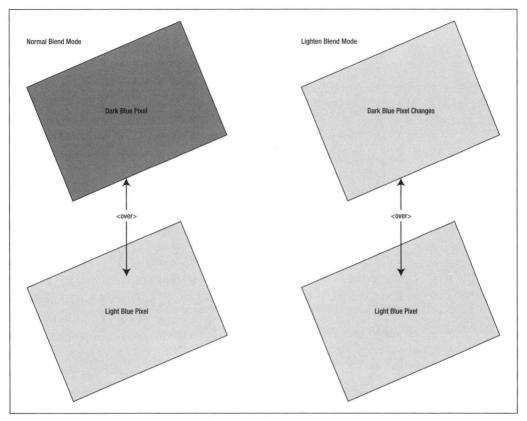

Figure 6-20. A Lighten blend mode is applied to two pixels.

If you take a look at the BlendMode *class documentation, "Huh?" might be your response. According to the docs, there are actually two ways of applying the blend mode:* BlendMode.NORMAL *or simply* "normal", *which includes the quotation marks because it is a string. If you want ActionScript to help you, go with the former, not the latter. Why? The word* NORMAL *will be colored in the ActionScript editor, indicating proper syntax. The other way of doing it will result in black lettering, which might not be much help if there are syntax issues.*

Let's get busy:

1. Open the BlendButtons.fla file. When the file opens, you will see that we have added a series of radio button components on the stage, added a Video object, and placed it over a colored image (see Figure 6-21). The video is over the image simply to demonstrate what the video will look like when a blend mode is applied to it. You'll now undertake that task.

167

Figure 6-21. The stage is set to explore blend modes.

2. Click once in the Actions layer and open the Actions panel.

3. Click once in the Script pane and add the following code:

```
var nc:NetConnection = new NetConnection();
nc.connect(null);

var ns:NetStream = new NetStream(nc);
videoMC.myVideo.attachNetStream(ns);

var listener:Object = new Object();
listener.onMetaData = function(md:Object):void{};
ns.client = listener;
ns.addEventListener(NetStatusEvent.NET_STATUS, statusHandler)

ns.play("Apple.flv");

function statusHandler(event:NetStatusEvent):void {
  switch (event.info.code) {
    case "NetStream.Play.Start":
      break;
    case "NetStream.Play.Stop":
      ns.seek(0);
      break;
  }
}
```

The Video object is wired up and ready to play. The new feature is the statusHandler function, which listens for the video to finish—NetStream.Play.Stop. When it does, the function uses the seek(0) method of the NetStream to go back to the start of the video and to replay it. This is a really good way to get an FLV file to loop.

> One of the authors is a firm believer in this axiom: Test early and test often. At this point you know that the video is wired up, and you might want to see whether the video plays by testing the movie. If the video doesn't show, it is obvious that the FLV file can't be found. What you don't want is to have the video fail to appear in a code block consisting of a few hundred lines because you will then have to poke through all that code looking for the issue. ActionScript works from top to bottom, running through each line of code sequentially, starting at line 1. This means you can do a bit and then test it as you go through the project you are working on. If there are issues, they can be quickly isolated, identified, and repaired.

4. Press Return (PC) or Enter (Mac) twice and enter the following lines:

```
addRB.addEventListener(MouseEvent.CLICK, blendClickHandler);
diferenceRB.addEventListener(MouseEvent.CLICK, blendClickHandler);
screenRB.addEventListener(MouseEvent.CLICK, blendClickHandler);
normalRB.addEventListener(MouseEvent.CLICK, blendClickHandler);
function blendClickHandler(event:MouseEvent):void {
  switch(event.target.name) {
    case "addRB":
      videoMC.blendMode = BlendMode.ADD;
      break;
    case"diferenceRB":
      videoMC.blendMode = BlendMode.DIFFERENCE;
      break;
    case"screenRB":
      videoMC.blendMode = BlendMode.SCREEN;
      break;
    default:
      videoMC.blendMode = BlendMode.NORMAL;
      break;
  }
}
```

Although you could just as easily write four separate functions for each radio button, that would be a waste of time because we Flash designers and developers are inherently lazy. If a simple and fast way of doing something can be found, we'll use it. This code block is a great example of what we call "effective laziness."

The use of the switch() statement is the key. What it does is test to see whether a radio button has been selected—the case matches the condition, which is the radio button's instance name. If it matches, it executes the function associated with the component. This statement doesn't work in isolation.

Notice the use of the case statement that contains what happens when the radio button is selected. The case statement is what defines the condition for the switch() statement. The other statement at play is break. This essentially stops the code from jumping to the next line and instead tells ActionScript, "The previous line is in play, so just skip everything else in the switch statement but still execute the function."

5. Press Return (PC) or Enter (Mac) twice and enter the following lines:

```
resetBTN.addEventListener(MouseEvent.CLICK, resetClickHandler);
function resetClickHandler(event:MouseEvent):void {
  videoMC.blendMode = BlendMode.NORMAL;
  normalRB.selected = true;
}
```

This function controls the Reset button on the stage. The first thing it does is to reset the blend mode of the video back to Normal. Then it makes sure the radio button with the Normal label is selected.

6. Test the video. Click a button, and the blend will be applied as shown in Figure 6-22.

Figure 6-22. The Add blend mode gives the video a bit of a transparent look.

If you are really feeling adventurous, feel free to add the remaining 10 blend modes to the movie.

What you've learned

We think you now understand what we mean when we tell people that the amount of fun you can have with the effects, filters, and blend modes in Flash CS3 Professional should be illegal. From drop shadows added to Alpha channel video, to video looking like it is projected onto a surface, the creative possibilities are there—and they are endless.

In this chapter you have discovered:

- How to apply simple effects to video
- How to use the Property Inspector to add filters and blend modes to video
- How to use ActionScript to loop video
- How ActionScript is used to programmatically add filters and blend modes to video

Just keep in mind that they can be processor-intensive, so keep the number of effects applied to any one video to a minimum. The other key to this chapter is that the filters and blend modes must be applied to video content in a movieclip. The fascinating thing about this is that content doesn't necessarily have to be the FLVPlayback component. They can be applied to content that is streamed into a Video object on the stage.

Finally, you discovered how to apply filters and blends to a video in a movieclip using ActionScript. You also saw that the filters and blend modes can be applied to video in movieclips through the Property Inspector or by using ActionScript. Which method is best? We leave that answer to you because, in the final analysis, a drop shadow was added to a talking head. Does anybody really care how it got there?

If you think filters and blends are cool, just wait and see what you can do when it comes to masking video. To find out, turn the page.

Chapter 7

MASKING VIDEO

To this point in the book, video has been treated like a television picture. It sits in a Video object or in the FLVPlayback component, and you watch it in a box. This isn't, as Martha Stewart would say, "A bad thing." Still, this is Flash, and there are a lot of other possibilities for the use of video beyond simply sticking it on the stage or manipulating it. Sometimes you might want it to actually appear inside an object, such as a circle, or framed within a custom viewer. In other instances, video is to be treated like a movieclip and otherwise manipulated in a series of creative ways. This is where masking comes in.

What we'll cover in this chapter:

- Creating a simple mask
- Applying a mask using ActionScript
- Creating feathered masks
- Generating masks at runtime
- Creating animation using the Tween class
- Creating and using an ActionScript class file

Files used in this chapter:

- BlackBackPack.flv (Chapter07\ExerciseFiles_Ch07\Exercise\BlackBackPack.flv)
- Mask_02.fla (Chapter07\ExerciseFiles_Ch07\Exercise\Mask_02.fla)
- Filters2.fla (Chapter07\ExerciseFiles_Ch07\Exercise\Filters2.fla)
- SimpleMask.ai (Chapter07\ExerciseFiles_Ch07\Exercise\SimpleMask.ai)
- ImageMask.fla (Chapter07\ExerciseFiles_Ch07\Exercise\ImageMask.fla)
- Phone.fla (Chapter07\ExerciseFiles_Ch07\Exercise\Phone.fla)
- Drag.fla (Chapter07\ExerciseFiles_Ch07\Exercise\Drag.fla)
- Trailer2.flv (Chapter07\ExerciseFiles_Ch07\Exercise\Trailer2.flv)
- Flashlight.fla (Chapter07\ExerciseFiles_Ch07\Exercise\Flashlight.fla)
- IllMaskt.fla (Chapter07\ExerciseFiles_Ch07\Exercise\IllMaskt.fla)
- Cigars.flv (Chapter07\ExerciseFiles_Ch07\Exercise\Cigars.flv)
- Drawing.fla (Chapter07\ExerciseFiles_Ch07\Exercise\Drawing.fla)
- StaticCutaway.fla (Chapter07\ExerciseFiles_Ch07\Exercise\StaticCutaway.fla)
- TransitionIn.fla (Chapter07\ExerciseFiles_Ch07\Exercise\TransitionIn.fla)
- MovingMask (Chapter07\ExerciseFiles_Ch07\Exercise\MovingMask)
- MovingMask_External.fla (Chapter07\ExerciseFiles_Ch07\Exercise\MovingMask\ MovingMask_External.fla)

Masking video is not exactly a complex subject. There really are only three methods of masking video. The first is to use a Mask layer in Flash, the second is to use an object with a hole in it that lets the video show through, and the third is to use an object's fill color as a mask. That's it. Real simple. The complexity happens when the mask is applied and used. Those techniques range from the very simple to the very complex.

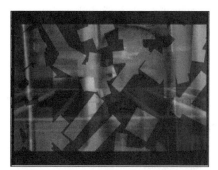

Which leads us to the point of this chapter: we'll cover a variety of techniques that start with the absolute basics and get more complex (see Figure 7-1) as you move through the exercises to the end of the chapter. Along the way, you'll learn which masking techniques work best in particular situations and you'll also discover a "gotcha" regarding the FLVPlayback component that is not exactly documented.

Let's get creative!

Figure 7-1. Dynamically generated movieclips and a color effect can turn a simple video into something spectacular.

Creating a simple mask

You will inevitably reach a point where you are literally trying to stick a "square video" into a "round shape." Obviously that won't work—you need to use a masking layer in Flash.

1. Open a new Flash document and use these settings:
   - Width: 320
   - Height: 240
   - Stage Colour: #333333

2. Add a layer and drag a copy of the FLVPlayback component into Layer 1.

3. Save the file as Mask_01 to the exercise folder and set the source parameter of the component to the BlackBackPack.flv file.

4. Select Layer 2 and draw a circle, with no stroke, on the layer. When it comes to masking, the color chosen for a fill doesn't matter, so pick what you like.

5. Right-click (PC) or Ctrl+click (Mac) on Layer 2 and select Mask from the context menu. When you do this, the icon for Layer 2 will change to show a mask. The Layer 1 icon will also change and the layer name will indent (see Figure 7-2), which means that the video in Layer 1 is being masked. You will also notice that both layers are locked.

6. Save and test the movie. The video (shown in Figure 7-2) will play inside the circle.

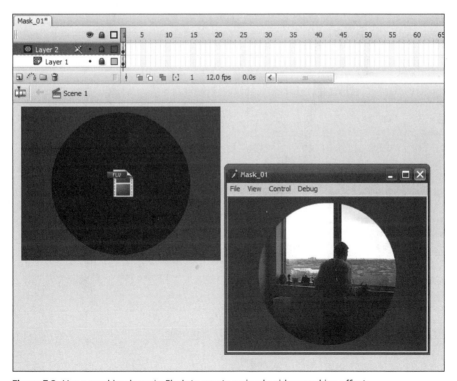

Figure 7-2. Use a masking layer in Flash to create a simple video masking effect.

175

Now that you know how to use a simple shape as a mask, let's look at how a complex shape can be used. In this example, we created a simple circle in Illustrator CS3, selected it, and applied the Roughen filter to give the shape a lot of odd nooks and crannies. Then we applied a Chalk Scribble brush stroke to the edges of the shape. This gave us the rather "funky" shape shown in Figure 7-3. It will make a perfect mask for the Back Pack video.

> *It is really important to understand that the content on any layer below a masking object will also be masked when associated with the* Mask *layer. This is why many Flash designers and artists will actually put mask effects in a separate movieclip. If you have multiple layers under a mask, simply drag the layer name a little to the left, and it will no longer be affected. Drag it to the right if you want it included in the mask.*

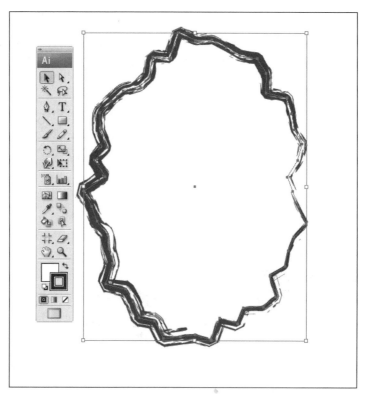

Figure 7-3. Illustrator CS3 has quite a few tools, filters, and effects that can be used to create masks.

With the mask containing a black stroke and a white fill created, we saved the image and simply dragged it from the Illustrator page to Layer 2 of the Flash stage.

The relationship between Flash and Illustrator is finally starting to become established. The suggested method of placing Illustrator images into Flash is to select File ➤ Import to Library. The Illustrator import dialog box that opens is a major improvement over previous versions of the dialog box. The big improvement is the capability to import Illustrator paths as either editable vectors or flattened bitmaps. As well, these paths can be imported into Flash as a series of movieclips. Finally, this dialog box also tells you if there are compatibility issues between Flash and earlier versions of Illustrator. All in all, a rather slick piece of work.

> *Be careful about creating artwork in Illustrator CS3 for placement in Flash CS3. The default color space for Illustrator is CMYK, whereas for Flash it is RGB. Before you save an Illustrator document, select* File ➤ Document Color Mode ➤ RGB Color. *Do this and Flash won't prompt you to return to Illustrator to change from CMYK to RGB.*
>
> *Most Flash designers and artists simply ignore the import and either copy and paste the drawing from Illustrator into Flash or use the drag-and-drop method.*
>
> *If you don't have Illustrator, all is not lost. This exercise, including the Illustrator image on* Layer 2, *can be found in the file named* SimpleMask.fla *in the Chapter 7 exercise folder. We have also included the Illustrator CS3 file,* SimpleMask.ai, *for those who want to try it out.*

With the mask in its proper location, we simply distorted it to fit the stage dimensions with the Auto transform tool, applied the mask to Layer 2 and, when we tested the movie, the Back Pack video played through the inside shape of the drawing (see Figure 7-4).

Figure 7-4. The mask from Illustrator is applied.

What about the cool strokes around the Illustrator shape? Where did they go? When an object is used as a mask, only the fill is used to determine the shape of the mask, so any stroke around the object used as a mask is essentially discarded. Let's bring the strokes back.

Now that you understand that any object used as a mask covers everything associated with the mask, you can see how to solve the lines issue. Simply place a copy of the mask object in a layer above the Mask layer. Here's how:

1. Open the Mask_02.fla file in the Chapter 7 exercise folder.

2. Unlock Layer 2 and select the mask on the stage. Copy the selection to the clipboard and relock the layer.

3. Add a new layer, select frame 1 in the new layer, and select Edit ➤ Paste In Place. The copy of the mask will be placed directly over the original.

4. What you don't want to do at this point is to test the video. It will be hidden by the white fill of the object in Layer 3. Instead, click once on the object in Layer 3 and press Ctrl+B (PC) or Cmd+B (Mac) to break the object apart. (You can also select Modify ➤ Break Apart. Pressing that combination once separates the object into fill and stroke.)

5. Click the Fill area of the broken apart object to select it—it looks cross-hatched—and then delete the selection. Just the stroke will be visible.

6. Test the movie, and the video (shown in Figure 7-5) is masked.

Figure 7-5. The strokes are placed on a layer above the mask.

Using an image as a mask

You have seen how vector line art can be used as a mask. Now we'll look at how images can be used for the same purpose. Images offer all sorts of possibilities. For example, if you take a photograph of the billboards in Times Square, New York, each of those billboards can be used to hold a video. This technique is more common than you might think. For example, Vodafone makes extensive use of this technique in its Future Vision site, in which it places video in wrist watches, rolled up Mylar, and other devices. It isn't only corporations that use this technique to great effect. Hit the home page of Wefail, a Flash design studio (www.wefail.com), and you will see a motion graphic, which in very simple terms is a collection of Flash movies and video framed in an image (see Figure 7-6).

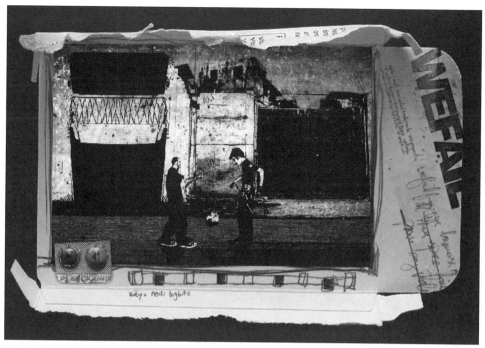

Figure 7-6. The Wefail home page

Images can't effectively be used as a mask without the help of ActionScript. Bitmaps can be used as long as the cacheAsBitmap *property is set to* true *for both the mask and the masked image. If this is the case, the* setMask() *method is applied to the object being masked (as you saw in Chapter 5). We'll also deal with this very issue later on in this chapter.*

For the purposes of this exercise, a bitmap can be used to mask or, for want of a better term, to "frame" the content under them. This is an important distinction because if you were to put an image on a masking layer, the image would disappear. Flash sees an image as being a bunch of pixels without a stroke around them. This means that the image is seen by Flash as nothing more than a fill, which is why it disappears. Instead, you have to cut the shape out of the image and then save the image using a format that supports transparency, such as a 24-bit PNG file. Saving an image in this format preserves the transparency that shows through the "hole" in the image.

If you're using Photoshop CS3, create the hole and save the image as a PSD file. If you're a Fireworks CS3 user, PNG is the native format for Fireworks. Just be aware that when you import a Fireworks PNG image into Flash, a copy of the image as a Flash movieclip will be added to the library, along with the bitmap.

If you are as big a fan of drag-and-drop as we are, use Fireworks for the task.

Finally, using an image as a mask requires you to ask a simple question: "Does this look real?" Sometimes sliding a video under an object looks . . . well . . . like you slid a video under an object. For example, slide a video under a hole in the image of a TV screen. It just doesn't look right because the designer didn't take the time to match the shape of the video to the hole, and the video has the wrong angles from a perspective point of view. Also televisions have glass screens, and inevitably a photo of a television screen will have a highlight or reflection on it. Take the time to match the geometry of the video to the shape of the mask and to incorporate any screen reflections or highlights. Your video will look more "real." In this exercise, we'll do just that with a TV screen.

1. Open the ImageMask.fla file in the Chapter 7 exercise folder. Notice that we have included an image with a hole in it on a separate layer.

2. Add an FLVPlayback component to the Video layer and set its source to the BlackBackPack.flv video. Place the component so that you can see the component's icon through the screen.

3. Select the Free Transform tool, click the component, and resize the component to fit the dimensions of the hole in the image (see Figure 7-7). Don't merrily start yanking corners here and there, or else you will distort the video. Instead, move the component so that the upper-left handle of the component is just a bit outside the upper-left corner of the hole. Move the center point—the white dot in the middle of the component—to the upper-left corner. Holding down the Shift key, drag the bottom-right corner up toward the top-left corner. This process will maintain the object's proportions.

> Don't worry if you can't get an exact fit. You rarely will. When scaling a video component or object, always leave a bit of the object covered. It looks more real that way because the video will fill the hole from edge to edge.
>
> Just because you can scale the component doesn't mean you should. All it does is reduce the dimensions of a video to fit the component. For example, if you have a video that is 360 x 240 and you scale it down, Flash will have to scale the FLV file on the fly to fit the component. It will still require the same bandwidth as the regular-sized FLV file, so you haven't done yourself or the user any favors. When using this technique in an actual production scenario, recompile the FLV file in the Encoder to the final size.

4. Save and test the movie. The mysterious backpackers should appear onscreen.

Now that you have done something rather simple, let's deal with something a bit more complicated.

One of the authors has a phone sitting on his desk that contains an information screen. He has wistfully looked at the phone on several occasions and wondered, "What would this look like if it were a video screen?" The great thing about Flash is it can be used to play these "What if . . ." games and turn a phone's information display into a video display.

Before we start, it is a good time for you to discover a "gotcha" that is a part of the FLVPLayback component: the component really hates it when it is distorted using the Free Transform tool. The component especially dislikes being skewed, as shown in Figure 7-8 (notice that the video seems to extend past the grab handles). The implication is that you'll be doing a lot of unnecessary fiddling and tweaking to get a video to fit into an oddly shaped area.

Figure 7-7. Scale the component to roughly fit the "hole" in the image. Note the placement of the center point in the upper-left corner, which ensures that scaling is done from or to that point.

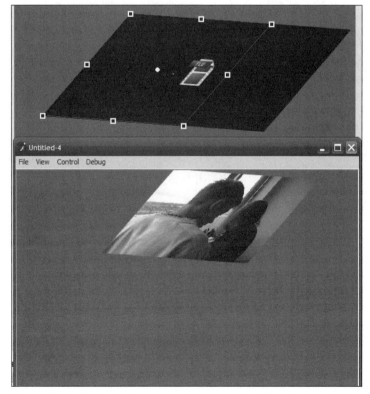

Figure 7-8. The FLVPlayback component is not exactly "distortion-friendly."

The solution is to use a Video object from the library instead of the component. Let's put a video in a phone, shall we?

1. Open the Phone.fla file in the Chapter 7 exercise folder. When the file opens, you'll notice that we have placed the phone and the screen on separate layers and left one layer open for the video and another for the actions (see Figure 7-9).

Figure 7-9. It starts with a phone.

Look at the screen in the phone and notice that it is a little wider at the bottom than the top, and the sides angle in as they move upward because of the perspective of the photograph. Playing a video that is rectangular in a trapezoidal area will simply not work. It will look a bit odd, which is why we suggest that you closely match the geometry of the video to that of the area covering it.

What you won't get is an exact fit because the component and the Video objects are not vector-based. The sides of the object, when manipulated by the Free Transform tool, can't be changed independently of each other. They all change. Moving the center point to a handle freezes only that side in place; the other three edges will move in relation to the center point.

> *Of course, for every issue there is an exception. In this case, holding down the* Alt/Option *key while dragging will allow you to change each side independently. In this exercise, we won't "fiddle" with the sides.*

There are two solutions to this problem. The first is to draw a shape in Flash that matches the shape of the cutout and to use that shape to mask the video. On the surface, this sounds like a great solution, but it is actually a duplication of effort because it will also be the purpose of the hole in the phone. The other solution is to change the shape of the Video object to approximate the shape of the cutout.

2. Move the Video layer above the Phone layer and turn off the visibility of the Screen layer. Open your library and select New Video from the library drop-down menu. When the dialog box appears, name the video (or use the name suggested) and click OK. You will see a small TV camera in the library.

3. Select the Video layer and drag the Video object from the library onto the Video layer. Give the Video object the instance name of myVideo in the Property Inspector.

4. With the Video object selected, click the Free Transform tool and manipulate the shape of the object to approximate the shape of the screen area, as shown in Figure 7-10. Don't forget to move the center point—that little white dot—to make changing the sides easier for you. After you finish, move the Video layer below the Phone layer and turn on the visibility of the Screen layer.

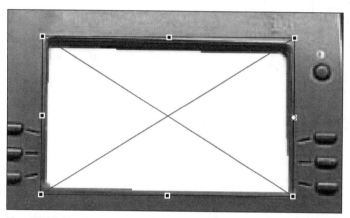

Figure 7-10. Use the geometry of the mask area to determine the shape of the Video object.

5. Save the file and then click once on frame 1 in the Actions layers. Press F9 (PC) or Option+F9 (Mac) to open the Actions panel.

6. Click once in the Actions pane and enter the following code:

```
var nc: NetConnection = new NetConnection();
nc.connect(null);
var ns: NetStream = new NetStream(nc);
myVideo.attachNetStream(ns);

var listener:Object = new Object();
listener.onMetaData = function(md:Object):void{};
ns.client= listener;

ns.play("Legend.flv");
```

183

If you test the piece right now, you won't see anything because the video is under the graphic of the screen. To fix that, select the screen, convert it to a movieclip, and reduce its Alpha value to 45% or 50%. Now test the movie. The video, shown in Figure 7-11, plays "through" the screen graphic.

Figure 7-11. The video phone

Even though the video is somewhat distorted, it still looks fine in the viewer. The reason? The end result is an optical illusion in many respects. The user's eyes will match the geometry of the video to the geometry of the hole. If you go to the Vodafone Future Vision web site (www.vodafone.com/flash/future/application/index.html), you will see this illusion used quite deliberately. For example, in the Entertainment section, Lisa has a "visual bracelet" that she uses to keep in touch with her friends (see Figure 7-12). If you select Experience, you will watch Lisa get invited out that evening by a couple of her friends. The video plays under the bracelet, and the curve of the bracelet also gives the illusion of the video being curved to follow that geometry as well.

There is obviously a small problem with your video. The words on the screen still show through. You can fix this by carefully using a variety of tools in either Photoshop or Fireworks to paint over the words with blank areas of the screen.

Another neat trick is to simply create a new movieclip and draw a square in the clip using the Rectangle tool in the toolbox, sample a green pixel in the screen, and fill the square with that color. Then all you need to do is to slide the Screen layer under the Phone layer and place the movieclip there. Resize it to fit the hole and apply 50% to 60% opacity. If you want to try it, replace the Screen1 movieclip with the ScreenVid movieclip in the library.

Figure 7-12. Notice how the video follows the geometry of the bracelet.

Video masks and ActionScript

With the release of Flash CS3 Professional, developers and designers are just now discovering that the manipulation of bitmap data can create some rather fascinating video effects. The exercises that finish this chapter are based upon ideas first unleashed upon an unsuspecting Flash World by Guy Watson in the UK In typical Flash fashion, others (such as Grant Skinner from Canada) have picked up on Guy's experiments and pushed the technique of bitmaps and video even further.

In this first exercise, you'll create a draggable mask. Let's get busy:

1. Open the Drag.fla file. When it opens, notice that we have supplied you with a movieclip named Mask and the Video object that is in that movieclip. We are also nice guys and have "wired up" the Video movieclip with the ActionScript that plays the Trail2.flv video.

The key to this technique is to understand that video can be masked, but in this case the mask will not be in a masking layer, but applied using ActionScript. The circle (which is in the Mask movieclip) that you see sitting over the video will be used as a mask (see Figure 7-13).

2. Click once in the Actions layer and open the Actions panel.

3. Scroll down the Script pane to line 21 of the code and enter the following line:

```
myVideo.mask = circle;
```

4. Save and test the movie.

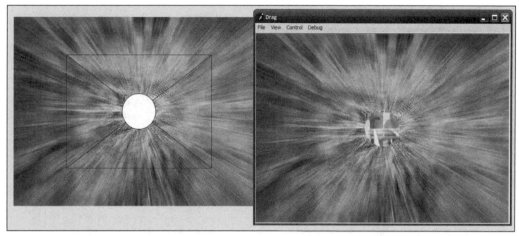

Figure 7-13. The mask is applied.

As you can see, you simply add the mask property to the object being masked and give the property the name of the object being used as the mask.

Now that you understand how that works, let's make the mask draggable.

1. Click once at the end of the line of code you just entered, press Return/Enter twice, and enter the following:

```
circle.addEventListener(MouseEvent.MOUSE_DOWN, mouseDownHandler);
circle.addEventListener(MouseEvent.MOUSE_UP, mouseUpHandler);
circle.buttonMode = true;
```

To move the circle around the stage, Flash needs to know what to listen for (MouseEvent.MOUSE_DOWN) and what to do when it "hears" it: execute the custom mouseDownHandler function.

2. Although Flash knows what to do, it doesn't know how to do it. This will be the purpose of the next two handlers. Press Return/Enter twice and enter the following code:

```
function mouseDownHandler(evt:MouseEvent):void {
  circle.startDrag();
}

function mouseUpHandler(evt:MouseEvent): void{
  circle.stopDrag();
}
```

3. Save and test the movie, and you should see the effect shown in Figure 7-13.

A flashlight effect

Now that you know how to drag a mask around the stage, let's take it to the next step and use a gradient fill instead of a solid fill. This will create the "illusion" of a flashlight shining on the video. Let's get started:

1. Open the Flashlight.fla file.

When the file opens, you'll see that we have placed a movieclip containing a gradient on the stage over the movieclip containing the Video object (see Figure 7-14). If this is starting to look somewhat familiar, it is. We'll use a technique used in the Reflection exercise from the previous chapter.

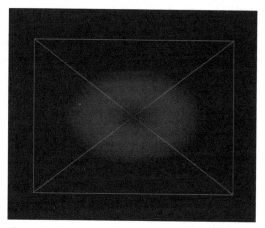

Figure 7-14. We start with a video and a gradient in a movieclip.

2. Select the gradient movieclip on the stage and give it the instance name of mcCircle.

3. Select the Video object on the stage and give it the instance name of mcVideo.

4. Select the first frame of the Actions layer and press F9 (PC) or Option+F9 (Mac) to open the Actions panel. You will see that the code is no different from that written in the previous exercise. You need to create the gradient mask.

5. Click once in line 1 of the code block and enter the following:

```
mcVideo.cacheAsBitmap = true;
mcCircle.cacheAsBitmap = true;
```

This might be a good place to describe what `cacheAsBitmap` does. This is a quote from a web site that explains it:

"Caching a movieclip as a bitmap at runtime provides significant performance enhancements for complex movieclips. It is less of a strain for your CPU to push pixels around the screen than to repeatedly recalculate the vector math and relevant properties (rotation, scale, alpha, etc.) that might be at work in your movieclips. In addition, caching a movieclip as a bitmap has other fun benefits. It allows a new level of compositing not possible in prior versions of Flash."

This quote is from `http://www.devx.com/webdev/Article/29296/0`. The topic is Flash 8, but it still applies to Flash CS3.

Our tech editor, David Stiller, read that quote and made the following very important comment: "The performance boost occurs only for movieclips with no animation in their own timelines. Setting the property to `true` means that Flash "takes a snapshot" of the vector art and displays it as a bitmap. If the movieclip has nested timelines, or animates on its own timeline, Flash has to continuously take new snapshots, which destroys the benefit. The movieclips in these examples happen to be acceptable, but this excerpt might mislead readers who want to, say, experiment with animated masks."

Thanks, David.

6. Save and test the movie. If you drag the mask around the stage, the edges of the gradient will actually feather the mask (see Figure 7-15), which gives the illusion of a flashlight.

If you remove the code that makes the mask draggable, you will have created a static feathered mask for the video.

Figure 7-15. Use a gradient to feather the edges of a mask.

Using ActionScript to dynamically add a masking object

You don't always have to pull an object out of the library and use it as a mask. You can let ActionScript handle the lifting on this one. In this exercise, you'll mask a video using an Illustrator drawing that is sitting in the library. Here's how:

1. Open the `IllMask.fla` file. As you can see in Figure 7-16, only the background image and the Video object are on the stage. The mask you'll use is in the MaskFinal.ai folder in the library.

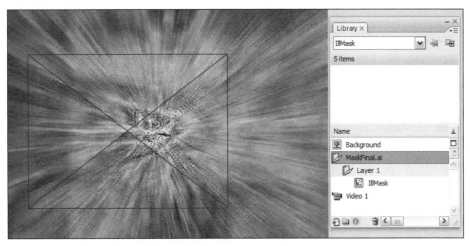

Figure 7-16. Masks can be pulled out of the library and added at runtime.

2. Click once on the `IllMask` movieclip in the library and select Linkage from the library drop-down menu. This will open the Linkage Properties dialog box.

3. Click the Export for ActionScript check box. When you do this, the name of the movieclip will appear in the Class area, and the Export in first frame selection will also be checked. The name you enter in the Class field is what ActionScript needs to find the movieclip in the library.

4. Click OK.

At this point you see the oddest dialog box (see Figure 7-17). You haven't made a mistake, but you have encountered a difference between ActionScript 2.0 and ActionScript 3.0. In ActionScript 3.0, the rules have changed. You need to create a custom class that will extend the `Movieclip` class. A class definition can be created by writing an ActionScript file with the same name as the Linkage class and placing it in the same folder as the SWF file. This opens the door for advanced custom programming that we don't need here, so letting Flash automatically generate one in this case is acceptable. Click OK and Flash will create a custom class named `IllMask` for you.

Figure 7-17. Ignore the warning.

189

5. Select the first frame of the Actions layer and open the Actions panel. Click once in line 23 of the code block and enter the following:

```
var maskMC:IllMask = new IllMask();
maskMC.x = 69;
maskMC.y = 79;
this.addChild(maskMC);
```

The first line of the code creates a movieclip using that class you just created. The next two lines position the movieclip on the stage, and the final line adds it to the display list of the stage.

6. Press Return/Enter twice and enter the final line of code:

```
myVideo.mask = maskMC;
```

7. Save and test the movie. The mask is pulled out of the library and placed over the video (see Figure 7-18).

Besides learning how to apply a mask at runtime, this is also a great technique to know. For example, you might have a variety of masks in the library and might want to apply different versions at various times in the Flash movie. This way, you avoid using layers and let the code do the work.

Figure 7-18. The mask is applied.

Drawing with ActionScript

In the next several exercises you will be constructing masked video movies that are composed of nothing more than a couple of objects in the library and ActionScript. In others, there is absolutely nothing in the library. You use a blank stage.

The most interesting aspect of these movies will be the blank stage you will use. The only "things" on the timeline will be several lines of code that use the objects in the library. ActionScript has come a long way since its earliest iterations, and in many respects a basic understanding of ActionScript is just as important as being able to move objects manually on the Flash stage.

In the first exercise, you will create a video on the blank stage and apply a mask to the video. The interesting thing about this exercise is that you won't be using a Video object or a movieclip; their creation will be done through ActionScript.

This is also a good time to introduce you to the Drawing Application Programming Interface (API). Although it sounds rather complex, it isn't. All the Drawing API really does is allow you to put down your mouse or pen and let ActionScript draw the lines, shapes, and other objects on the stage. By letting Flash "draw" these shapes at runtime, you wind up with a smaller SWF file because the objects aren't in the library.

The Drawing API, which was introduced in Flash MX, is nothing more than a subset of methods accessible to movieclips. The major thing they do is to allow you to draw stuff—lines, circles, and shapes—within the confines of a movieclip. The best way of wrapping your mind around the Drawing API is to approach its use as though you were drawing with a pencil. In the exercise that follows, you will actually draw the mask using code. So let's take a few minutes to review or learn how to use the Drawing API.

We always tell our students that essentially everything you can do with your mouse and the Flash interface you can also do with ActionScript (for example, drawing lines, rectangles, and so on). Instead of defining all your properties using the Properties window, you do it with ActionScript.

When you draw a line on a blank sheet of paper, you place the pen or pencil on the paper where the line is to be drawn and draw a line. The whole thing can be done without needing to think about it much at all. When you use code to draw that same line, it takes a bit more thought. You actually have to tell Flash the problem:

- The start point of the line on the x- and y-axis
- The thickness of the line
- Its color
- The opacity of the line
- Where the line ends on the x- and y-axis

If you open Drawing.fla in the Chapter 7 complete folder, you will see how a line is drawn. When you open the file, select the code frame and open the Actions panel. You will see the following code:

```
var newMC:MovieClip = new MovieClip();
newMC.graphics.lineStyle(15,0x990000);
newMC.graphics.moveTo(10,10);
newMC.graphics.lineTo(300,350);
this.addChild(newMC);
```

If you test it, you will see that a burgundy line has been drawn from the top of the screen downward (see Figure 7-19). That happens through the use of the Drawing API.

The first line of code creates an empty movieclip named newMC on the main timeline. The next line of code tells Flash that the line to be created—the lineStyle() method—is 15 pixels thick and is a burgundy (0x990000) color.

> If you want the line to be somewhat transparent, say 50%, the lineStyle() method would be newMC.graphics.lineStyle(15,0x990000,.5). The Alpha percentages in ActionScript 3.0 are expressed as decimals between 1 and 0.

Now that Flash knows what to draw, you have to tell Flash where to draw it. The moveTo() method tells it to put the pen 10 pixels across and 10 pixels down from the registration point of the movieclip. The lineTo() method, which actually draws the line, says the line ends 350 pixels from the edge of the stage and 300 pixels from the top of the stage.

If you were to draw a triangle, there would be three lineTo() methods used, and a square would use four lineTo() methods.

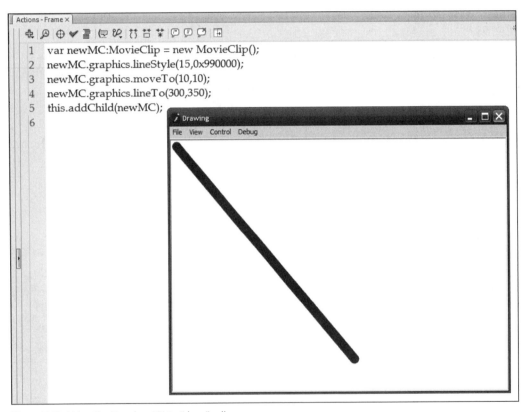

Figure 7-19. Using the Drawing API to "draw" a line

Now that you understand the basics of the Drawing API, let's relate what it can do to the use of Flash video.

As you saw earlier in this chapter, a mask is really nothing more than a graphic shape that gets placed over a video. Everything outside of the shape is hidden, meaning only the part of the video, directly under the shape, is visible. That shape can just as easily be an object drawn on the stage or an object drawn using ActionScript in a movieclip.

This is an important concept because there really is no distinction between whether a mask is an object you can see or one that is created programmatically. This means that masks can be shapes drawn into movieclips at runtime and disposed of when they are finished. These movieclips contain all the properties of movieclips, so they can move, replicate themselves, fade in, fade out, change color, and so on.

So all you really need to do is create a movieclip that contains a virtual Video object linked to an FLV file, place a shape created by the Drawing API over it, and then use that movieclip as a mask using the mask property of ActionScript.

Before you get all excited, all you know how to draw is a line. Let's draw a square and actually fill it with a color. This square you will draw will form the basis for some rather fascinating video-masking effects.

1. Open Flash and create a new ActionScript 3.0 document.

2. Select the first frame in Layer 1 and open the Actions panel. When the editor opens, enter the following code into the Script pane:

```
import flash.geom.*;
import flash.display.*

var videoMask:MovieClip = new MovieClip();
videoMask.graphics.beginFill(0x990000,1);
videoMask.graphics.moveTo(10,10);
videoMask.graphics.lineTo(320,10);
videoMask.graphics.lineTo(320,60);
videoMask.graphics.lineTo(10,60);
videoMask.graphics.lineTo(10,10);
videoMask.graphics.endFill();

this.addChild(videoMask);
```

If you test the movie, you will see that you have created a burgundy rectangle on the stage.

We start by importing all the classes in the geometry (flash.geom) and flash.display packages, which explains the asterisk. It is called a wild card and is used here as a shortcut to bring in all the classes in a given package. Although not technically needed in this particular code sample, it is a common best practice to use import statements.

The fill is created through the beginFill() method, and the two parameters used in the method are the fill color and its opacity (remember that 1 is equivalent to 100% opacity). If you place the beginFill() method in front of a series of lineTo() commands, you are telling the API to get ready to fill the shape about to be drawn. How does it know when to stop filling the shape? That is the purpose of the endFill() method. The result is shown in Figure 7-20.

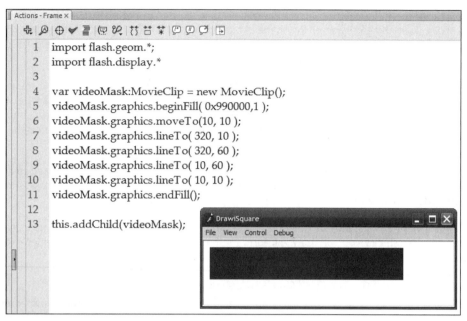

Figure 7-20. The endFill() method tells Flash to fill a shape with a solid color.

Now let's try something a bit different. Remove the endFill() or "comment it out" by putting // in front of it. Test the movie.

How about that? The same object, even though the line of code that closes the shape is missing. The Drawing API is not exactly stupid. When an endFill() method is not present, a line is automatically drawn back to the starting point where the beginFill() method was called. Still, you might choose to draw several shapes and want to keep them distinct, so keep the endFill() method in the back of your mind.

Let's use what you have learned to create some masks.

Where did everything go?

This exercise is designed to show you that when it comes to video, you can actually create everything you have used to this point in the book using a few simple lines of code. New to ActionScript 3.0 is the capability to create an instance of a Video object from the library entirely in code. What you'll do is to mask a video using a circular mask. Let's get busy.

1. Open a new ActionScript 3.0 document and save it to the Chapter 7 exercise folder.

2. In the Property Inspector set the stage size to 350 pixels wide by 300 pixels high and set the stage color to #666666 (medium gray).

3. Select the first frame in Layer 1 and open the Actions panel.

4. Click once in the Script pane and enter the following code:

```
import flash.media.Video;
import flash.net.NetConnection;
import flash.net.NetStream;
```

Although not required for this particular exercise, importing the classes at the start of the code is a good habit to develop because you'll need those import statements if you ever write your own external class files. Even though the vast majority of the exercises in this book are "timeline-based," ActionScript 3.0 is heavily reliant on classes.

The first line imports the Video class into the movie, and the other two lines import the NetConnection and NetStream classes from the flash.net package. The Video class that is included in the flash.media package is the display object used for displaying video files and is needed to create a virtual Video object.

> A class contains all the common characteristics that an object created from it should contain. The easiest way to recognize a class is that its name always starts with an uppercase letter. This is a quick way to find a class in the ActionScript 3.0 Help menu.

5. Press Return/Enter twice and enter the following code:

```
// Define Net Connection
var nc:NetConnection = new NetConnection();
nc.connect(null);

// Define Net Stream
var ns:NetStream = new NetStream(nc);

// Listen for the metaData
var listener:Object = new Object();
listener.onMetaData = function(md:Object):void{};
ns.client = listener;
ns.play("Cigars.flv");
```

Now that we have the NetConnection and the NetStream in place, let's turn our attention to feeding the stream containing the Cigars video into a virtual Video object.

6. Press Return/Enter twice and add the following code:

```
var myVideo:Video = new Video();
myVideo.attachNetStream(ns);
addChild(myVideo);
```

As you can see, the Video object is created using that first line of code. The second line "hooks" the stream into the object, and the last line places it on the stage. In this example, the video will be tucked up into the upper-left corner of the stage. What if you want the object to start 10 pixels down and 20 pixels in from the right edge of the stage?

7. That last line is what places the object on the stage, so you can add those positions between the second and third lines of the code. Click once after that second line, press Return/Enter and add the following:

```
var myVideo:Video = new Video();
myVideo.attachNetStream(ns);
myVideo.x = 10;
myVideo.y = 20;
addChild(myVideo);
```

If you test the movie at this point (see Figure 7-21), you will see the video playing on the stage and positioned where you wanted it.

> *The new* Video *object will always default to a size of 320 x 240, unless given specific width and height values. We have always regarded this as a bit odd because if you pull the same object from the library and physically add it to the stage, its default size is 160 x 120.*

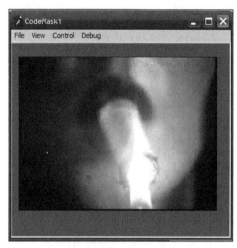

Figure 7-21. The invisible Video object becomes visible at runtime.

8. Let's now turn our attention to the mask. Click once at the end of the previous code block, press Return/Enter twice, and enter the following code to create a circular mask:

```
var mask_mc:MovieClip = new MovieClip();
mask_mc.graphics.beginFill(0x000000);
mask_mc.graphics.drawCircle(160,120,100);
addChild(mask_mc);
myVideo.mask = mask_mc;
```

The first line of code creates the movieclip named mask_mc, which will hold the mask. We know that masks use the Fill color to create the mask, and the second line of code fills the movieclip with a black color. The third line sets the shape of the mask. The three parameters (drawCircle(160,120,100);) determine the x and y location of the circle's center point, and the third number is the diameter of the circle.

The third line puts the mask on the stage over the video, and the last line (as you saw in the Reflection exercise) turns the movieclip into a mask.

9. Go ahead; test the movie. The square video is playing in a circle (see Figure 7-22).

Figure 7-22. Add a "virtual" mask and you have a rather interesting technique on your hands.

> You can also use this technique to create a square mask. The following line:
>
>   mask_mc.graphics.drawCircle(160,120,100);
>
> will be replaced with this one:
>
>   mask_mc.graphics.drawRect(10,10,200,120);
>
> The parameters for the drawRect() method are, in order of appearance, the x and y position of the rectangle based on its upper-left corner and the width and the height of the rectangle. As well, the Help menu should start to become your best friend. For a full listing of Drawing API functionality, see the Graphics class entry of the ActionScript 3.0 Language Reference in the Help docs. In particular, see the Public Methods heading.

Playing with masking colors

In this exercise, you'll create a mask that trims the video while still providing a backdrop for a masking effect. The idea actually came from wedding photographs. The loving couple is in full focus while the background is either faded or washed out. It is sort of like putting the subject in a window and giving the illusion of the subject being behind the washed-out area of the image. We thought, "Hey, why should the Photoshop guys have all the fun?" and then went to work.

We went to work, but there is a twist. There will be two copies of the video playing simultaneously. One copy will be masked, and the other will play outside of the mask. The user can change that video's color based on the position of the mouse over the unmasked video. You can accomplish this by understanding a fundamental rule of streaming Flash video: only one stream per Video object can be played at any one time. After you understand that rule, the project becomes somewhat easier to understand. You simply need to create two Video objects and feed a stream into each one. Let's get to work.

1. Open the StaticCutaway.fla file. Select the code in frame 1 and open the Actions panel. The code is not much different from the code written to this point in the book. The main difference is that we created two movieclips (myVideoOutside and myVideoInside) that will be used to create the effect.

2. Scroll down to line 36 of the code and enter the following:

```
var mask_mc:MovieClip = new MovieClip();
mask_mc.graphics.beginFill(0x000000);
mask_mc.graphics.drawRect(50,50,220,140);
this.addChild(mask_mc);

myVideoInside.mask = mask_mc;
```

Use the Drawing API to create the mask, which is nothing more than a simple rectangle filled with black. The last line takes that object and uses it as a mask for the video that will play in the myVideoInside movieclip.

3. Press Return (Mac) or Enter (PC) twice and enter the following code:

```
var insideFilters:Array = new Array();

var bevel:BevelFilter = new BevelFilter();
bevel.distance = 5;
bevel.angle = 45;
bevel.shadowAlpha = 0.3;
bevel.highlightAlpha = 0.3;
bevel.blurX = 5;
bevel.blurY = 5;
bevel.strength = 5;

insideFilters.push(bevel);

myVideoInside.filters = insideFilters
```

Now that we have created the mask, this code simply applies a Bevel filter to the masking object. As you might notice, the various values for the filter match those that would appear in the Filters panel in the Property Inspector. In fact, we actually created a movieclip containing a black rectangle with the same dimensions as the mask_mc movieclip and applied a Bevel filter to it. Once we got a "look" that satisfied us, we wrote down the values and added them to the code. Having done that, we simply deleted the movieclip from the library.

We then used the push() method of the Array class to store our first filter in the insideFilters array. This technique actually makes a lot of sense. Although you could just as easily write the first line of the filter code block this way:

```
var bevel:BevelFilter = new BevelFilter(5,45,.3,.3,5,5,);
```

You really don't have any idea of what those values mean. If things don't look the way you want when you test the movie, it is much easier to fix if the values are given "meaning" than to try to figure out what that second value of .3 really means, for example.

Having dealt with the video that will be masked and beveled, we can now turn our attention to the second video that will be placed into the movieclip named myVideoOutside. This one will be a bit different. As it plays, the color of the video will change based upon the position of the mouse on the stage.

4. Press Return (Mac) or Enter (PC) twice and enter the following code:

```
stage.addEventListener(MouseEvent.MOUSE_MOVE, onMouseMoveHandler);

function onMouseMoveHandler(evt:MouseEvent):void {
  var xPercent:Number = new Number(mouseX / 320);
  var yPercent:Number = new Number(mouseY / 240);

  var colorMatrixArray:Array = [xPercent,0,0,0,0,
                                0,yPercent,0,0,0,
                                0,0,xPercent*yPercent,0,0,
                                0,0,0,1,0];

  var colorMatrix:ColorMatrixFilter = new ColorMatrixFilter();
  colorMatrix.matrix = colorMatrixArray;

  var outSideFilters:Array = new Array();
  outSideFilters.push(colorMatrix);

  myVideoOutside.filters = outSideFilters;
};
```

Although this might look complex, in actual fact there is nothing here you haven't encountered to this point in the book. The color change is accomplished through the use of the Array used by ColorMatrixFilter.

The first step in the process is to tell the stage what to listen for (MOUSE_MOVE) and what to do when it hears it: execute the onMouseMoveHandler function.

The next step is to capture the mouse's x and y positions on the stage and to turn those numbers into percentage values. Those numbers are tossed into an Array, which is then used by the ColorMatrixFilter class to change the color of the video in the movieclip.

5. Save the movie and test it, as shown in Figure 7-23.

Now it's time to have fun. Change the color multiplier values and those in the matrix and see what happens when you test the movie. Remove the mouse movement and play with the multiplier values or change the multipliers from xPercent to yPercent values, and vice versa. As we've said, the amount of fun you can have with this should be illegal!

Figure 7-23. Note the position of the cursor and the color of the area of the video outside of the mask.

Tweening and easing = Swiss cheese

In this final exercise, before we turn you loose on your own project, we'll explore the use of the Tween and easing classes that are used by the TransitionManager class to create a rather interesting intro for a video.

The Tween class lets you use ActionScript to move, resize, and fade movieclips by specifying a property of the target movieclip to animate over a number of frames or seconds. In this exercise, you'll create a series of growing circles that will act as a mask for the video.

The Tween class also lets you specify a variety of easing methods. Easing refers to gradual acceleration or deceleration during an animation, which helps your animations appear more realistic. The fl.transitions.easing package provides many easing classes that contain equations for this acceleration and deceleration, which change the easing animation accordingly. In this exercise, the easing will be used to control how fast the circles grow on the stage. Let's get busy.

1. Open the TransitionIn.fla file. When it opens, select the first frame of the Actions layer and open the Actions panel.

2. Click once in line 1 of the script and enter the following code, which imports the classes being used in the exercise:

```
import fl.transitions.Tween;
import fl.transitions.easing.*;
```

These two lines of code actually kicked off a rather interesting discussion among the authors and our tech editor, David Stiller. When Tom saw the original code, these two lines were buried later on in the script. This struck him as a bit odd because he was used to importing classes right at the start of the code. The question was: is it a "best practice" to put these things at the start of the code, or can they appear later on?

Adam's position was simple: everything you have done so far in the book is based on the Flash timeline, so putting them at the top or in the middle of the code was not an issue. He was absolutely correct. Stylistically, their placement is not going to break the code. David agreed with this and the decision was to put them at the top to remain consistent with industry best practice.

But it really doesn't answer the question you might be asking, "Why is this best practice?" David ruminated on this for a couple of days and sent this rather brilliant response:

"As long as no harm is done, let the computer do the work. Back in ActionScript 1.0/2.0, variables didn't need to be declared, so people got lazy and didn't declare them. Let the computer do that, right? Well, in that case the laziness was detrimental because it led down the slippery slope of sloppy coding. (Does this variable have a null value or is it undefined? Where/when is it initialized? Is it initialized?) But I'll argue that import statements are another matter. In ActionScript 3.0 class files, if you don't have import statements, your code doesn't work at all. It's that simple. Likewise, in ActionScript 3.0, if you don't declare your variables, your code doesn't work. Boom. That said, in ActionScript 3.0 timeline code, Flash takes care of many (but not all) import statements for you. I personally feel that omitted import statements don't lead to sloppy code in the way nondeclared or nontyped variables can. Why? Well, nothing is especially clarified by their presence. It's not as if a developer is going to wonder if a variable was initialized somewhere; it'll be obvious what classes are in use because their very names will state their arrival. In ActionScript 3.0, if you want to attach something, you have to actually subclass the object it will be used for (that is, extend MovieClip to attach a movieclip symbol). Thankfully, Flash takes care of that by issuing a click-through warning when you set the Linkage class. I'm thankful for the helping hand because it would suck to have to write a full ActionScript 3.0 class file (a standalone text file) just to have to attach something. In the same way, I say let the automatic import statements do their automatic thing. The only dicey price for the convenience is the nebulous question of which import statements are actually needed. Here's a note I added to a recent CommunityMX article on the subject:

First, you'll notice an import statement, right off the bat. In ActionScript 3.0, as in 2.0, there are two paradigms for where code can be placed: in the FLA file itself or in external text files. When going the route of external text files—which in ActionScript 3.0 must be classes (files with an .as file extension, structured with the package and class keywords)—you'll find yourself typing import quite a lot. In fact, you'll do it once, for practically every object needed, at the top of each class. In contrast, when going the route of internal FLA file code, you'll find that Flash implicitly "understands" most of the import statements without your having to type them. While the definitive line is a bit blurry, a general rule of thumb is that "commonly used objects," such as text fields, movieclips, events, and MouseEvent objects, tend to work just fine without an accompanying import statement. (Remember, this applies to in-FLA code only.)

For the sort of code used in this book—not full-on applications, but more along the lines of handy scripts (for the most part)—I think it's okay to leave off the import statements. This approach has a precedent in Flash 8's ActionScript 2.0, where lesser-used classes like BitmapData and StyleSheet require imports, but most classes do not."

Thanks, David.

3. Click once in line 26 of the code block and enter the following:

```
var mask_mc:MovieClip = new MovieClip();
var counter:Number = 0;
```

We start the project by giving a new movieclip an object reference (mask_mc) and creating a variable that will hold the value of a number (counter) that will be constantly changing. The 0 is the initial value for the counter variable.

4. Press Return/Enter twice and enter the next two lines of code:

```
var myTimer:Timer = new Timer(50,63);
myTimer.addEventListener(TimerEvent.TIMER, onTick);
```

The Timer object is created because we need the mask to appear as a series of circles being drawn over the video. If we didn't have the timer, the mask would be drawn all at once and defeat the purpose of the effect.

The Timer class is extremely useful for ensuring that code—in this case, the function that draws circles—occurs at the frequency you set. Just be clear on one aspect of this class: if your operating system or the Flash movie is busy at the time the function is to be executed, it will be delayed.

The parameters for the Timer object simply tell Flash to "fire" the Timer every 50 milliseconds and to stop firing after 63 events have been completed. We choose 63 because we'll create 7 rows of 9 circles.

If you're having a hard time wrapping your mind around the Timer parameters, feel free to change the code line var myTimer:Timer = new Timer(50,63); to this:

```
var myTimer:Timer = new Timer();
myTimer.delay = 50;
timer.repeatCount = 63;
```

The next line (myTimer.addEventListener(TimerEvent.TIMER, onTick);) adds the event listener and tells Flash that when it detects the TIMER event to execute the custom onTick function you're about to write.

5. Press Return/Enter twice and write the function that creates the circles:

```
function onTick(event:TimerEvent):void {
    var circle_mc:MovieClip = new MovieClip();
    circle_mc.graphics.beginFill(0x0000);
    circle_mc.graphics.drawCircle(0,0,1);
    circle_mc.x = (counter%9)*40;
    circle_mc.y = Math.floor(counter/9)*40;
    mask_mc.addChild(circle_mc);
```

If you carefully walk through this code block, you will see how the first circle is drawn. After that is done, the circle is placed on the stage at 0,0 with a diameter of 1 pixel, and the movieclip containing the circle is nested in the mask_mc movieclip. The next row puts nine circles beside each other, and the next line puts each row of nine under the previous one.

This is all well and good, but we need to have 62 more circles appear on the stage and we want them to "zip" in as they appear on the stage.

6. Press Return/Enter twice and add the following code:

```
circle_mc.tween1 = new Tween(circle_mc,"width",Strong.easeOut,➡
circle_mc.width,70,10,true);
circle_mc.tween2  = new Tween(circle_mc,"height",Strong.easeOut,➡
circle_mc.width,70,10,true);
counter++;
}
```

Let's look at that first line to understand what is going on.

The Tween class lets you use ActionScript to move, resize, and fade movieclips by specifying a property of the target movieclip, in this case circle_mc, to animate over a number of frames or seconds. This class also lets you specify a variety of easing methods.

You might be aware of how tweens are eased using the Property Inspector, but now you know that easing can also be accomplished programmatically. Easing refers to gradual acceleration or deceleration during an animation, which helps your animations appear more realistic. The fl.transitions.easing package (imported at the start of this code block) provides many easing methods that contain equations for this acceleration and deceleration, which change the easing animation accordingly.

We start by creating a new Tween object. The parameters determine how the animation occurs. Here's what they mean:

- Object: The tween will be applied to the movieclip named circle_mc.
- Property: The value "width" is always written as a string and could be any settable property of the MovieClip class, such as height or alpha.
- Function: The Strong.easeOut method applies a faster-than-normal ease out to the width of the circle_mc object.
- Start: This number, the current value of circle_mc.width, indicates the start value for the effect.
- End: This number (70) indicates the ending value for the effect.
- Duration: This number (10) tells Flash to perform the tween over a time period of 10 seconds.
- Duration Type: This Boolean value (true) tells Flash to use seconds as the time unit instead of frames (otherwise, the duration of 10 in the previous parameter would depend on the frame rate of the movie).

You then apply this same Tween to the height property of the movieclip named circle_mc. The incremented counter variable (counter++) affects the x and y positions of the circles, which creates the needed number of circles on the stage. Note that tweens are added as a pair of dynamic properties to each new circle movieclip, so that each can manage its own tween.

7. Now that the circles are roaring onto the stage, you need only three lines of code to create the mask effect. Press Return/Enter twice and enter the following:

```
this.addChild(mask_mc);
myTimer.start();
myVideo.mask = mask_mc;
```

8. Save and test the movie. The circles shown in Figure 7-24 will build across the video.

Figure 7-24. Holey video, Batman!

Your turn: Masks in motion

We conclude this chapter by bringing together everything we have discussed and you have learned so far into one final exercise.

As you know, movieclips can be created using ActionScript and they have properties, such as position and size, that can be manipulated. In this exercise, we'll have a quite a few masks (up to 30 at any given time) moving across the screen, and the color of the video will change based upon the position of the mouse onscreen.

Where the masks will differ from what was done previously is that, as they pass over the video, the ColorTransform is removed from within the mask area. To make this even more interesting, the masks will actually be a variety of shapes.

Finally, you're about to be introduced to a new best practice, in which the code that drives the project is located on the timeline and within a separate ActionScript document.

Packages

As the name suggests, a package is the "holder" for a group of classes. In the case of this project, the package will be used to add to the MovieClip class. This process is called extending the class. The beauty of this way of working is that you have more flexibility (instead of having to write code on the timeline). By having the code that defines the shapes of the objects and what they do external to the main FLA file and SWF file, you can easily make changes to the project without having to concern yourself with opening Flash and making the change.

These files can be created using a word processor, including TextEdit on the Mac and WordPad on the PC, or they can be created in an HTML editor such as Dreamweaver CS3. These files always contain the file extension .as.

> There are other ActionScript editors out there that you can use, including SEPY (www.sephiroth.it/python/sepy.php), *Flex Builder 3 from Adobe, and FlashDevelop* (http://osflash.org/flashdevelop). *You can even use Flash by selecting the* ActionScript *file from the* New Document *dialog box when you select* File ➤ New.

So why a separate ActionScript document if you can do the same thing on the timeline? ActionScript is an object-oriented programming (OOP) language. The beauty of this concept is that you can encapsulate (a fancy word for reuse) your code, eliminating the need to write the same thing over and over. The result is less code-writing time and reduced debugging time. Another great advantage is centralization. The code is all in one place instead of spread out along the timeline, inside various movieclips, or even inside various Flash documents.

What does all of this have to do with video? To this point you have seen that Flash video projects can range from dead simple code-free playback applications to projects that are quite complex. There is a real danger that as you become more confident and proficient with this subject, your code will be spread all over the movie and, in many cases, the same code is written in a number of spots. This is called "spaghetti code," and you will spend an inordinate amount of time hunting through the project looking for code errors if you use this approach. OOP forces you to encapsulate certain functions into classes or even extend class functionality, as we will do in a minute. So much for the pep talk, let's have some fun.

1. Open a new text document, name it TetrisShape.as, and immediately save it to the MovingMask folder in the chapter's exercise folder.

2. Click once on the page and add the classes you will need by entering the following text:

```
package {
    import flash.display.MovieClip;
    import flash.utils.Timer;
    import flash.events.TimerEvent;
```

3. Press Return/Enter twice and enter the following:

```
public class TetrisShape extends MovieClip{
    private var shapeMovie:MovieClip;
    private var shapeNumber:Number;
    private var shapeSpeed:Number;
    private var shapeRotation:Number;
```

What is with the public and private stuff? When a class is created or extended, you can choose to have it available to other movies or code blocks outside of the package. This is the use of the public attribute. Anything that is to remain solely in the package has the private attribute. In this case, you'll create a class named TetrisShape that will be an extension of the MovieClip class and will be available to other Flash movies. The variables will be used to set some properties for the TetrisShape and are given the private attribute because they will only be used by this class.

The attributes in ActionScript 3.0 are the following:

- Public: The change is available to anything that needs to use it.
- Private: The change is available only to the class. It can't be used by the subclasses.
- Protected: The change is available to both the class and the subclasses.
- Internal: The change is available to any class in the package.

4. Press Return/Enter twice and enter the following:

```
public function TetrisShape() {
    shapeNumber = Math.floor(Math.random() * 4);
    shapeRotation = 0;
    shapeMovie = new MovieClip();
    shapeMovie.graphics.beginFill(0x000000);

    switch(shapeNumber) {
      case 0:
        shapeMovie.graphics.drawRect(-20,-20,40,40);
        break;

      case 1:
        shapeMovie.graphics.drawRect(-10,-40,20,80);
        break;

      case 2:
        shapeMovie.graphics.moveTo(-30,-20);
        shapeMovie.graphics.lineTo(-10,-20);
        shapeMovie.graphics.lineTo(-10,00);
        shapeMovie.graphics.lineTo(30,00);
        shapeMovie.graphics.lineTo(30,20);
        shapeMovie.graphics.lineTo(-30,20);
        shapeMovie.graphics.lineTo(-30,-20);
        break;

      case 3:
        shapeMovie.graphics.moveTo(-10,-30);
        shapeMovie.graphics.lineTo(10,-30);
        shapeMovie.graphics.lineTo(10,-10);
        shapeMovie.graphics.lineTo(30,-10);
        shapeMovie.graphics.lineTo(30,10);
        shapeMovie.graphics.lineTo(10,10);
        shapeMovie.graphics.lineTo(10,30);
        shapeMovie.graphics.lineTo(-10,30);
        shapeMovie.graphics.lineTo(-10,10);
        shapeMovie.graphics.lineTo(-30,10);
        shapeMovie.graphics.lineTo(-30,-10);
        shapeMovie.graphics.lineTo(-10,-10);
        break;
    }
    shapeMovie.graphics.endFill();
```

```
        addChild(shapeMovie);
        resetShape();
        startAnimation();
    }
```

The code starts by paying strict attention to one of the ActionScript fundamentals: all classes, TetrisShape in this case, should have a function with the same name as the class associated with them. This function, called the constructor, is automatically executed when the class is used.

The next three lines set a random shape, set its default rotation value to zero, and create the movieclip in which the shape will be drawn. The next big code block draws the various shapes in response to a switch statement. The final three lines put the shape in the movieclip named shapeMovie, set the properties for the shapeMovie movieclip, and start it animating across the screen.

5. Press Return/Enter twice and enter the following:

```
        private function shapeStep(timeEvent:TimerEvent):void {
            x += shapeSpeed;
            rotation += shapeRotation;
            if (x > 320) resetShape();
        }

        private function startAnimation():void {
            var moveTimer:Timer = new Timer(20);
            moveTimer.addEventListener(TimerEvent.TIMER,shapeStep);
            moveTimer.start();
        }

        private function resetShape():void {
            shapeSpeed = Math.random() * 5;
            x = -width;
            y = Math.random() * 240;
        }

        public function setRotation(newRotation:Number):void {
            shapeRotation = newRotation;
        }
    }
}
```

These four functions determine how the shape will animate and how often they occur: every 20 milliseconds.

6. Take a minute to carefully review this code and pay close attention to ensuring that things are spelled correctly and that the number of opening and closing brackets is equal. When you finish, save the document.

Now that the class file has been created, we can turn our attention to pulling the project together in Flash. The plan is to have about 100 of the shapes that will be created by the .as file move and tumble across the screen. Not only that, but these shapes will also act as a mask, and the color of the video will change when you move the mouse around the screen. Sound like a lot of work? Not really. Let's get started.

1. Open the `MovingMask_External.fla` file, click once on the first frame of the movie, and open the Actions panel.

2. Click once in line 21 of the Script pane and enter the following code:

```
var mask_mc:MovieClip = new MovieClip();

var maskTimer:Timer = new Timer(100,50);

maskTimer.addEventListener(TimerEvent.TIMER,maskTimerHandler);
function maskTimerHandler(timeEvent:TimerEvent):void {
  var myTetrisShape:TetrisShape = new TetrisShape();
  myTetrisShape.setRotation(Math.random()*3);
  mask_mc.addChild(myTetrisShape);
}

maskTimer.start();

addChild(mask_mc);
```

A new movieclip, mask_mc, is created to hold the shape created in the external .as file. The timer is told to create 100 of the shapes, and the function tells ActionScript to grab the shape from that external .as file, start it rotating, and add the movieclip containing the shape to the Flash stage.

The remainder of your coding chores will add the functionality to the movie.

3. Click once in line 55 of the code in the Script pane and enter the following:

```
stage.addEventListener(MouseEvent.MOUSE_MOVE, onMouseMoveHandler);

function onMouseMoveHandler(evt:MouseEvent):void {
  var xPercent:Number = new Number(mouseX / 320);
  var yPercent:Number = new Number(mouseY / 240);

  var colorMatrixArray:Array = [ xPercent,0,0,0,0,➡
                                 0,yPercent,0,0,0,➡
                                 0,0,xPercent*yPercent,0,0,➡
                                 0,0,0,1,0 ];

  var colorMatrix:ColorMatrixFilter = new ColorMatrixFilter();
  colorMatrix.matrix = colorMatrixArray;
  var outSideFilters:Array = new Array();
  outSideFilters.push(colorMatrix);

  video_mc.filters = outSideFilters;
};
```

Nothing new here. This code block simply changes the video color based upon the location of the mouse on the stage.

4. Carefully review your code and save and test the movie. The Tetris shapes move across the screen (see Figure 7-25), and the video changes color as you move the mouse.

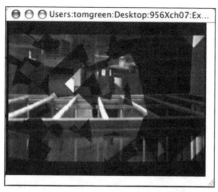

Figure 7-25. Using an external .as file to create the masking shapes

What you've learned

This chapter took masking from its most basic use—a shape on the stage over a video—to some rather advanced applications of masked video driven only by ActionScript. As you have discovered, video can be used as a straight presentation, but the careful use of a mask also offers you a wide range of creative possibilities that range from playing video through the screen on a phone, using shapes created in Illustrator, to creating the mask using the Drawing API to draw the mask and an external ActionScript class file to create and apply the mask.

In this chapter you have discovered:

- How to create a variety of masks
- How to use ActionScript to create and apply masks and masking effects
- How to create feathered masks and masks that are generated when the movie plays
- How to use the Tween class to animate masks
- How to create and use an ActionScript class file

The other subtext to this chapter is that masking can serve to place a video in context. Want to demonstrate video on a cell phone? Use the cell phone as a mask. Want video to serve strictly as an artistic medium? Let ActionScript do the heavy lifting. Your only constraint is the limit you place on your creativity and a relentless attention to detail.

Speaking of creativity and attention to detail, the next chapter focuses solely on some of the creative things you can do with video.

Chapter 8

FLASH VIDEO TRICKS, TIPS, AND SPECIAL EFFECTS

We don't deny that there has been quite a bit of material covered to this point in the book. So far, each chapter has focused on a specific creative aspect of working with Flash video. In this chapter, we let you take a bit of a "breather" and present a number of little exercises that will both further your knowledge of this fascinating subject and also allow you to apply several techniques that don't exactly fit the chapter themes to this point (or in subsequent chapters).

What we'll cover in this chapter:

- Rotoscoping video
- Ageing video
- Using SWFObject
- Creating looping video
- Visualizing the audio track in a video
- Letting the user resize video at runtime
- Adding a poster frame to the FLVPlayback component

Files used in this chapter:

- Roto.mov (Chapter08\ExerciseFiles_Ch08\Exercise\Roto\Roto.mov)
- iPod.fla (Chapter08\ExerciseFiles_Ch08\Exercise\iPod.fla)
- TaxiTurvey.flv (Chapter08\ExerciseFiles_Ch08\Exercise\TaxiTurvey.flv)
- Ageing.fla (Chapter08\ExerciseFiles_Ch08\Exercise\AgeingVideo\Ageing.fla)
- SWFObject.html (Chapter08\ExerciseFiles_Ch08\Exercise\SWFObject\SWFObject.html)
- Ageing.fla (Chapter08\ExerciseFiles_Ch08\Exercise\SWFObject\Ageing.fla)
- expressinstall.as (Chapter08\ExerciseFiles_Ch08\Exercise\SWFObject\expressinstall.as)
- ShutEye_Popeye.flv (Chapter08\ExerciseFiles_Ch08\Exercise\PosterFrame\ShutEye_Popeye.flv)
- BigBadSinbad.flv (Chapter08\ExerciseFiles_Ch08\Exercise\Interactive\BigBadSinbad.flv)
- Follow_Legend.flv (Chapter08\ExerciseFiles_Ch08\Exercise\Loop\Follow_Legend.flv)
- tortoise.flv (Chapter08\ExerciseFiles_Ch08\Exercise\Visualization\tortoise.flv)
- DWFlashVideo (Chapter08\ExerciseFiles_Ch08\Exercise\DWFlashVideo)

Rotoscoping video

In early 2000, one of the authors was in New York. Although he was there to get "trained up" on Dreamweaver, a visit to the inaugural meeting of the New York Macromedia user group was on the agenda. This meeting, held in Apple's office, was to feature one of the stars of the Flash industry, Hillman Curtis.

It was a difficult evening for Hillman. He was there to talk about Flash, whereas the majority of the attendees were Director users who had a tendency to absorb everything Hillman said through a "Director filter." In the middle of Hillman's presentation, he explained how to add video to a Flash movie, and it was this presentation that started the author on the path to the book you are currently reading.

Until that point in time, video in Flash was squarely in the realm of "wouldn't it be cool if..." Video was a dream, and yet here was Hillman demonstrating how it could be added to Flash. The technique drew on history. If you look at a piece of movie film, you will see that it is nothing more than a series of still images in a straight line. Video that's composed of a series of still images is said to be **rotoscoped**. Rotoscoping is no different from those flip books you had as a kid. As you flip through the pages, things seem to be in motion.

If you are a stickler for precise terminology, the rotoscoping exercise does not fit the precise definition of the term. Animators used this technique in the early days of film to create life-like movement in animations. For example, Prince Charming in Snow White looks rather life-like thanks to this technique. Animators filmed live actors in the scene. They would then output that film as a series of still images and draw the characters (such as Prince Charming) over the actors. We won't be doing that in this exercise. Instead, we'll show you how to output a video clip as a series of still images and then use them in Flash. Let's get started.

1. Open the Roto folder; a series of 40 sequentially numbered images are included in the Images folder. These images were created by copying a small clip from the Tortoise video.

> *The rest of this tutorial will focus on how the images were exported from QuickTime Pro and manipulated in Fireworks CS3. If you have neither application, we have included a folder named Thumbnails in the Roto folder; the images needed by Flash to complete this exercise can be found there.*

2. Double-click the Roto.mov file to open the QuickTime Player.

3. Select File ➤ Export and select Movie to Image Sequence in the Export drop-down menu.

4. Navigate to the Images folder and click Open. This tells QuickTime where to place the image sequence.

5. Click the Options button to open the Export Image Sequence Settings dialog box. Select JPEG from the Format drop-down menu and set the Frames per second value to 30 (see Figure 8-1). Click OK to close the dialog box.

6. Click the Save button. You will see a progress bar showing the process. When it closes, quit QuickTime. If you open the Images folder, you will see 40 sequentially numbered JPG images.

Figure 8-1. Creating the images in QuickTime

It's great to have the images, but a Flash button that is 320 pixels wide and 240 pixels high is unacceptable. Let's use Fireworks CS3 to scale the images to a size of 64 x 48. You can use Photoshop for this task as well, but the batch-processing feature of Fireworks CS3 is a real time-saver when it comes to this task.

1. Launch Fireworks CS3.

2. When the Start page opens, select File ➤ Batch Process to open the Batch Process dialog box shown in Figure 8-2.

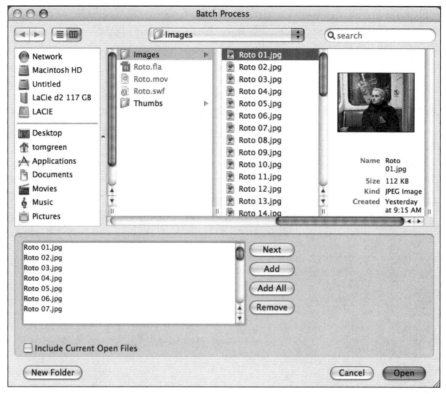

Figure 8-2. Fireworks CS3 is great for batch processing.

3. Navigate to the folder containing the images created earlier and open it. Click an image in the list and click the Add All button to add all the images in the folder to the batch processing list. When the image is added, click Next to open the list of Batch Options shown in Figure 8-3.

4. Click the Scale option and click the Add button to add scaling to the batch processing list. The Scale options will appear at the bottom of the dialog box.

5. From the Scale drop-down menu, select Scale to Percentage and set the value to 20%. This will give you an image that is 64 pixels wide by 48 pixels high. This size is somewhat large for a button, but it fits our needs for this exercise.

6. Click Next to open the Saving Files options shown in Figure 8-4. Click Browse and navigate to the folder where the original images are located and add a new folder named Thumbs. This is the folder in which the scaled images will be placed. When you see the Thumbs folder in the path, click Batch. Fireworks will show you a progress bar, and you will be notified when the process is finished. Click OK and quit Fireworks CS3.

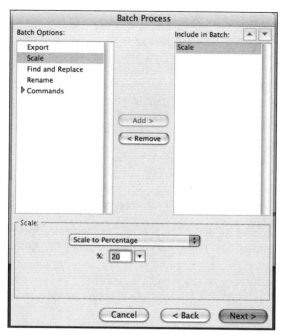

Figure 8-3. All the images will be scaled to 20% of their original size.

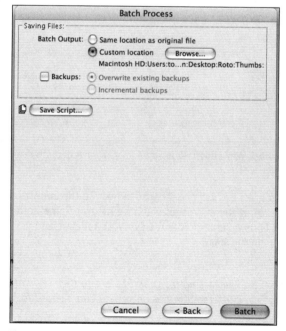

Figure 8-4. All the scaled images are then moved to a separate folder.

You were probably looking at the Save Script *button and wondering, "Hmmmm, what does this do?" Glad you asked. If you'll be repeating this process, clicking that button will create a batch script that will be placed in the Fireworks commands folder on your hard drive. The exact location of this folder varies from system to system and depends on whether you want the command to be available to all users or only to your user profile. Commands folders are located in the configuration folder in the Fireworks application folder and also in your user-specific Fireworks configuration folder. Here's the neat thing: the next time you want to scale all the images in a folder to 20% size, simply open Fireworks CS3 and select* Commands ➤ Run Script. *Locate the script, click* Open *to run it, and then navigate to the folder containing the files to be processed.*

Having created the assets, let's now create the rotoscoped video button in Flash CS3.

1. Open a new ActionScript 3.0 document in Flash CS3. When the document opens, create a new movieclip symbol named Tort. When you click OK to create the symbol, the Symbol editor will open.

2. Select File ➤ Import ➤ Import To Stage and navigate to the Thumbs folder. Select the first image in the sequence and click Import. The images will import to the symbol's timeline, not the main timeline.

3. You will next see the dialog box shown in Figure 8-5. It tells you that the file you are importing is a part of an image sequence and asks whether you want to import all the images in the sequence. The answer is a resounding yes. When you click Yes, all 40 images will be placed on individual frames on the timeline and added to the library. Best of all, they will all be in the register, meaning that they will all align with each other.

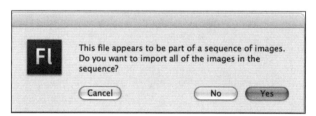

Figure 8-5. Why import 40 separate images when the software will do it for you?

4. Click Yes, and a progress bar will appear that shows you the import progress. When it finishes, you will see that each of the 40 images will have its own frame in the movieclip and they will also appear in the library. Scrub across the symbol's timeline and you will see that you have a short video playing on the stage.

You might want to consider tossing the thumbnails into their own folder in the library. We're not huge fans of cluttered libraries because it can be hard to find things.

5. Click the Scene 1 link to return to the main timeline. Create a new button symbol named Roto. Button symbols can be regarded as four-frame movieclips. The first three frames (Up, Over, and Down) are not that difficult to understand. Up is what the user sees before using the mouse, Over is what the user sees when the mouse is over the button, and Down is what the user sees when the mouse is pressed. The frame named Hit is the hot spot for the button.

6. When the Symbol editor opens, drag a copy of the first image in the sequence to the Up frame. In the Property Inspector, set its x and y coordinates to 0,0.

7. Click once in the Over frame of the Symbol editor and add a key frame. Delete the image that appears and replace it with a copy of the Tort movieclip from the library, as shown in Figure 8-6. Set the x and y position in the Property Inspector to 0,0.

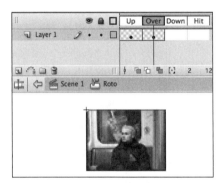

Figure 8-6. Put the movieclip in a button symbol and you have a video in a button.

8. Click the Scene 1 link. When you return to the main timeline, drag a copy of the Roto button to the stage. Save and test the movie. The video inside the "Over" key frame will "play" when you roll over the button.

Before we move on to the next exercise, let's get really clear about a couple of things:

- This technique works best when you have only a couple of seconds (30 to 50 Flash frames) of video that is rotoscoped. Don't try to place a few hundred images on the timeline.
- Do what we did and resize the images to fit the dimensions of the button before importing them.
- If you want the video to have a "jerky" feel, simply remove five or six of the key frames in the movieclip.
- If you need audio for the video clip, it needs to be added to either symbol. In this case, you would add an audio layer to the button symbol and place the audio clip in the Over key frame. If you use the movieclip, the audio would be added between the key frames in an audio layer.
- If you need the audio track from the video, don't use this technique. Instead consider creating an FLV file that matches the dimensions of the button and using a Progressive Download into a Video object to play the video in the button.
- If you need a Down state, consider converting the first image of the sequence to a movieclip and then changing its color using either the Color or Blend features of the Property Inspector.

Create your own iPod ad

You have to admit that when an Apple iPod ad hits your TV, there is no doubt that it is an iPod ad. People dance and otherwise cavort, but what makes the ads so noticeable is they are one color: black. Be careful here because we will be using an Alpha channel video. If you use a video without an Alpha channel, the technique will affect the entire screen.

In this exercise, you'll discover that the effect used is really not that difficult to achieve. Here's how:

1. Open the iPod.fla file and create a new movieclip symbol named iPod.

2. When the Symbol editor opens, add a Video object to the stage and use these values in the Property Inspector:

   - Instance Name: myVideo
   - Width: 160
   - Height: 210
   - X: 0
   - Y: 0

3. Add a new layer named Actions. Select the first frame of the Actions layer and open the Actions panel by selecting Window ➤ Actions.

4. When the Actions panel opens, enter the following code:

```
var nc:NetConnection = new NetConnection();
nc.connect(null);
var ns:NetStream = new NetStream(nc);
myVideo.attachNetStream(ns);

var listener:Object = new Object();
listener.onMetaData = function(md:Object):void{};
ns.client = listener;

ns.play("Reflect.flv");
```

5. Click the Scene 1 link to return to the main timeline and drag the movieclip from the library to the stage.

6. Click the movieclip once and select Brightness in the Color drop-down menu in the Property Inspector.

7. Set the Brightness value to -100.

8. Save the movie to the same folder as the FLV file and test the movie. As shown in Figure 8-7, you have just created your own iPod ad.

Figure 8-7. Change the brightness—you have an iPod ad!

Letting video show its age

Sometimes you might require your video to look rather old (with sort of a sepia color) and contain a few scratch marks to indicate age. This is easily accomplished in Flash. What better video to use to demonstrate this technique than an old Popeye cartoon named Taxi Turvey that was created in 1954?

> This video is squarely in the realm of public domain, thanks to the efforts of Rick Prelinger, who founded the Prelinger Archive in 1983. This collection, which was obtained by the U.S. Library of Congress in 2002, contains more than 2,000 videos that are freely available to the general public at www.archive.org/details/prelinger. Even though the digital source files are available, the authors are including only FLV versions of the clips that they created in this book.

Let's age some video.

1. Open the `Ageing.fla` file. When it opens, you will see we have placed a movieclip containing the Video object that will play the cartoon.

2. Click the movieclip on the stage to select it and click the Filters tab on the Property Inspector to open the Filters panel.

3. Open the filter list by clicking the + icon on the panel and selecting Adjust Color. When the Adjust Color panel opens, reduce the Saturation value to -100. This has the effect of removing the color and leaving you with a black-and-white video.

4. Click the Properties tab and, with the movieclip on the stage selected, select Color ➤ Tint and use the following values:

- R: 204
- G: 102
- B: 0
- Opacity: 40%

This process applies the sepia tone shown in Figure 8-8.

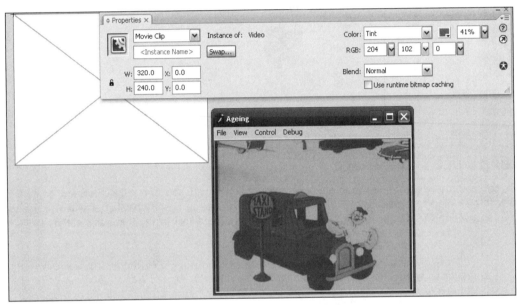

Figure 8-8. Add a sepia tone to the video after desaturating the video's color.

5. Create a new movieclip named Scratches. When the Symbol editor opens, add a gray box that is 320 by 240 and set its x and y coordinates to 0,0. Add a frame in frame 10 of this clip's layer. Lock the layer.

6. Add a new layer and add key frames in frames 2 to 10 of this layer.

7. Select the Pencil tool. In the Property Inspector set the stroke color to white (#FFFFFF) and the stroke width to .25. In frame 1 of the new layer, draw three or four random squiggles. Repeat this step for the remaining key frames in the layer. Be sure to draw the lines in random locations in each new frame.

8. Delete the layer containing the gray box and click the Scene 1 link to return to the main timeline.

9. Add a new layer and place the Scratches movieclip in this layer. Be sure that the movieclip matches the dimensions of the video below it. Save and test the movie. Your video has developed some scratches (see Figure 8-9).

Figure 8-9. The video looks a little beat up.

Now let's make the video flicker. Follow these steps:

1. Add a new layer to the main timeline and lock Layer 2.

2. Select the Rectangle tool and draw a gray box: #999999. In the Property Inspector, set the dimensions of the box to 320 by 240 and set its x and y coordinates to 0,0.

3. Select the box on the stage and convert it to a movieclip named Flicker.

4. When the Symbol editor opens, select the box on the stage and convert it to a movieclip named FlickerBox. By creating this movieclip, you can use the Property Inspector to manipulate the box.

5. Add a key frame in frame 2 of the Flicker movieclip. Select the box on the stage and select Brightness from the Color drop-down menu in the Property Inspector. Set the Brightness value to 86%. The box appears to get brighter.

6. Select the object in frame 1 of the Flicker movieclip and reduce its Brightness value to 36%. The box will appear to darken.

7. Return to the main timeline, save the movie, and test it. The video appears to flicker.

Ageing through code

Some of you might have gone through this exercise and thought: "Hang on, can this be done using only ActionScript?" Absolutely, but there's a hitch: there is no AdjustColorFilter class in Action-Script 3.0.

To get around this odd omission, we'll use a custom class written by Matthew Lloyd (www.devslash. com), who has graciously permitted its use in this book. Matthew's class uses the built-in ColorMatrixFilter class, which you first encountered in Chapter 6, to perform hue and saturation transformations that can be added to the filters property of movieclips or any other object that accepts filters.

> *Fortunately, you don't have to be as math-savvy as Matthew to benefit from his work. All you have to do is import his* HueColorMatrixFilter *class and make sure to include his class file in the same folder as your FLA file, complete with its com/deviant sub-folders. Or include the class file and its subfolders in another location on your hard drive and make a note of its path in the classpath preferences:* Edit ➤ Preferences ➤ ActionScript ➤ ActionScript 3.0 Settings.

Here's the code:

```
import fl.motion.Color;
import com.deviant.HueColorMatrixFilter;

var myVideo:Video = new Video();

var videoContainer:MovieClip = new MovieClip();
addChild(videoContainer);

videoContainer.addChild(myVideo);

var nc:NetConnection = new NetConnection();
nc.connect(null);

var ns:NetStream = new NetStream(nc);
myVideo.attachNetStream(ns);

var listener:Object = new Object();
listener.onMetaData = function (md:Object):void{};
ns.client = listener;

ns.play("TaxiTurvey.flv");

// Desaturate
var sepia:HueColorMatrixFilter = ➥
new HueColorMatrixFilter();
sepia.Saturation = 0;
videoContainer.filters = [sepia.Filter];

// Add tint
var ct:Color = new Color();
ct.setTint(0xDD9900, 0.5);
videoContainer.transform.colorTransform = ct;

// *********************************************************
// Create a Mask
var mask_mc:MovieClip = new MovieClip();
mask_mc.graphics.beginFill(0x000000);
```

```
    mask_mc.graphics.drawRect(0,0,318,238);
    addChild(mask_mc);

    // ***********************************************************
    // Set the mask_mc as the mask for myVideo
    myVideo.mask = mask_mc;

    var scratches:Sprite = new Sprite();
    addChild(scratches);

    // Add random alpha
    videoContainer.addEventListener(Event.ENTER_FRAME, ➥
    enterFrameHandler);
    function enterFrameHandler(evt:Event):void {

      // Set a random alpha
      this.alpha = 0.6 + (Math.random() * 0.2);

      // Set a random x and y position from -1 to 1

      this.x = (Math.random() * 2) - 1;
      this.y = (Math.random() * 2) - 1;

      // Draw a random scratch at a random time

      scratches.graphics.clear();
      if (Math.random() < 0.2) {
        scratches.graphics.lineStyle(1, 0xFFFFFF, 0.2);
        scratches.graphics.moveTo(Math.random() * 318, ➥
    Math.random() * 238);
        scratches.graphics.lineTo(Math.random() * 318, ➥
    Math.random() * 238);
      }
    };
```

There are a couple of things in the bold code that are new. First is the inclusion of the custom HueColorMatrixFilter class. It gets used in the next bold area, where it is instantiated, its Saturation property is set to 0, and it is then added to the filters array of the movieclip that holds the Video object (videoContainer). Without this desaturation, the next part, the setTint() method, doesn't look as good as the nonscripted approach because the original colors of the video still show through.

The second is how the tint is applied to the video. setTint() is a method from the Color class that accepts two parameters. The first parameter is the actual tint color; the second, using a value between 0 and 1, is the percentage of the tint to be applied. A value of 0 returns the object to its original color, and a value of 1 completely tints the object (none of its original color is visible). By applying a 50% tint—ct.setTint(0xDD9900,0.5)—a sepia effect is produced. Or if you chose not to use HueColorMatrixFilter for desaturation, some of the cartoon's original color shows through.

The third new technique is how the flicker and scratches are applied. A new Sprite named scratches is created to act as the canvas on which the scratches are drawn. Then, in an ENTER_FRAME event handler, the alpha, x, and y properties of videoContainer are adjusted to random values within a limited range. This simple change to the alpha is what starts the flicker as the video randomly receives an alpha value of any number between 60% and 80%. The x and y movement causes the flicker.

The last lines of the ENTER_FRAME handler move the scratches around in a random manner. The code generates a random number between 0 and 1. If that number is less than 0.2, a random scratch is drawn in the Sprite instance (scratches) within the boundaries of the video.

The complete version of this file can be found in the chapter download. The path is Chapter08\ ExerciseFiles_CH08\Complete\Ageing_AS3\aged.fla.

Using SWFObject to deploy a SWF file

If you have published Flash content, you will be quite familiar with the HTML option in the Publish Settngs dialog box. What this option does is create the HTML wrapper for your video, and a small JavaScript file will appear in the Scripts folder that is created at the same time. If you're a Dreamweaver user, you also might have experienced Dreamweaver asking you whether you want to update the JavaScript that makes your SWF file play when you place a SWF file in a Dreamweaver document. If you were to create an HTML document using the last exercise, you would see an HTML page and a JavaScript file (AC_RunActiveContent) sitting in the same directory as your SWF file (see Figure 8-10).

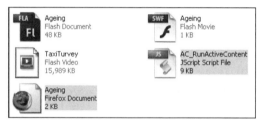

Figure 8-10. Select the HTML option when you publish a SWF file and you create two files.

If you open the HTML file, you will see an <object> tag and an <embed> tag, which are the default for placing a SWF file into an HTML page. In this version of Flash, Flash CS3, Adobe modified the code for the EOLAS workaround (see the following for more info), which was first introduced in the Dreamweaver 8.03 update. Here's the default embed code in the HTML document:

```
<object classid="clsid:d27cdb6e-ae6d-11cf-➡
96b8-444553540000" codebase="http://download.macromedia.com/pub/➡
shockwave/cabs/flash/ ➡
swflash.cab#version=9,0,0,0" width="320" ➡
height="240" id="Ageing" align="middle">
<param name="allowScriptAccess" value="sameDomain" />
<param name="allowFullScreen" value="false" />
<param name="movie" value="Ageing.swf" />➡
<param name="quality" value="high" />➡
<param name="bgcolor" value="#ffffff" />
<embed src="Ageing.swf" quality="high" bgcolor="#ffffff" ➡
```

```
    width="320" height="240" name="Ageing" align="middle" ➥
    allowScriptAccess="sameDomain" allowFullScreen="false"➥
     type="application/x-shockwave-flash" ➥
    pluginspage="http://www.macromedia.com/go/getflashplayer" />
    </object>
```

Thankfully, you don't need to really understand this code other than to know that it embeds a SWF file into the HTML document. Many Flash developers aren't finding Adobe's workaround to be as bulletproof as they might expect. Before we get into dealing with this, let's quickly review what got us to this point.

The EOLAS patent dispute

In 1998 the EOLAS company (EOLAS is an acronym for Embedded Objects Linked Across Systems) was granted a patent that "relates to a distributed hypermedia method for automatically invoking external application providing interaction and display of embedded objects within a hypertext document." This is a mouthful for the simple concept of a browser's capability to support plug-ins.

Up until 1999, Internet Explorer would use an ActiveX control to launch these plug-ins, one of which was the Flash Player. In that year, the EOLAS company asked Microsoft to license the technology. Microsoft declined and found itself in court. In 2003, the court made its decision, and Microsoft was the loser. Naturally, the decision was appealed, and Microsoft arrived at the end of the road in October 2005, when the US Supreme Court refused to hear the appeal. Facing a potential payout of more than half a billion dollars, Microsoft decided that it could get a bigger bang for that money by simply changing how Internet Explorer handled plug-ins. In April 2006, Microsoft changed Internet Explorer to sidestep the EOLAS patent by requiring users to click once on an ActiveX control to activate it.

This, of course, is not exactly user-friendly, which is why there is now a JavaScript-based workaround that plays interactive content without user interaction.

Even though the Adobe Dreamweaver solution is quite useful, it still has some issues, including the following:

- **Duplication of `<object>` and `<embed>` tags**: If you need to make a change to the code, you must make the change in both places. In addition, revisions made by hand to the code don't necessarily show up in Design view, and vice versa.

- **Version detection**: The code doesn't allow for alternate HTML content if the necessary Flash Player isn't installed. Flash CS3 does have this capability if you choose the HTML Publish option and select this feature in the HTML Publishing Options panel.

One of the most popular solutions to this was developed by Geoff Sterns. It is called SWFObject, and you can freely access it from http://blog.deconcept.com/swfobject/. What it does is to simplify Flash Player detection and essentially replaces all the `<object>` and `<embed>` tags in the HTML and writes it to the browser via JavaScript after the HTML document loads into the browser. Unlike Flash, it is search-engine friendly and can be configured to include Adobe's ExpressInstall, which allows the user to upgrade to the latest Flash Player version without having to manually download and launch the installer. If you use a Mozilla browser such as Firefox, you have also experienced the nastiness of having to close the browser while the installation takes place. Unfortunately, this issue still remains with no solution on the horizon.

Using SWFObject

Using SWFObject is rather simple.

1. Launch Dreamweaver CS3 or another HTML editor of your choosing. Open the SWFObject. html file in the SWFObject folder found in the Chapter 8 exercise folder.

2. If you are in Dreamweaver CS3, click the Code button to open Code view.

3. Select line 6 of the code and replace it with the following:

```
<script src="Scripts/swfobject.js" type="text/javascript"></script>
```

If you follow that path in the exercise folder, you will see a file named swfobject.js inside the Scripts folder. This file allows the browser to know how the SWFObject object is defined, as referenced later in the code. Put it in whatever folder you like as long as you reference its path correctly.

4. Select all the code between the opening <body> tag and the closing </body> tag. Press Delete to remove it.

5. Add the following code between the <body> and </body> tags:

```
<div id = "flashcontent">
    <p>The swf file will automatically appear here when the page ➥
    loads into the browser. Some developers use this text as alternate ➥
    content for those users without the Flash plug-in or ➥
    who have turned off JavaScript.</p>
</div>
<script type = "text/javascript">
    var so = new SWFObject("Ageing.swf",➥
    "myMovie","320","240", "9", "#FFFFFF");
    so.write("flashcontent");
</script>
```

The key to working with SWFObject is to give the video (that is, the SWF file that contains the video) its own <div> tag on the page. The video gets inserted on the page by the code block under the closing </div> tag, replacing whatever content is inside that <div> tag. This could be explanatory text (as shown), a stand-in graphic file, or whatever you like. For SWFObject to know which <div> tag you mean, it must contain an ID (such as flashcontent) that is referenced later by the write() method.

The important line is the SWFObject constructor:

```
var so = new SWFObject("Ageing.swf","myMovie",➥
"320","240", "9", "#FFFFFF");
```

It identifies the SWF file to be played, gives it an ID ("myMovie") that allows JavaScript to reference the SWF file if you ever need it to, sets the width and height of the SWF file, sets the minimum version of the Flash Player needed to see the content (you can also specify minor releases, such as 9.0.45), and gives it a background color: #FFFFFF (white).

6. Save and test the file by opening it in a browser. The video shown in Figure 8-11 will play, and you won't see the Click to activate warning in Internet Explorer.

If you are feeling lazy and aren't in the mood to constantly write the code in an HTML page, CommunityMX has developed a Dreamweaver extension that will do the work for you. You can purchase it here: www.communitymx.com/content/article.cfm?cid=D982E.

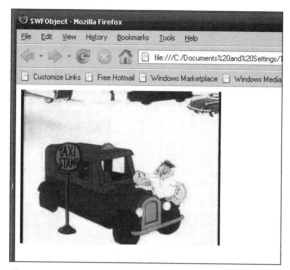

Figure 8-11. Using SWFObject

Using ExpressInstall

When Macromedia (now Adobe) released Flash Player 8, it included a new feature called ExpressInstall. What it did was to automatically prompt everyone with Flash Player version 6 or higher to upgrade to the latest version of the Flash Player. What made this so remarkable was that the user didn't have to manually download and launch the installer to upgrade. Unfortunately, Mozilla-based browser users must still close the browser while installing the update.

Follow these steps to add ExpressInstall functionality to your web page:

1. Click once at the end of the constructor (line 16) of the HTML code and press Return/Enter.

2. Add the following line of code:

```
var so = new SWFObject("Ageing.swf","myMovie","320","240", "7",➥
"#FFFFFF");
so.useExpressInstall("expressinstall.swf");
so.write("flashcontent");
```

3. Save the file.

When you downloaded the file from Geoff's site, a file named expressinstall.swf was included in the download. When the page loads, SWFObject first checks for the presence of Flash Player. If the user needs to upgrade, the expressinstall.swf file is loaded instead of the SWF file containing the video. When expressinstall.swf loads, users see a dialog box asking whether they want to upgrade to the latest version of the Flash Player. If the user approves the installation of the new Flash Player, it quietly loads in the background, and the user is shown the download progress.

There is a second method that doesn't involve HTML code, which you can use to add ExpressInstall to a SWF file:

1. Open the Ageing.fla file in the SWFObject folder. When it opens, you'll notice that the first frame of the movie is empty.

2. Select frame 1 of the movie and open the Actions panel.

3. Click once in the Script pane and enter the following code:

```
#include "expressinstall.as";
var ExpressInstall = new ExpressInstall();
if (ExpressInstall.needsUpdate){
  ExpressInstall.init();
  stop();
}
```

The first line of code is what "loads up" the expressinstall.as file. If you do use this technique, be sure that the expressinstall.as file is in the same folder as the SWF file that is calling it—or supply the relevant path in your #include directive. The remainder of the code checks to see whether an update is needed. If so, it starts the process.

Using a preview image as a video placeholder

It is quite common to be handed a video that starts with a black screen for the first second or two before the actual content starts to play. Place this on a web page, and the user will see a black box with video controls under it. This is obviously a worst-case scenario. A more common one is this: you don't want the video to start playing as soon as the FLVPlayback component appears on the stage. Instead, you want to load a thumbnail image, commonly referred to as a poster frame, from the video into the component and have that thumbnail disappear when the user clicks the play button.

In this exercise, we'll show you how to create that thumbnail from within Flash CS3 and then add the thumbnail and the FLVPlayback component at runtime.

Follow these steps to create the thumbnail:

1. Open a new Flash CS3 document and drag a copy of the FLVPlayback component to the stage.

2. Save this file to the PosterFrame folder found in your Chapter 8 exercise folder.

3. Drag a copy of the FLVPLayback component from the Components panel to the stage and set the source parameter to ShutEye_Popeye.flv in the component parameters.

4. Double-click the preview parameter; the Select Preview Frame dialog box (shown in Figure 8-12) will open, and the video will start to play.

This dialog box actually serves three functions:

- Allows you to preview an FLV file
- Acts as a timecode source for cue points or other events
- Creates a runtime preview image

If you roll the mouse over the video, you'll see a set of fully functioning video controls.

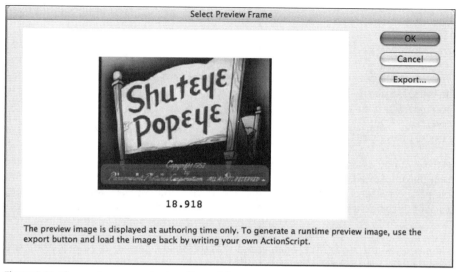

Figure 8-12. The preview parameter is quite useful.

5. Click OK, and the dialog box will close. The frame of the video that was playing when you clicked the OK button appears in the component on the stage. This is a great feature if you want more than a black box with an FLV icon on the Flash stage. This image is there only as a placeholder and does not appear when the video is played through the component.

6. Click the preview parameter again to open the Select Preview Frame dialog box. Roll over the image and use the scrubber in the video control to get yourself to the 137.504 mark of the video. You should see an image of Popeye about to toss the mouse out of the front door. The Select Preview Frame timecode uses only seconds and milliseconds.

7. Click the Export button to open the Export Image dialog box. Name the image ShutEye and save it to the PosterFrame folder in your Chapter 8 exercise folder. The image appears in the component and in the PosterFrame folder. The image format used for the exported images is PNG.

8. Click once on the component on the stage and delete it. Save the file.

The amazing virtual FLVPlayback component

In the previous chapter, you learned how to add a video to the stage through the use of ActionScript (and nothing else). You might have gone through that exercise ("Where did everything go?") and wondered, "Can I do the same thing with the FLVPlayback component?" The answer: absolutely. Here's how:

1. If you closed the previous example, open it. If you open the library you will see an instance of the FLVPlayback component in the library. You need to have the component in the library, not on the stage, for this technique to work.

2. Rename Layer 1 as Actions, select the first frame, and open the Actions panel.

3. Click once in the Script pane and enter the following code:

```
import fl.video.FLVPlayback;
var myVideo:FLVPlayback = new FLVPlayback ();
myVideo.skin = "SkinOverAll.swf";
myVideo.skinBackgroundColor = 0x999999;
myVideo.source = "ShutEye_Popeye.flv";
myVideo.x = 100;
myVideo.y= 20;
addChild(myVideo);
```

The first thing you do is import the FLVPlayback class into the movie. From there, the rest of the code is relatively uncomplicated. You create an instance of the component in the library and reference it by a variable named myVideo. Add a skin, give the skin a color, and tell Flash which FLV file to use and where to put the component on the stage. The last line is how the component is actually "put" on the stage.

4. Save and test the movie. The video appears, as shown in Figure 8-13, exactly where specified, and the skin appears in the movie as well.

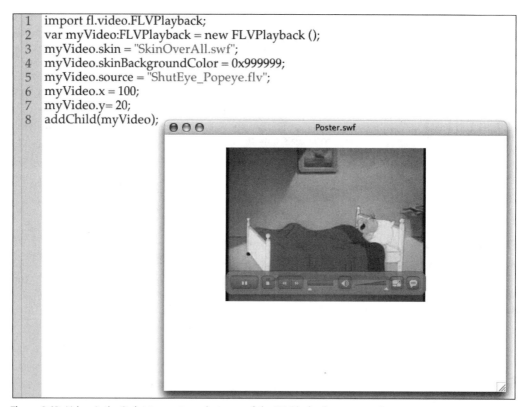

Figure 8-13. Using ActionScript to create an instance of the FLVPlayback component

Now that the video is playing, let's dynamically add that PNG image created earlier. Even though we are using a PNG image, you can also use JPG and GIF images to load a thumbnail for the cartoon. Follow these steps:

1. Close the SWF file. When you return to Flash, open the Actions panel containing the code entered earlier.

2. Click once at the end of line 1 in the Script pane and press Return/Enter.

3. Enter the following code, which imports the classes needed to complete the exercise:

```
import fl.video.VideoEvent;
import flash.net.URLRequest;
import flash.display.Loader;
```

4. Obviously, a video that plays as soon as it loads defeats the purpose of this exercise. Let's deal with that. Click once after the line that sets the y position of the component on the stage, press Return/Enter, and enter the following:

```
myVideo.autoPlay = false;
```

5. Now that the video is paused, let's use the Loader class to identify the image to be placed into the component. This occurs when the video loads, so we need to tell Flash what to listen for and what to do when the Play button on the skin is clicked. This is followed by a preparatory instance of the Loader class and a call to the custom loadImage() function, which we'll define in just a moment. Press Return/Enter once after the line just entered and then add the following:

```
myVideo.addEventListener(VideoEvent.PLAYING_STATE_ENTERED, playVideo);
var thumbImage:Loader = new Loader();
loadImage(thumbImage,"ShutEye ");
```

6. You can now add the video and thumbnail functionality to the component. Click once after the last line of the code, press Return/Enter twice, and enter the following function, which "turns off" the image when the Play button is clicked:

```
function playVideo(evt:VideoEvent):void {
  thumbImage.visible = false;
}
```

7. The final function loads the image into the Loader and places it into the display list of the FLVPlayback instance. Press Return/Enter twice and enter the following:

```
function loadImage(loader:Loader, imageURL:String):void {
  var urlRequest:URLRequest = new URLRequest(imageURL);
  loader.load(urlRequest);
  myVideo.addChild(loader);
}
```

8. Check your code, save the movie, and test it. The poster frame shown in Figure 8-14 appears inside the FLVPlayback component. Click Play; the image disappears, and the video starts to play.

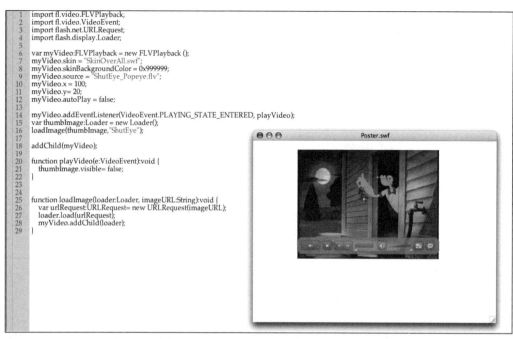

```
1   import fl.video.FLVPlayback;
2   import fl.video.VideoEvent;
3   import flash.net.URLRequest;
4   import flash.display.Loader;
5
6   var myVideo:FLVPlayback = new FLVPlayback ();
7   myVideo.skin = "SkinOverAll.swf";
8   myVideo.skinBackgroundColor = 0x999999;
9   myVideo.source = "ShutEye_Popeye.flv";
10  myVideo.x = 100;
11  myVideo.y= 20;
12  myVideo.autoPlay = false;
13
14  myVideo.addEventListener(VideoEvent.PLAYING_STATE_ENTERED, playVideo);
15  var thumbImage:Loader = new Loader();
16  loadImage(thumbImage,"ShutEye");
17
18  addChild(myVideo);
19
20  function playVideo(e:VideoEvent):void {
21      thumbImage.visible= false;
22  }
23
24
25  function loadImage(loader:Loader, imageURL:String):void {
26      var urlRequest:URLRequest= new URLRequest(imageURL);
27      loader.load(urlRequest);
28      myVideo.addChild(loader);
29  }
```

Figure 8-14. Creating an instance of the FLVPlayback component and adding a poster frame

Letting the user "play" with the video

Media pundits and those who study the field of media will tell you that video is a passive medium. They are quite correct in this observation because you passively sit somewhere and watch a video. In this exercise, you'll create a project that lets the user interact with (or "play" with) the video. In this example, the user will be using the mouse to pause and play the video and also to scale the video.

The core concept underlying this exercise is this: the user doesn't interact with the video; the user interacts with the stream. This a hard concept to grasp and the authors have spent countless hours beating this point into the heads of their students. You don't pause a video; you pause the stream of information into the Flash Player. You don't play a video; you start the flow of information into the Flash Player and let it go to work.

Thus, as you move through this exercise, you'll discover that you need to suspend the stream before you can actually play with the video.

1. Open a new Flash ActionScript 3.0 document. This whole project will be code driven, so save the file to the interactive folder and open the Actions panel.

2. Declare the variables to be used. Click once in the Script pane and enter the following:

   ```
   var nc:NetConnection = new NetConnection();
   var ns:NetStream;
   var listener:Object = new Object();
   ```

The only really "new" thing here is the creation of the `listener` variable. You have usually created this variable and then created the onMetaData event handler in the next line. The neat thing about variables is they can be declared whenever you need them to be. But in this case, we decided to keep things neat and tidy and created the `listener` variable well before the onMetaData event handler.

3. This project will require the user to click and drag the bottom-right corner of the video to resize it while it is playing. This means that you need to not only create a Video object but also the movieclip into which it will be placed (because a Video object can't be scaled on the fly). Wrap it in a movieclip and it becomes possible. Press Return/Enter twice and enter the following:

```
var videoMC:MovieClip = new MovieClip();
var myVideo:Video = new Video(320,240);

nc.connect(null);
ns = new NetStream(nc);
myVideo.attachNetStream(ns);

listener.onMetaData = function(md:Object):void{};
ns.client = listener;

ns.play("BigBadSinbad.flv");
```

Having created the objects that will hold the video and wire the Video object up for playback, you can turn your attention to the interactivity. Remember that this will occur with the mouse (and you know that the mouse will be used to control the stream of data into the Flash Player). As soon as a mouse action is undertaken, the stream will be paused. The mouse will be used to do the following:

- Start the video playing through a mouse click
- Start the video playing when it rolls out of the movieclip holding the video
- Use the video when the mouse rolls over the video
- Scale the video by dragging a corner of the video
- Have the resized video "drop" into place and start playing when the mouse is clicked

To accomplish these tasks, Flash needs to listen for a series of mouse events.

4. Press Return/Enter twice and enter the following listeners:

```
videoMC.addEventListener(MouseEvent.CLICK, playMovie);
videoMC.addEventListener(MouseEvent.MOUSE_OUT, playMovie);
videoMC.addEventListener(MouseEvent.MOUSE_OVER, pauseMovie);
videoMC.addEventListener(MouseEvent.MOUSE_DOWN, dragMovie);
videoMC.addEventListener(MouseEvent.MOUSE_UP, dropMovie);
```

5. With the housekeeping out of the way, let's get the video onto the stage. Press Return/Enter twice and enter the following code:

```
videoMC.x = 25;
videoMC.y = 25;
addChild(videoMC);
videoMC.addChild(myVideo);
```

6. The final step is to simply write the functions called in the listeners. Let's start with the easy ones: playMovie and pauseMovie. Press Return/Enter twice and type in the following code:

```
function playMovie(evt:MouseEvent):void {
  ns.resume();
}

function pauseMovie(evt:MouseEvent):void {
  ns.pause();
}
```

The remaining functions are where the magic happens. One function, dragMovie(), will make sure that the dragging responds only when the user clicks within 50 pixels of the bottom-right corner of the video to resize the video. The next one, dropMovie(), will "drop" the resized video into place on the stage. Let's get busy:

7. Press Return/Enter twice and type in the following function:

```
function dragMovie(evt:MouseEvent):void {
    if (videoMC.mouseX >= videoMC.width - 50 && videoMC.mouseY >=➡
videoMC.height - 50) {
        ns.pause();
        videoMC.removeEventListener(MouseEvent.MOUSE_OUT, playMovie);
        videoMC.removeEventListener(MouseEvent.MOUSE_OVER, pauseMovie);
        videoMC.addEventListener(Event.ENTER_FRAME, resizeMovie);
    }
}
```

The first line tells Flash that this function is tied to a MouseEvent. The next one checks to see whether the mouse is within 50 pixels of the bottom-right corner of the movieclip holding the video (this explains the expression – 50). If the mouse is indeed within that range, the video is paused. If the mouse is in that "golden zone" of 50 pixels, Flash is also told to stop listening for MOUSE_OVER and MOUSE_OUT events. Even so, if the user releases the mouse outside of the golden zone, the video will play. If the mouse is released outside of the golden zone and is over the video, the video will pause. The last line of the code uses an ENTER_FRAME event to allow the user to resize the video on the screen.

8. Having paused and resized the video, you need to turn your attention to "dropping" the resized movieclip into place and getting the video inside of it to play. This is done by simply telling Flash to stop listening for the resizeMovie function and reassigning the rollover and rollout events. Press Return/Enter twice and enter the following:

```
function dropMovie(evt:MouseEvent):void {
  ns.pause();
  videoMC.addEventListener(MouseEvent.MOUSE_OUT, playMovie);
  videoMC.addEventListener(MouseEvent.MOUSE_OVER, pauseMovie);
  videoMC.removeEventListener(Event.ENTER_FRAME, resizeMovie);
}
```

> *This function is the same as the previous one in step 7. If you are faced with this situation on a regular basis, simply copy and paste the code instead of retyping it. From there, you can make the minor changes.*

9. The final step is to write the `resizeMovie` function. Press Return/Enter twice and enter the following code:

```
function resizeMovie(evt:Event):void {
  ns.pause();
  myVideo.width = videoMC.mouseX;
  myVideo.height = myVideo.width * .75;
}
```

We start by telling Flash that this function is tied to an `ENTER_FRAME` event and, as such, to pause the video. The next two lines resize the video.

Movieclips have a number of properties, including the two used here: `width` and `height`. The first line is what sets the width of the movieclip to equal the x position of the mouse in relation to the upper-left corner of that movieclip. If the mouse is within that 50-pixel golden zone and the mouse is clicked and dragged inward to the 200-pixel mark on the x-axis, the movieclip's width will be adjusted to 200 pixels.

The second line is actually quite clever. The bulk of the videos we use have a 4:3 aspect ratio, which means the height of any video used with this ratio is 75 percent of the width. For example, the FLV file is 320 x 240. Seventy five percent of 320 is 240, so if the movieclip's width is changed to 500 pixels, its height will change, in proportion, to 375 pixels.

This works really well for videos that use the 4:3 aspect ratio. Then again, as you will discover in Chapter 12, HD video and ratios such as 16:9 and so on come into play. If you have an odd-sized video, consider changing the last line of the code `myVidep.height = myVideo.width * .75` to `myVideo.scaleY = myVideo.scaleX`.

Figure 8-15. The `resizeMovie()` function is used to shrink the video by dragging the mouse inward.

10. Check your code and save the movie. Test the movie and, as you see in Figure 8-15, you can use your mouse to play with the video.

Looping video

This is a rather short but important exercise. You need to know how to do loop video because at some point you will be asked to set up an FLV file so that it automatically rewinds and starts to play when the video finishes.

We'll show you how to loop video using the FLVPLayback component and then we will show you how to loop it using the Video object and ActionScript. Let's get started:

1. Open a new Flash ActionScript 3 document and save it to the looping folder in this chapter's exercise folder.

2. Open the Components panel and drag a copy of the FLVPlayback component to the stage.

3. Select the component and, in the Property Inspector, give it the instance name of player.

4. With the component selected on the stage, click the Parameters tab and set the source parameter to Follow_Legend.flv.

5. In the FLVPlayback parameter, set the skin parameter to None.

6. Add a new layer named Actions, open the Actions panel, and enter the following code into the Script pane:

```
import fl.video.VideoEvent;

player.addEventListener(VideoEvent.COMPLETE, playAgain);
function playAgain(evt:VideoEvent):void {
  player.seek(0);
  player.play();
}
```

This code is rather uncomplicated. To control the component with ActionScript, you need to import the VideoEvent class from the fl.video package because that is exactly what the code will look for: an event in the metadata of the FLV file. The package contains the classes you need to work with the FLVPlayback and FLVCaptioning components.

The next line tells ActionScript to listen for an event from the FLVPlayback component named player. The event being listened for is a COMPLETE event, which means exactly what it says: the video is finished or complete. When the player instance detects that event, it is then instructed to do the custom playAgain() function. The function does two things: it first uses the seek() method to return the FLV file to its zero point and then uses the play() method to start the video playing again.

The seek() method is rather interesting because you don't just use it to go to the start of a video. The parameter is always a number expressed in milliseconds. Therefore, if you want to go to the 1-minute point in the video, use player.seek(60000).

> Be careful with the seek() method because you won't go to that precise time in the Progressive Download method used here. The seek() method goes to the first video key frame after the point in time specified. Also, Progressive Download cannot seek to key frames that haven't yet loaded. If you need absolute precision, you'll need to deploy the video using Flash Media Server 3.

7. Save and test the movie.

In this next exercise, you'll create a code-driven looping video. Here's how:

1. Open a new Flash ActionScript 3.0 document and save it to the looping folder.

2. Select the key frame in frame 1 and open the Actions panel.

3. Click once in the Script pane and enter the following code:

```
var myVideo:Video = new Video();
addChild(myVideo);

var nc: NetConnection = new NetConnection();
nc.connect(null);
var ns: NetStream = new NetStream(nc);
myVideo.attachNetStream(ns);

var listener:Object = new Object();
listener.onMetaData = function(md:Object):void{};
ns.client = listener;

ns.addEventListener(NetStatusEvent.NET_STATUS, statusHandler);

function statusHandler(evt:NetStatusEvent):void{
  if (event.info.code == "NetStream.Play.Stop") {
    ns.seek(0);
  }
}
ns.play("Follow_Legend.flv");
```

There is not a lot here that's new. In fact, only the code block following the assignment of `listener` to `ns.client` is new, and that's where the action happens.

The first line simply tells Flash what to listen for. In this case, it is a NET_STATUS event and to execute the `statusHandler()` function when a particular event is detected. A NET_STATUS event is how a NetConnection or a NetStream object reports its status. In this case, we'll tell Flash to keep an eye on the NetStream and, when it detects the event that turns off the stream, to replay the video.

The heavy lifting is done by the `statusHandler()` function. In this case, Flash will keep its ears peeled for a NetStream.Play.Stop message that indicates the end of the video has been reached. When it hears the message (by way of the `info.code` property of the event's incoming parameter, `evt`), it simply scoots the video playhead back to the start of the video, just as you did in the previous example using the component.

4. Save and test the movie.

If you can watch the video, why not watch the audio?

There are times in this crazy business when the engineers at Adobe toss a new feature into Flash that is so cool you have an overwhelming urge to slip on the shades, dress in black, and head for the trendiest joint in town. When Flash CS3 was released, this is exactly what happened. Adobe added audio visualization, which meant that you could toss a tune into Flash and actually see a graphic representation of the tune. If you have ever turned on the visualization feature of Windows Media Player you know what we're talking about.

We found this technique to be absolutely fascinating, and one of the authors even started demonstrating sound visualization at conferences and lectures from Toronto to Beijing. The inevitable response is "Cool!" In preparing for this chapter, we thought, "Wouldn't it be really cool if you could apply audio visualization to the audio track of an FLV file?" Guess what? You can.

Before we start, it might not be a bad idea to take a moment and understand how visualization works in Flash. In simple terms, you read the audio amplitude and create a series of shapes using ActionScript, which grow or shrink in step with the changes in the audio track's amplitude. We can do this because the audio track is independent of the video track in Flash video (as you discovered when you created an FLV file). Knowing this, we used the soundTransform class to turn down the volume of the audio track, but we also used the new SoundMixer class to create the visualization effect and the new computeSpectrum() method that will create the actual graphics. From there, what you do with the visualization is limited only by your creativity. In this exercise, you won't create bars that bounce up and down with the audio track; you'll make them reflections as well.

Sound cool? Great. Slip on your shades and let's get to work:

1. Open a new Flash ActionScript 3.0 document and set the stage color to black: #000000. Save this file to the visualization folder in this chapter's exercise folder.

2. Select the first frame of Layer 1 and open the Actions panel. What you'll do is to get this video playing.

3. Click once in the Script pane and enter the following code:

```
var myVideo:Video = new Video();
addChild(myVideo);

var nc:NetConnection = new NetConnection();
nc.connect(null);
var ns: NetStream = new NetStream(nc);
myVideo.attachNetStream(ns);

var listener:Object = new Object();
listener.onMetaData = function(md:Object):void{};
ns.client = listener;

// Sound
var videoSound:SoundTransform = new SoundTransform();
videoSound.volume = 0.5;
ns.soundTransform = videoSound;

// Play Video
ns.play("Tortoise.flv");
```

Almost nothing new here. All you're doing is creating the Video object and feeding a stream into it to get the video to play. Just before the ns.play("Tortoise.flv"); line, a SoundTransform instance is used to adjust the volume of the video by way of the soundTransform property of the NetStream instance. If you save and test the video at this point, it will play in the upper-left corner of the SWF file, as shown in Figure 8-16. The area underneath the video will be used for the audio visualization. Let's get started.

What we'll do is to create a visualizer that looks rather familiar. We'll use bars, just as with audio equalizers, which will rise and fall based upon the amplitude of the sound.

Figure 8-16. We can watch the video; now let's watch the audio.

4. Press Return/Enter twice and enter the following code that will do the following:

- Create a ByteArray for the raw audio data
- Create a ByteArray for the frequency data
- Determine the height of the bars in the visualization
- Create a sprite to hold the data

```
// Define an array to store the data returned
// by the computeSpectrum function

var bytesFrequency:ByteArray = new ByteArray();
var bytesRaw:ByteArray = new ByteArray();

// Define height of the eq bars
var egHeight:Number = 200;

// Create a sprite for the raw data
var eqTopRaw:Sprite = new Sprite();
eqTopRaw.x = 0;
eqTopRaw.y = 350;
addChild(eqTopRaw);
```

5. The next step is to create four movieclips that will hold the bars and their reflections. Press Return/Enter twice and enter the following:

```
// Create four sprites for the main eq and reflection and the blur
// of the main eq and reflection
var eqTopBlur:Sprite = new Sprite();
eqTopBlur.x = 0;
```

239

```
eqTopBlur.y = 350;
addChild(eqTopBlur);

var eqTop:Sprite = new Sprite();
eqTop.x = 0;
eqTop.y = 350;
addChild(eqTop);

var eqBottomBlur:Sprite = new Sprite();
eqBottomBlur.x = 0;
eqBottomBlur.y = 355;
addChild(eqBottomBlur);

var eqBottom:Sprite = new Sprite();
eqBottom.x = 0;
eqBottom.y = 355;
eqBottom.alpha = 0.2;
addChild(eqBottom);
```

6. Now you have to apply the blur to the four sprites. Press Return/Enter twice and enter the following:

```
// Define an array to store the blur filter
var eqFilters:Array = new Array();
var blur:BlurFilter = new BlurFilter();
blur.blurX = 10;
blur.blurY = 10;
blur.quality = BitmapFilterQuality.MEDIUM;
eqFilters.push(blur);

// Add blur to top and bottom blur eq
eqTopBlur.filters = eqFilters;
eqBottomBlur.filters = eqFilters;
```

Up to this point in the exercise, there really is nothing new. Everything you have done has been covered at some point in the chapters and exercises preceding this one.

7. Press Return/Enter twice and enter the following code:

```
addEventListener(Event.ENTER_FRAME, onEnterFrame);
function onEnterFrame(evt:Event):void {
// Get computeSpectrum data
  SoundMixer.computeSpectrum(bytesFrequency, true, 1);
  SoundMixer.computeSpectrum(bytesRaw, false, 1);
```

There will be a lot more to this function, but let's take a second to understand the computeSpectrum() method before we move on.

As you know, SoundMixer is a class, and computeSpectrum() is a method of that class. This method takes a snapshot of the sound wave and places it in the ByteArray object created in step 3.

A ByteArray is a series of numbers between -1 and 1, and the object can have up to 512 values. If you divide that number in half, you get one of the magic numbers of computing: 256. Although we commonly use this number when referring to audio (8-bit audio) or color (8-bit color), each audio channel can have its own 8-bit sound. This means that the left channel and the right channel can each have values of 256, which are the numbers that will give the graph its motion. High frequencies will be shown on the right side of the graph, and low frequencies will appear on the left side. This explains the first parameter.

The second parameter (true or false) is called the FFTMode. If you are heavily into math, you know that FFT is a Fourier transform calculation. Simply put, it is a calculation that turns the audio frequency into a graph instead of a sound wave. If the value is true, as it is for bytesFrequency, you get a wave; if it is false, as it is for bytesRaw, you get a graph.

The final parameter is the stretchFactor. This number is what sets the resolution of the audio. If you use a value of 0, the audio is sampled at a rate of 44.1kHz—CD resolution. If you use a 1, which we do here, the audio is sampled at a rate of 22.05kHz. As the stretchFactor numbers increase, the sound quality rapidly degrades.

8. Having determined how the visualization will look, we can now turn our attention to actually drawing it. Press Return/Enter twice and enter the following code:

```
// Define a counter
var i:int;

// Define fill colours for each of the four movies
eqTopBlur.graphics.clear();
eqTopBlur.graphics.beginFill(0xDDDDDD);
eqTopBlur.graphics.moveTo(0, 0);

eqTop.graphics.clear();
eqTop.graphics.beginFill(0xFF0000);
eqTop.graphics.moveTo(0, 0);

eqBottomBlur.graphics.clear();
eqBottomBlur.graphics.beginFill(0xDDDDDD);
eqBottomBlur.graphics.moveTo(0, 0);

eqBottom.graphics.clear();
eqBottom.graphics.beginFill(0xFF0000);
eqBottom.graphics.moveTo(0, 0);

// Define line style for raw data
eqTopRaw.graphics.clear();
eqTopRaw.graphics.lineStyle(1,0x111111);
eqTopRaw.graphics.moveTo(0, 0);

// Loop through computeSpectrum data
for (i=0; i<512; i++) {
  var t:Number = bytesFrequency.readFloat();
  var n:Number = (t * egHeight);
```

```
        var t2:Number = bytesRaw.readFloat();
        var n2:Number = (t2 * egHeight);
        if (n > 0) {

            // Draw eq lines
            eqTopBlur.graphics.drawRect(i, 0, 1, -n);
            eqTop.graphics.drawRect(i, 0, 1, -n);
            eqBottomBlur.graphics.drawRect(i, 0, 1, n);
            eqBottom.graphics.drawRect(i, 0, 1, n);

            // Draw eq dots
            eqTopBlur.graphics.drawRect(i, -n * 2, 1, 1);
            eqTop.graphics.drawRect(i, -n * 2, 1, 1);
            eqBottomBlur.graphics.drawRect(i, n * 2, 1, 1);
            eqBottom.graphics.drawRect(i, n * 2, 1, 1);

        }
        // Draw raw data lines
        eqTopRaw.graphics.lineTo(i, -n2 * 2);
    }
};
```

This code uses the Drawing API to draw the lines used in the visualization. In fact, as you can see, the lines are thin rectangles instead of lines. The height of those rectangles is dependent on the value of the computeSpectrum() method, as shown here:

```
    var t:Number = bytesFrequency.readFloat();
    var n:Number = (t * egHeight);
```

> You don't have to use rectangles. You can just as easily use the drawCircle method and replace the lines with a sequence of pulsating circles.

9. Save and test the movie. When the video starts to play, the audio track will be shown under the video (see Figure 8-17).

> If you are new to this and find the code presented to be a bit overwhelming, we have included a completed version of this exercise in the Complete folder of this chapter. What you should do is to open the code and start playing with the colors and other values from the code in step 7 to see what they do. If you make a mistake or otherwise mess things up, select File ➤ Revert and you will be returned to your starting point.

Figure 8-17. Now you can watch audio and video!

Adding Flash video to Dreamweaver CS3

If you are a Dreamweaver user, you might have noticed the inclusion of a Flash Video selection in the Insert ➤ Media menu. This feature was added to Dreamweaver back in 2004. Although we have spent practically every moment in this book focusing on outputting video that uses either the skin from the FLVPLayback component or a custom controller, you can add an FLV file to Dreamweaver CS3 by selecting Insert ➤ Media ➤ Flash Video.

The obvious question is, "Why?" The answer is that you might have an intimate understanding of Flash video, but there are a lot of web designers and developers who have never touched this application. This feature is tailor-made for them. As well, the Flash video feature of Dreamweaver is a great way of rapidly deploying an FLV file for client approval or allowing a web designer or developer to add video to a site.

Here's how to use this Dreamweaver CS3 feature:

1. Launch Dreamweaver CS3 and create a new HTML page. Save this page to the DWFlashVideo folder.

2. Click once on the page and select Insert ➤ Media ➤ Flash Video. This will open the Insert Flash Video dialog box shown in Figure 8-18.

Let's go through the options:

- Video type: Select Progressive Download Video if the FLV file is to be streamed from a web server. Select Streaming Video if the video is to be played from a Flash Media Server (FMS). If you do choose the Streaming Video option, the interface will change to include the RTMP address for the server and the name of the video.

- URL: Click the Browse button and navigate to the folder containing the FLV file. In this case, select ShutEyePopeye.flv in the folder where you saved the HTML page.

243

- Skin: You get three choices—Clear, Corona, and Halo. These skins are based on the Halo skin style, which was the only choice available in Flash prior to the release of Flash 8. Keep in mind that each one has a minimum width, and a preview of the skin will appear under the Skin selection. Be aware that you can't control the placement of the skin. All skins in Dreamweaver CS3 appear over the video.

- Width and Height: These settings allow you to manually change the width and height of the Flash Player. If you click the Detect Size button, Dreamweaver will obtain the dimensions by looking in the FLV file's metadata for these values.

- Auto play and Auto rewind: Select these settings and the video will do exactly what you selected.

- Message: This is the message that will appear if the user needs to upgrade the Flash Player version or if there is no Flash Player on the user's system. You can add your own message here.

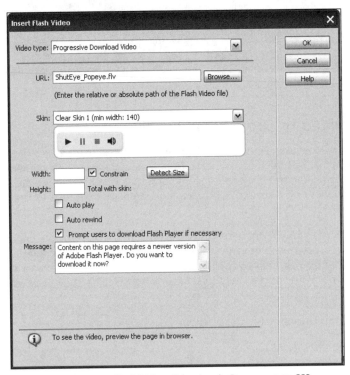

Figure 8-18. The Insert Flash Video dialog box in Dreamweaver CS3

3. Click OK to save the changes in the dialog box. When the dialog box closes, a placeholder that contains a Flash video icon will appear on the page.

4. To test the video, press F12 to launch the page in a browser. Press Play and the video will start to play, as shown in Figure 8-19.

Figure 8-19. The video and the skin

What you've learned

This chapter showed you a lot of professional techniques that you can use in your everyday efforts. Starting with showing you how to add a rotoscoped video to Flash, we wandered through a variety of simple to complex techniques before finally stopping at putting a video in Dreamweaver CS3.

In this chapter you did the following:

- Used the color tools and filters to create an iPod ad
- Wrote the ActionScript that will loop a video
- Aged a video by adding tints, scratches, and flickers to its playback
- Discovered how the audio track of a video can be used as a design element
- Learned about the ActionScript needed to resize, pause, and play a video when no controls are used
- Used SWFObject to place a Flash SWF file in a web page

The key to all these techniques is that they don't have to work in isolation. You can age a video that the user is enlarging on the screen. You can add a rotoscoped video to a Flash movie, create the SWF file, and then use SWFObject to place it in a Dreamweaver CS3 page. In short, you learned a lot of creative techniques whose use will be limited only by your creativity.

Now that we've had a bit of a rest, let's pick up our gear and move on to the next chapter, in which you'll discover how to create video applications that involve using multiple videos.

Chapter 9

PLAYING WITH MULTIPLE VIDEOS

Inevitably, you'll be asked to work not only with one video but also with many videos. The question then becomes how to present them. This chapter shows you a number of ways of managing the playback of multiple video files. Ranging from simply embedding the call to the video in a button to using XML to manage multiple videos, you will learn a variety of techniques. The most important thing you will learn, though, is this: there is no best way of managing the playback of multiple videos. Why? The reason is simple: when users select a video, they don't care how it got there. They simply expect their selection to play.

What we'll cover in this chapter:

- Using components to choose among multiple videos
- Using XML with Flash video
- Adding animation to Flash video
- Playing a sequence of videos
- Making video interactive

Files used in this chapter:

- ComboBox.fla (Chapter09\ExerciseFiles_CH09\Exercise\ComboBox\ComboBox.fla)
- Puppetji_Gossip.flv (Chapter09\ExerciseFiles_CH09\Exercise\ComboBox\Puppetji_Gossip.flv)
- Puppetji_One.flv (Chapter09\ExerciseFiles_CH09\Exercise\ComboBox\Puppetji_One.flv)
- Puppetji_Seeing.flv (Chapter09\ExerciseFiles_CH09\Exercise\ComboBox\Puppetji_Seeing.flv)
- Puppetji_TruthAccording2Puppetji.flv (Chapter09\ExerciseFiles_CH09\Exercise\ComboBox\Puppetji_TruthAccording2Puppetji.flv)
- ComboBoxXML.fla (Chapter09\ExerciseFiles_CH09\Exercise\ComboBox\ComboBoxXML.fla)
- videos.xml (Chapter09\ExerciseFiles_CH09\Exercise\ComboBoxXML\videos.xml)
- Deck.fla (Chapter09\ExerciseFiles_CH09\Exercise\Deck\Deck.fla)
- deckvideos.xml (Chapter09\ExerciseFiles_CH09\Exercise\Deck\deckvideos.xml)
- Sequence.fla (Chapter09\ExerciseFiles_CH09\Exercise\Sequence\Sequence.fla)
- SequenceCpt.fla (Chapter09\ExerciseFiles_CH09\Exercise\Sequence\SequenceCpt.fla)
- VideoClock.fla (Chapter09\ExerciseFiles_CH09\Exercise\VideoClock\VideoClock.fla)
- VideoSet1 (Chapter09\ExerciseFiles_CH09\Exercise\VideoClock\VideoSet1)
- VideoSet2 (Chapter09\ExerciseFiles_CH09\Exercise\VideoClock\VideoSet2)
- SlapGuy.fla (Chapter09\ExerciseFiles_CH09\Exercise\SlapGuy\SlapGuy.fla)

Using a ComboBox component

The ComboBox component is a great place to start this chapter because it has both a label and a data identifier requirement. The label is used to place text in the drop-down menu, whereas the data will be used to "link" a selection to a particular FLV file.

Speaking of FLV files, this chapter introduces you to the infamous Puppetji (see Figure 9-1). Puppetji is a character with a huge Internet following because he is a guru who dispenses pearls of advice (usually irreverent advice) to his followers. We are honored that our guru permitted us the use of four videos, and if you want to find more, the series can be found at puppetji.blogspot.com. The master can also be found on YouTube.

The authors want to express their deep gratitude for permission to use these videos in this chapter. It is not often you encounter a production company whose sense of collective humor matches that of the writers and editors of this book. Puppetji is the creation of James Murray, who also performs. Kevin Susman and James Murray produce the series. The production company is 2 Funny Films.

Figure 9-1. Meet your guru: Puppetji (or "PJ," as he is known in his off hours).

We have four Puppetji films. Let's make them available to the master's adoring public.

The plan is to use code to load in the ComboBox component and to use the data portion of the component's parameters to load the videos into a Video object that will also be created.

1. Open the ComboBox.fla file in your exercise folder, in which we have placed a background image and added a static text block on the stage (see Figure 9-2).

Figure 9-2. We start with a very simple stage.

2. Select the Actions layer and open the ActionScript editor. Enter the following code:

```
import fl.controls.ComboBox;
import fl.data.DataProvider;

var videos:Array = new Array(
  {label:"Select a Video",data:""},
  {label:"Gossip",data:"Puppetji_Gossip.flv"},
  {label:"One",data:"Puppetji_One.flv"},
  {label:"Seeing", data:"Puppetji_Seeing.flv"},
  {label:"Truth", data:"Puppetji_TruthAccording2Puppetji.flv"}
);
```

We start by importing the ComboBox class from the controls package. The next line imports the DataProvider class from the data package. The second one, DataProvider, is important because of the nature of the ComboBox component.

By leaving the first data property empty, you can use that first item in the Array as the component's default label at runtime. This is why there is nothing between the quotation marks in the first item's data property in the Array.

Place a ComboBox component on the stage and then click the Parameters tab in the Property Inspector. This component needs a dataProvider, which is actually composed of two pieces: label and data (see Figure 9-3). The label is what will appear in each strip of the component and is visible when the user clicks the component and the drop-down menu appears. The data is the data associated with the label and is used when the user clicks the label in the component.

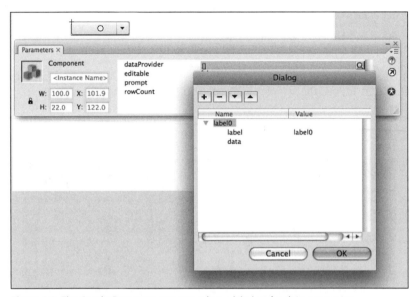

Figure 9-3. The ComboBox component requires a label and a data parameter.

This is the purpose of the Array you entered. Notice that it contains the words that will appear in the label and the video that is associated with that label.

The ComboBox component is stone cold stupid. You need to tell it what to do with the data parameter. We'll get to that in a minute, but first we have to get the ComboBox out of the library and onto the stage.

3. Press Return/Enter twice and type in the following:

```
var moviesCB:ComboBox = new ComboBox();
moviesCB.dropdownWidth = 200;
moviesCB.width = 200;
moviesCB.move(335, 80);
moviesCB.dataProvider = new DataProvider(videos);
addChild(moviesCB);
```

We start by creating an instance of the ComboBox moviesCB class. With that housekeeping out of the way, the next four lines tell Flash that the width of the drop-down menu will be 200 pixels, the width of the component will also be 200 pixels, the component is to be placed on the stage at 335,80, and the all-important dataProvider for the component will be the list just created. The final line of the code actually puts the component on the stage.

Now that the component is on the stage, we need to tell Flash what to do when one of the items in the drop-down menu is clicked.

4. Press Return/Enter twice and add the following code:

```
moviesCB.addEventListener(Event.CHANGE, changeHandler);

function changeHandler(evt:Event):void {
  if (ComboBox(evt.target).selectedItem.data != "") {
    ns.play(ComboBox(evt.target).selectedItem.data);
  }
};
```

This code should now be familiar. We simply tell Flash what to listen for (a CHANGE event), to use the data portion of the item that has just been clicked (an FLV file), and to play that FLV file through the stream. Notice that this happens only when the data property isn't an empty string. In fact, let's get that stream going.

5. Press Return/Enter twice and add the following code:

```
var myVideo:Video = new Video();
addChild(myVideo);

var nc:NetConnection = new NetConnection();
nc.connect(null);

var ns:NetStream = new NetStream(nc);
myVideo.attachNetStream(ns);

var listener:Object = new Object();
listener.onMetaData = function (md:Object):void{};
ns.client = listener;
```

6. Save the file and test the movie. The component will contain the labels from the list (see Figure 9-4). When you click a label, the video plays.

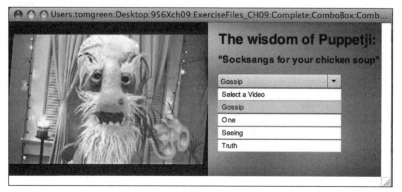

Figure 9-4. Pick your wisdom.

XML and the ComboBox component

That last exercise was pretty cool, but it contains a fatal flaw. What will happen if Puppetji decides that the video series is so popular that he wants to add more videos?

The initial answer is "a lot more work" because you "hard-wired" the data used by the component into the ActionScript. If you need to add videos to (or remove videos from) the list, you need to open the original FLA file and make the changes to the ActionScript. This can be a time-consuming process and assumes that you will have access to the original FLA file (which is not always the case). In this case, the power of the relationship between XML and Flash becomes self-evident.

> We won't get deep into this subject. If you are new to XML and Flash, we suggest that you check out Foundation Flash CS3 for Designers (friends of ED, 2007), written by author Tom Green and technical editor David Stiller, for a complete overview of this important subject.
>
> We wrote the following in Foundation Flash CS3 for Designers:
>
> "The remarkable thing about XML is that it can basically be whatever you want it to, provided you stick by its rules. The main purpose of XML is to expedite the sharing of data. In fact, XML is so flexible that newcomers are often baffled on where to even begin. On paper—or rather, on the screen—XML looks a lot like HTML, except instead of predetermined tags and attributes, you organize your content into descriptive tags of your own design. The combination of familiar, hierarchical format and completely custom tags generally makes XML content easy to read, both to computers and humans. By separating your data from the movie, you give yourself the opportunity to change content from the outside, affecting SWF files without having to republish them."

In the hands of an experienced Flash developer or designer, Flash can become a rather robust tool when it comes to dynamic data—data that can or will change over time—because Flash can reach out from the SWF file to data located on the web server with the URLLoader and URLVariable classes of ActionScript 3.0. In this exercise, we use only the URLLoader class.

> Although we use the ComboBox component in this exercise, don't forget the ListBox component. It also requires label and data parameters, and is really handy if you need to hand the user a scrollable list of choices instead of a drop-down menu.

Let's use XML to load the videos:

1. Open the ComboBoxXML.fla file in the exercise folder. You're starting with the same interface used in the previous exercise.

2. Select the first frame of the Actions layer and open the ActionScript editor. When it opens, click once in the Script pane and enter the following:

```
import fl.controls.ComboBox;
import fl.data.DataProvider;
```

Now that you have imported the ComboBox and DataProvider classes into the SWF file, you can now concentrate on using the XML file video.xml (found in the exercise folder) as the dataProvider for the ComboBox component. Here's how:

3. Press Return/Enter twice and add the following code:

```
var videosXML:XML = new XML();
var loader:URLLoader = new URLLoader();
var request:URLRequest = new URLRequest("videos.xml");

loader.addEventListener(Event.COMPLETE,loaderOnCompleteHandler);
loader.load(request);
```

To use an XML document in Flash, the first thing you need to do is to create a new XML object. In this case, the XML object has the instance name of videosXML.

The next line creates the loader for the XML document, and the third line tells Flash which XML document (videos.xml) will be loaded by using a URLRequest with the instance name of request.

As is standard practice when using ActionScript, Flash needs to be told what to listen for and what to do when it hears it. In this case, Flash will wait for the XML file to load. When it finishes (signaled by the COMPLETE event), it will execute the loaderOnComplete function.

Before you write the loaderOnComplete function, it might be a good idea to look at the XML file you will be using:

```
<?xml version="1.0" encoding="utf-8"?>
<videos>
  <video>
    <name>Gossip</name>
    <url>Puppetji_Gossip.flv</url>
  </video>
  <video>
    <name>One</name>
    <url>Puppetji_One.flv</url>
  </video>
  <video>
    <name>Seeing</name>
    <url>Puppetji_Seeing.flv</url>
  </video>
  <video>
    <name>Truth</name>
    <url>Puppetji_TruthAccording2Puppetji.flv</url>
  </video>
</videos>
```

As you can see, the document structure closely resembles the one used in the Array from the last exercise. The major differences are that the data is within the videos root node and each element, called video, contains the name for the list part of the ComboBox parameters; and the name of the file used, including the extension, is contained in the <url></url> tag. The purpose of the function, therefore, is to pull those two bits of information out of each element and use them as the parameters for the component.

4. Press Return/Enter twice and add the following code:

```
function loaderOnCompleteHandler(evt:Event):void {
  videosXML = new XML(evt.target.data);
  var videos:Array = new Array({label:"Select a Video", data:""});
  for each (var video:XML in videosXML.video){
    videos.push({label:video.name.toString(),➡
data:video.url.toString()});
  }
  moviesCB.dataProvider = new DataProvider(videos);
}
```

The function starts by creating a new XML object that uses the data in the XML document as its parameter. The next line creates an Array that will be used for the label and data parameters required by the component. The first label, Select a Video, is the user instruction that will appear in the ComboBox at runtime.

The for loop steps through each video in the XML document and, using E4X notation, pulls the name and the url data out of the XML document and adds it as text to the ComboBox. The toString() method lifts that text from its XML trappings. Without it, Flash will try to add the url and name parameters to the ComboBox, but will have trouble passing the data property to the play() method of the NetStream class.

Now that the data has been fired into the ComboBox, it's time to add the component to the stage and to tell Flash what to do when an item in the component is clicked.

5. Press Return/Enter twice and enter the following code:

```
var moviesCB:ComboBox = new ComboBox();
moviesCB.dropdownWidth = 200;
moviesCB.width = 200;
moviesCB.move(335, 50);
addChild(moviesCB);

moviesCB.addEventListener(Event.CHANGE, changeHandler);
function changeHandler(evt:Event):void {
  if(ComboBox(evt.target).selectedItem.data != ""){
    ns.play(ComboBox(evt.target).selectedItem.data);
  }
};
```

Nothing new here. The final step is to "wire up" the Video object:

6. Press Return/Enter twice and enter the following code:

```
var myVideo:Video = new Video();
addChild(myVideo);

var nc:NetConnection = new NetConnection();
nc.connect(null);
```

```
var ns:NetStream = new NetStream(nc);
myVideo.attachNetStream(ns);

var listener:Object = new Object();
listener.onMetaData = function (md:Object):void{};
ns.client = listener;
```

7. Check your code. If there are no mistakes, test the video.

If you really want to see the power of XML and Flash, try this bonus round:

1. Add an FLV file of your choosing to the exercise folder.

2. Open the videos.xml document in any text editor or in Dreamweaver CS3.

3. Copy the last video element—from <video> to </video>—and paste it between the final </video> and </videos> tags.

4. Change the name and the url to reflect the new videos just added and save the document.

5. Double-click the SWF file. The video you have just added appears in the component and plays when it is clicked.

A video deck

This exercise builds upon what you have learned and takes it in a different direction. Until now, users' choices have been somewhat restricted to the use of a conventional drop-down menu. This exercise harnesses the animation prowess of Flash CS3. The choices will be images that scroll from side to side, and the image scales up. When users make their decision and click an image, the video plays and a control deck moves onto the screen. When users finish viewing the video, they simply click the Close button in the deck. The control slides off the screen and the side scrolling images reappear. Sounds like a lot of work? Not really. Let's roll up our sleeves and get started.

> A quick heads-up. A lot of the code is stuff you have written previously. We have left the "holes" in the ActionScript where you will add the functionality. This way, we don't repeat a lot of what we have said previously, and you aren't subjected to a glorified typing lesson.

1. Open the Deck.fla file in the Chapter 9 exercise folder. When the file opens, you'll see that we have added the control deck off the stage and included the background image from the previous two exercises (see Figure 9-5).

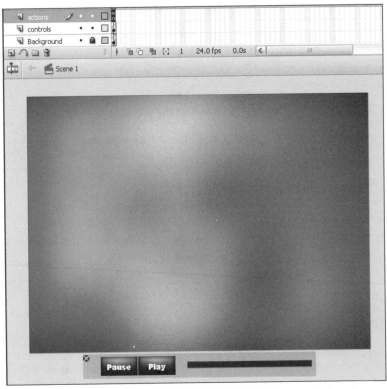

Figure 9-5. The interface is preassembled. All you need to do is to "wire it up."

2. Select the first frame in the Actions layer and open the Actions panel.

The first 20 lines of the code get things started. Start by importing the classes needed in this exercise:

```
import fl.transitions.Tween;
import fl.transitions.easing.*;
import fl.transitions.TweenEvent;
import flash.display.Sprite;
import flash.display.DisplayObject;
```

The new stuff involves the transitions package. Although it might sound rather mysterious, the transitions package is not that hard to comprehend. You know that you can animate objects between key frames on the timeline. The transitions package allows you to do the same thing using code. The package uses the TransitionManager class, which defines animation effects. It allows you to apply one of ten preset animation effects to movieclips.

In this case, you'll use the Tween and TweenEvent classes and the easing package of the TransitionManager to move and resize the movieclips you'll be using to select the videos. Here are descriptions of what they do:

- The Tween class lets you use ActionScript to move, resize, and fade movieclips by indicating the property of the target movieclip, which will be animated between frames or over a specified amount of time.

- The TweenEvent class is the way a tween event is broadcast by the Tween class. For example, a property of the TweenEvent class is position. If an object is in motion when a tween event is occurring, the position of the object on the stage will, in very simple terms, be communicated by the event. Strictly speaking, position refers to the current location of the tween along its journey, so even an alpha tween, which might not physically move, changes its "position" from 0 (transparent) to 1 (opaque).

- The easing package contains a number of classes that allow you to apply easing effects to movieclips. They are the same effects that can be applied using the Property Inspector, plus a few more. If you are unfamiliar with this technique, **easing** is the gradual acceleration or deceleration of movement. For example, a ball dropped from the top of the stage would accelerate on its way to the bottom of the stage, but decelerate (because of gravity) when it bounces back upward.

The next block defines the variables used throughout the project:

```
// Define Variables
var totalVideos:Number;

var selectedThumbnail:DisplayObject;
var selectedThumbnailID:int = -1;
var overThumbnail:DisplayObject;
var overThumbnailID:int = -1;

var i:int;
var xMousePercent:Number;
var totalWidth:Number;
var targetX:Number;
var rangeOfMotion:Number;

// Video Dimensions
var videoFullSize:Number = 320;
var videoRollOutScale:Number = 0.6;
var videoRollOverScale:Number = 0.8;
var videoMouseUpScale:Number = 1;
var spacing:Number = 20;
```

These variables control such things as the ID number of a thumbnail, how many videos are used in the movie, and the size and scale percentage applied to a video. This example is coded to make it very easy to tweak. For example, if you want more videos, you can just add them to the XML. Or if you want to increase the display size of the videos, you can change the videoFullSize variable, and everything else should adjust.

257

3. Locate the empty text block for Step 3: in the code block and now get the movieclips onto the stage. Enter the following code:

```
var imageContainerMC:MovieClip = new MovieClip();
imageContainerMC.x = spacing;
imageContainerMC.y = 50;
addChild(imageContainerMC);
```

When the movie plays, a series of movieclips containing thumbnails of the videos will slide across the stage. This code block creates the movieclips for those thumbnails, spaces them out, and has them appear 50 pixels from the top of the stage.

4. Scroll down to the empty space for Step 4: in the code, click once, and add the following:

```
movieClip.x = counter * (videoFullSize * videoRollOutScale + spacing);
movieClip.scaleX = 0.6;
movieClip.scaleY = 0.6;
```

If you scroll through the code to this point, all it does is load the XML data into the movie and toss the thumbnails into their movieclips.

The code just entered determines their position on the x-axis and their scaleX and scaleY values.

5. Scroll down to the empty space for Step 5: in the code, click once, and add the following:

```
function movieClipMouseUpHandler(evt:Event):void {
    selectedThumbnail = imageContainerMC➡
.getChildByName(evt.target.parent.name);
    selectedThumbnailID = imageContainerMC➡
.getChildIndex(selectedThumbnail);
    var tweenScaleX:Tween = new Tween(selectedThumbnail, ➡
"scaleX", Strong.easeOut, selectedThumbnail.scaleX, 1, 12);
    var tweenScaleY:Tween = new Tween(selectedThumbnail, ➡
"scaleY", Strong.easeOut, selectedThumbnail.scaleX, 1, 12);
    var tweenY:Tween = new Tween(selectedThumbnail, ➡
"y", Strong.easeOut, selectedThumbnail.y, -29, 12);
    selectedThumbnail.removeEventListener(➡
MouseEvent.MOUSE_OVER, movieClipMouseOverHandler);
    selectedThumbnail.removeEventListener ➡
(MouseEvent.MOUSE_OUT, movieClipMouseOutHandler);

    var controlsInTweenX:Tween = new Tween(controlsMC, ➡
"y", Strong.easeOut, controlsMC.y, 300, 12);
}
```

Not much new here other than the creation of a new Tween() object. The parameters used by a tween are object, property, function, begin, finish, and duration. If we walk through the first one, you can see how this all works. The first time it is used is in this line:

```
var tweenScaleX:Tween = new Tween(selectedThumbnail,➡
  "scaleX", Strong.easeOut, selectedThumbnail.scaleX, 1, 12);
```

We start by creating a variable for the scaling on the x-axis. We then tell Flash which object is affected by the tween (in this case, it is the thumbnail the user clicked). We specify the scaleX property and then tell Flash that the scaling will tween using the easeOut tween of the Strong class contained in the easing package imported earlier. Strong simply means that the effect occurs faster than normal. The final two values determine the starting and ending values of the tween. It starts at its current scaleX value (selectedThumbnail.scaleX) and grows to 100% (1). The last value is duration, which, in this case is 12 frames. The duration can be set as seconds or frames. If you choose seconds, you must add one final parameter: true.

6. Press Return/Enter twice and, still in the Step 5: space, enter the remaining functions:

```
function movieClipMouseOverHandler(evt:Event):void {
  overThumbnail = imageContainerMC➥
.getChildByName(evt.target.parent.name);
  overThumbnailID = imageContainerMC➥
.getChildIndex(overThumbnail);

  var tweenScaleX:Tween = new Tween(overThumbnail, ➥
"scaleX", Strong.easeOut, overThumbnail.scaleX, 0.8, 12);
  var tweenScaleY:Tween = new Tween(overThumbnail, ➥
"scaleY", Strong.easeOut, overThumbnail.scaleX, 0.8, 12);
  var tweenY:Tween = new Tween(overThumbnail, ➥
"y", Strong.easeOut, overThumbnail.y, -14, 12);
}

function movieClipMouseOutHandler(evt:Event):void {
  overThumbnailID = -1;

  var tweenSaleX:Tween = new Tween(overThumbnail, ➥
"scaleX", Strong.easeOut, overThumbnail.scaleX, 0.6, 12);
  var tweenScaleY:Tween = new Tween(overThumbnail, ➥
"scaleY", Strong.easeOut, overThumbnail.scaleX, 0.6, 12);
  var tweenY:Tween = new Tween(overThumbnail, "y", ➥
Strong.easeOut, overThumbnail.y, 0, 24);
}
```

All this code does is to put things in motion. If you are new to this process, we suggest you carefully review this important code block to understand what is going on.

7. The final step is to put the controls into motion. Scroll down to the empty space for Step 7: in the code, click once, and enter the following:

```
controlsMC.thumbnailsMC.buttonMode = true;
controlsMC.thumbnailsMC.addEventListener(MouseEvent.MOUSE_UP, ➥
thumbnailsMCMouseUpHandler);

function thumbnailsMCMouseUpHandler(evt:Event):void {
  // Reset selected video
  selectedThumbnailID = -1;
```

```
// Tween selected thumbnail back to original size and location
var tweenSaleX:Tween = new Tween(selectedThumbnail, ➡
"scaleX", Strong.easeOut, selectedThumbnail.scaleX, 0.6, 12);
var tweenScaleY:Tween = new Tween(selectedThumbnail, ➡
"scaleY", Strong.easeOut, selectedThumbnail.scaleX, 0.6, 12);
var tweenY:Tween = new Tween(selectedThumbnail, "y", ➡
Strong.easeOut,selectedThumbnail.y, 0, 12);

// Remove controlstweens
var controlsOutTweenX:Tween = new Tween(controlsMC, ➡
"y", Strong.easeOut, controlsMC.y, 400, 12);
```

We start by making the movieclip containing the video controls "clickable." By setting the buttonMode property of the movieclip to true, the user will be given a visual clue (the pointing finger), showing that the controls are "live."

The remainder of the code puts everything back when the Close button on the control deck is clicked and moves the deck off of the stage.

8. Save and test the movie. When it starts, the thumbnails will slide across the screen (see Figure 9-6). They will also move and scale as you move your mouse from left to right, or vice versa.

Figure 9-6. The thumbnails appear on the stage and react to the user's mouse movement.

Click a thumbnail. As shown in Figure 9-7, the thumbnails disappear, the control deck slides onto the stage, and the selected video plays.

Figure 9-7. Click a thumbnail to play the video. Click the Close button to hide the control deck and return to the sliding thumbnails.

Playing videos sequentially

When writing a book of this sort, authors and editors totally understand each other or else their egos clash and they start bellowing at each other like mastodons across the primordial ooze. Thankfully, the former is the case with this book,

In creating this chapter, the authors were pretty satisfied with the lineup. There was quite a bit of meat here until one of the authors asked this question as the chapter was being written: what is missing? He ruminated on it for a couple of days, and the answer became apparent in one of his classes when a student mentioned that she was trying to get a series of videos to play in sequence.

This is one of those things that are quite common, but we tend not to pay a lot of attention to. You see this quite a bit on sites that bracket videos with ads. Click the play button, an ad plays; as soon as the ad finishes, the video plays; when it finishes, another ad plays. Realizing that this was omitted, we started thinking about how to do this. In the course of the discussions, we discovered that technical editor David Stiller had dealt with this very issue in his blog in October 2007. The blog entry is here: quip.net/blog/2007/flash/actionscript-20/how-to-play-video-files-sequentially.

We naturally contacted David and asked if we could use his solution in this book. Per David, here's how to get a series of videos to play—one after the other:

1. Open the Sequence.fla file in the exercise folder. When it opens, you'll see that we have tossed a Video object with the instance name of myVideo onto the stage.

2. Select the first frame in the Actions layer and click once in the Script pane of the Actions panel. Enter the following code:

```
import flash.events.NetStatusEvent;

var videos:Array = new Array("Puppetji_Gossip.flv",➥
 "Puppetji_Seeing.flv", "Puppetji_One.flv");
var currentVideo:uint = 0;
var duration:uint = 0;
var ready:Boolean = true;

var nc:NetConnection = new NetConnection();
nc.connect(null);
var ns:NetStream = new NetStream(nc);
myVideo.attachNetStream(ns);
ns.play(videos[currentVideo]);

var listener:Object = new Object();
listener.onMetaData = function(evt:Object):void {
  duration = evt.duration;
  ready = true;
};
ns.client = listener;
```

The key to playing a sequence of videos is to wait for the currently playing video to finish, and when it does, to fire up the next video in the lineup. This tells you that the technique is tied to an event triggered by an FLV file playing on the NetStream. This is why we import the flash.events package and use the NetStatusEvent class from that package.

The next step is to identify the videos and get them into an Array named videos. The next two lines of code ensure that the number of videos is set to 0, that it is always a positive number (uint), and that the duration value used is also a 0. Finally, a Boolean variable, ready, is declared and set to true. More on that in a moment.

> If you are interested in discovering the difference between an int and a uint, David Stiller deals with it quite neatly in this blog entry: www.quip.net/blog/2007/flash/actionscript-30/mind-your-ints-and-uints.

The remainder of the code block is nothing you haven't seen before, except that the onMetaData event handler actually does something this time (it resets ready to true). The reason for this variable is described in the NET_STATUS handler notes that follow.

With the videos "queued up" and ready to go, the rest of the code concerns itself with getting the next item in the list ready to go.

3. Press Return/Enter twice and enter the following:

```
function nsHandler(evt:NetStatusEvent):void {
  if (ready && ns.time > 0 && ns.time >= (duration - 0.5)) {
    ready = false;
    currentVideo++;
```

```
            if (currentVideo < videos.length) {
              ns.play(videos[currentVideo]);
            } else {
              ns.removeEventListener(NetStatusEvent.NET_STATUS, nsHandler);
            }
          }
        };
```

The magic happens with this function and a NetStatusEvent. Flash will be constantly checking the FLV file to keep an eye on the current status of the FLV file. As you know, you can keep an eye on the current time of the video. In this case, we check to make sure that the time is somewhere between the start of the video—ns.time > 0—and just before the end of the video—ns.time>= (duration - 0.5). If the time is between those two numbers, Flash is told to ignore the function. There's one more condition, though, and that's the ready variable. The NET_STATUS event often fires more than once during important changes in a video's behavior, such as when a video ends. The ready variable ensures that the event handler function does its thing only once—otherwise, it might increment the currentVideo variable repeatedly while the other two conditions are true. That wouldn't be good, so the first time all three conditions are met, ready is set to false. It is reset to true when the next video loads, thanks to the onMetaData handler.

When the time is about one-half second before the end of the video, the next video in line is pulled out of the Array—currentVideo++. Naturally, we need to make sure that it is a part of the Array. If it is, put it on the stream and start playing it—ns.play(videos[currentVideo]).

4. Save and test the movie. The videos will play in the order in which they appear in the list.

> *Yes, you can (and should) skip "hard-wiring" the videos into the code and use XML instead. Regardless of the method used—internal vs. external—the key to this exercise is the function in step 3.*

Playing sequential videos through the FLVPlayback component

For those who prefer to use the FLVPlayback component, follow these steps:

1. Open the SequenceCpt.fla file in the Chapter 9 exercise folder.

2. Select the first frame in the Actions layer and open the ActionScript editor.

3. Click once in the Script pane and enter the following code:

```
var videos:Array = new Array("Puppetji_Gossip.flv", ➡
"Puppetji_Seeing.flv","Puppetji_One.flv");
var currentVideo:uint = 0;

myVideo.mouseChildren = false;

function playCurrentVideo():void {
  myVideo.source = videos[currentVideo];
  myVideo.play();
```

```
  }
  playCurrentVideo();

  myVideo.addEventListener(Event.COMPLETE, completeHandler);

  function completeHandler(evt:Event):void {
    currentVideo++;
    if (currentVideo > 0) {
      myVideo.mouseChildren = true;
    }
    if (currentVideo < videos.length) {
      playCurrentVideo();
    }
  }
```

We start by creating an Array of the videos to be played. After that, a currentVideo variable is declared to keep track of which video is the one currently playing. Then we have an optional line that disables the buttons of the FLVPlayback skin. The third line, which will appeal to control freaks, will keep users from being able to pause, seek, change the volume, and so on during the first video. Many developers are responsible for placing commercials in front of the requested content, and this provides a way to keep viewers from skipping past the ad.

The purpose of the first function, playCurrentVideo(), is to update the source property of the FLVPlayback instance and tell it to play. After the function is defined, it is immediately called and starts playing the first video in the Array.

The completeHandler function is practically the same as the first one. The difference is that it calls playCurrentVideo() and listens for the end of the video, which kicks out a COMPLETE event. When that is detected, the line currentVideo++ gets the next item in the Array, turns on the controls, and starts playing the video.

A video clock

One of the authors once attended a Flash conference at which he saw Flash pushed to its extremes by the presenter. In a conversation with the presenter afterward, the author asked the presenter why he did it. The response was succinct: "Because I can."

On the surface, this comment might just reek of arrogance or extreme self-confidence, but in fact, it was the exact opposite. Sometimes you like to play with Flash to see what it can do. When you discover something interesting that initially has no practical use, you take solace in the fact that you actually did it. In this exercise, you'll create something new: a clock that uses video to show the time on the user's computer. Why use video to show the time when you can just as easily use a dynamic text field and number? Easy. Because you can. Let's get started.

1. Open the VideoClock.fla file in the exercise folder. When it opens, you'll see that we have added a series of Video objects and a series of dynamic text boxes (see Figure 9-8). Moving from left to right, the first two video and text boxes represent the hours. The next two will be used to show minutes, and the last two will display the seconds. If you click each item, you'll also see that we have added an instance name for each object.

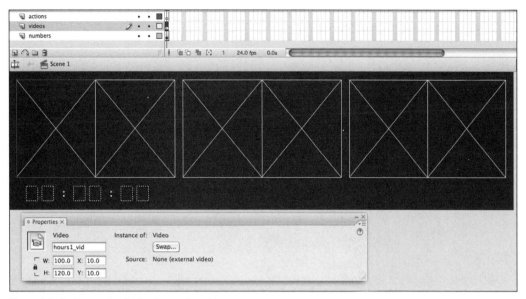

Figure 9-8. Setting up to display time using videos

2. Click once in the first frame of the Actions layer and open the Actions panel. Click once in the Script pane and add the following code that identifies the location of the videos to be used, sets up the NetConnection, and creates the listener for the metadata in the FLV file.

```
var videoDirectory:String = new String("videoSet1/");
var nc:NetConnection = new NetConnection();
nc.connect(null);

var listener:Object = new Object();
listener.onMetaData = function(md:Object):void{};
```

3. To this point in the chapter, multiple videos have played individually on the stage. If you want to play multiple videos at the same time, each video will need its own NetStream. This is a fundamental rule of Flash video: one video, one stream. Let's create the six streams used for the videos. Press Return/Enter twice and enter the following:

```
var seconds1_ns:NetStream = new NetStream(nc);
seconds1_vid.attachNetStream(seconds1_ns);
seconds1_ns.client = listener;

var seconds2_ns:NetStream = new NetStream(nc);
seconds2_vid.attachNetStream(seconds2_ns);
seconds2_ns.client = listener;

var minutes1_ns:NetStream = new NetStream(nc);
minutes1_vid.attachNetStream(minutes1_ns);
minutes1_ns.client = listener;
```

```
var minutes2_ns:NetStream = new NetStream(nc);
minutes2_vid.attachNetStream(minutes2_ns);
minutes2_ns.client = listener;

var hours1_ns:NetStream = new NetStream(nc);
hours1_vid.attachNetStream(hours1_ns);
hours1_ns.client = listener;

var hours2_ns:NetStream = new NetStream(nc);
hours2_vid.attachNetStream(hours2_ns);
hours2_ns.client = listener;
```

> We know that is a lot of typing. Here's a little "teacher trick": simply type the first one, copy it, and paste it into the code. Just keep in mind that the instance names do change.

4. Having created the streams, let's create the variables that will be used by the rest of the code. These variables will store the digits, including seconds, found in a typical digital clock. Press Return/Enter twice and enter the following:

```
var secondOnes:String = "";
var secondTens:String = "";
var minuteOnes:String = "";
var minuteTens:String = "";
var hourOnes:String = "";
var hourTens:String = "";
```

5. With the variables out of the way, we can now concentrate on creating the timer that will control the videos and the text. Press Return/Enter twice and enter the following:

```
var myTimer:Timer = new Timer(1000);
myTimer.addEventListener(TimerEvent.TIMER, onTick);
function onTick(evt:TimerEvent):void {
  var now:Date = new Date();

  var seconds:String = new String(now.getSeconds().toString());
  if(seconds.length < 2){
    seconds = "0" + seconds;
  }
```

We start by creating a new Timer object that fires every 1,000 milliseconds, or once each second. Having done that, we listen for a TIMER event. When it is detected, the onTick() function takes over.

You need to capture the current date from the user's computer by creating a Date object and using the methods and properties in the Date class. The Date class represents date and time information. An instance of the Date class, in this case now, represents a point in time for which the properties such as year, month, day, hours, minutes, seconds, and milliseconds can be accessed. You can grab this information as either Universal Time (Greenwich Mean Time or, in Flash, UTC) or the local time on the user's computer.

For those of you who are trivia buffs or, like us, have a wealth of useless information, the times represented by the Date object are expressed as "the number of milliseconds since January 1, 1970." It is known as Unix time.

Now that we know the date, we need to pull some information—hours, minutes, and seconds—out of the Date object and put it to work. If the String.length property of the seconds variable is less than 2—that is, if there's only a single character in this string (numerals less than 10)—the variable's current character is preceded by 0. All this means is that 1 will be rendered as 01, 2 as 02, and so on.

6. Having dealt with the individual seconds, press Return/Enter twice, and write the code that loads up the video and adds the text:

```
secondOnes = seconds.substring(1,2);
seconds2_tb.text = secondOnes
seconds2_ns.play(videoDirectory+secondOnes+".flv");
```

We start by creating a variable for this particular bit of information and giving it a range of values: seconds.substring(1,2). These values represent the second character in the string. Thus if the string were to be 25, only the 5 would be used.

After we have that information, the value is tossed into the dynamic text box and is used to retrieve and play the video containing that value in its file name in the videoDirectory folder.

7. Now that you know how to feed video and text into the interface, press Return/Enter twice and enter the remaining code, which is nothing more than a variation of the code entered in the previous two steps:

```
if (secondOnes == "0" || secondTens == "") {
  secondTens = seconds.substring(0,1);
  seconds1_tb.text = secondTens;
  seconds1_ns.play(videoDirectory + secondTens + ".flv");

  var minutes:String = new String(now.getMinutes().toString());
  if (minutes.length < 2) {
    minutes = "0" + minutes;
  }

  if (secondTens == "0" || minuteOnes == "") {
    minuteOnes = minutes.toString().substring(1,2);
    minutes2_tb.text = minuteOnes;
    minutes2_ns.play(videoDirectory + minuteOnes + ".flv");

    if (minuteOnes == "0" || minuteTens == "") {
      minuteTens = minutes.toString().substring(0,1);
      minutes1_tb.text = minuteTens;
      minutes1_ns.play(videoDirectory + minuteTens + ".flv");

      var hours = now.getHours().toString();
    if (hours.length < 2) {
```

```
                    hours = "0" + hours;
                }

            if (minuteTens == "0" || hourOnes == "") {
                hourOnes = hours.toString().substring(1,2);
                hours2_tb.text = hourOnes;
                hours2_ns.play(videoDirectory + hourOnes + ".flv");

                if (hourOnes == "0" || hourTens == "") {
                    hourTens = hours.toString().substring(0,1);
                    hours1_tb.text = hourTens;
                    hours1_ns.play(videoDirectory+hourTens+".flv");
                }
            }
        }
      }
    }
}

    myTimer.start();
```

There is a lot of code here, but it is simply the same thing over and over. Each time we change the seconds digit, and if the seconds digit is 0, we change the tens of seconds. If the tens of seconds is 0, we change the minutes digit, and so on.

8. Save and test the movie. The videos play and the text changes (see Figure 9-9).

> *If you are interested in using a different set of videos, we have included them in the VideoSet2 folder. They were created by Raymond Dowe, a very talented student at Humber College in Toronto.*

Figure 9-9. A video clock

Your turn: Interactive video

When we were planning this chapter, Tom wanted to end it with something original that used multiple videos in a rather creative manner. Adam, who had just returned from a teaching sojourn in Mexico, mentioned that he had completed a rather interesting project with the students at the school where he was teaching. In essence, the user uses the mouse to smack people around. When Tom saw it, the project immediately "made the book."

The thing about video is it is generally a passive medium. You really don't interact with it, apart from clicking a button to get a video to play. This exercise goes in the opposite direction. Depending on how fast you move your mouse, the direction it is moving, and where it passes over the poor soul in the project, you can do everything from gently smacking the subject to knocking him completely off his feet.

1. Open the SlapGuy.fla file in the exercise folder. When it opens (see Figure 9-10), you will see there isn't much to it: a couple of dynamic text boxes with instance names and a couple of labels and layers. All the magic is contained in the code you will write.

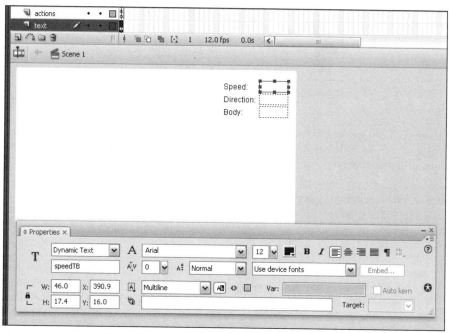

Figure 9-10. Not much to the stage; the magic happens in the code.

2. Before you start, now would be a good time to take a look at what you are working with. Minimize Flash and open the SlapGuy folder in your exercise folder. Inside this folder are 14 very short FLV files. If you check out the file names (see Figure 9-11), you get a very strong clue about how this project will function.

Each FLV file is named for a specific mouse speed, direction, and location. If the user moves the mouse slowly to the right across the victim's (er, subject's) torso, the `rightchestslow.flv` will play. Move it quickly to the left, and the `leftchestfast.flv` will play. The net effect will be the ability to have a rather interesting interactive video project by the end of the exercise. Let's "wire it up."

Figure 9-11. Your raw material is a series of 14 very short FLV files.

3. Maximize Flash, select the first frame of the Actions layer and open the Actions panel. Scroll down to line 24 of the code and enter the following variables, which are used to track the mouse speed, direction, and body area the mouse will pass over:

```
var xPositionLastFrame:Number = stage.mouseX;
var xPositionCurrentFrame:Number = stage.mouseX;
var mouseSpeed:Number;
var mouseSpeedText:String = "";
var mouseDirectionText:String = "";
var mouseDirectionText:String = "";
```

4. Now that you have created the variables, regularly check the location of the mouse on the stage using a MOUSE_MOVE event. What will happen is that the mouse's x position at the current moment will be compared with where it was previously. By subtracting one from the other, you can set the limits for the various speeds. Enter the following code:

```
stage.addEventListener(MouseEvent.MOUSE_MOVE, mouseMoveHandler);

function mouseMoveHandler(evt:MouseEvent):void {
  xPositionLastFrame = xPositionCurrentFrame;
  xPositionCurrentFrame = stage.mouseX;
  mouseSpeed = xPositionLastFrame - xPositionCurrentFrame;
  if ((mouseSpeed > 20) || (mouseSpeed < -20)) {
    mouseSpeedText = "fast";
```

```
    } else {
      mouseSpeedText = "slow";
  }

  speedTB.text = mouseSpeedText;
```

The mouseSpeed variable is just that—a variable. If you want to use a higher or lower number than 20, be our guest. As you can see, however, that number is also "translated" into the words fast and slow, which are then fed into the text box on the stage.

5. It isn't only the speed of the mouse that is critical; it is also the location of the mouse from the top of the stage. Each video is 240 pixels high. To determine which of the head, chest, and feet FLV files get played, you need to divide the stage into three areas, as shown in Figure 9-12. To do this, click once in the Step 5: section of the code and enter the following:

```
if ((stage.mouseY > 25) && (stage.mouseY <60)) {
    bodyText = "head";
} else if ((stage.mouseY > 60) && (stage.mouseY <140)) {
    bodyText = "chest";
} else if ((stage.mouseY > 140) && (stage.mouseY <220)) {
    bodyText = "feet";
}
bodyTB.text = bodyText;
```

Figure 9-12. The stage is "divided" into three distinct areas.

6. The last step in this project is designed to grab the direction of the mouse movement and trigger the relevant video. Click once in the Step 6: area of the code and enter the following:

```
if ((xPositionLastFrame < 150) && (xPositionCurrentFrame > 150)) {
    mouseDirectionText = "left";
    ns.play(mouseDirectionText + bodyText + mouseSpeedText + ".flv");
} else if ((xPositionLastFrame > 150) &&➥
(xPositionCurrentFrame < 150)) {
    mouseDirectionText = "right";
    ns.play(mouseDirectionText + bodyText + mouseSpeedText + ".flv");
}
directionTB.text = mouseDirectionText;
}
```

271

In this case, we use the width of the video to determine the direction of the mouse movement. Each FLV file is 360 pixels wide. By setting an arbitrary point on the x-axis, in this case 150 pixels, you can determine whether the mouse is moving right or left (see Figure 9-13). That value is then fed into the relevant Text box and is used in the FLV file name used in the NetStream play() method. If you look at how the stage is divided, you can see how we came up with the names of the 12 FLV files.

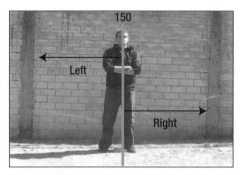

Figure 9-13. The stage is bisected to determine the direction of the mouse movement.

7. Save and play the movie. Notice that the videos swap out, depending on how fast the mouse is moving and where it is on the stage (see Figure 9-14).

Figure 9-14. Our victim (subject) is having a bad day.

What you've learned

As you might have noticed, there are a lot of ways to play multiple videos. Ranging from simply choosing from a list to actually interacting with video, there's a lot you can do if you have multiple videos to play. In this chapter, you have done the following:

- Used a ComboBox component with and without XML to allow the user to choose from a number of videos
- Used a series of movieclips to trigger FLV file playback
- Discovered how to play a sequence of videos
- Learned how to play multiple videos on the stage
- Learned how to make video an interactive experience

The techniques presented ranged from the simple to the rather complex. This chapter is in no way to be considered as the end of your creative explorations with Flash video. We have presented a series of techniques that are designed to introduce you to the basics of multiple video selection and playback, and nothing more. There are two major "takeaways" from this chapter. The first is that XML gives you the flexibility to add to and subtract from a list of videos. Change the XML and you don't need to root around the Flash file. The second is that each video playing on the stage must have its own NetStream. If you "get" those two, you "get" working with multiple videos in Flash.

In the next chapter, you'll explore live video instead of working with FLV files that we created earlier. We'll show you how to work with the Camera object. From there, we'll answer the inevitable question: "What else can I do with a webcam?"

Turn the page to find out. See you there.

Chapter 10

THE CAMERA OBJECT AND FLASH VIDEO

One of the authors is fond of saying this to anybody who will listen: "The amount of fun you can have in this business should be illegal." When it comes to connecting a web camera (webcam) to your computer and seeing what you can do in Flash, his statement takes on even more importance. It is both easy and fun to connect a web camera to a Flash movie. The only problem is that after you do it, you will discover that the creative possibilities are unlimited and that you are facing a life sentence.

How easy is it? A webcam and two lines of ActionScript get you into the game. Really!

In this chapter we will start slowly with simply connecting a webcam to a Flash movie. After that, we kick out the jams and explore some of the more interesting things you can do with a webcam.

What we'll cover in this chapter:

- Creating a Camera object
- Using the web camera in Flash CS3
- Adding a live camera feed to images in Flash CS3
- Using the Flash Media Encoder

Files used in this chapter:

- Flip.fla (Chapter10\ExerciseFiles_CH10\Exercise\Flip.fla)
- DundasSquare.jpg (Chapter10\ExerciseFiles_CH10\Exercise\DundasSquare.jpg)
- DundasSquare.fla (Chapter10\ExerciseFiles_CH10\Exercise\DundasSquare.fla)
- BitmapVideo.fla (Chapter10\ExerciseFiles_CH10\Exercise\BitmapVideo.fla)
- Cigars.flv (Chapter10\ExerciseFiles_CH10\Exercise\Cigars.flv)
- BitmapWebcam.fla (Chapter10\ExerciseFiles_CH10\Exercise\BitmapWebcam.fla)
- Gotcha.fla (Chapter10\ExerciseFiles_CH10\Exercise\Gotcha.fla)

Flash and the Camera object

The first thing to understand about using the Camera object is that its primary purpose is to broadcast a video feed from your camera through Flash Media Server 3 to a SWF file in a web page. So if you have a Flash Media Server (FMS) account, you can wave at Aunt Millie in Manchester, UK from your computer, and if she has a webcam, you can see her wave back at you. Although that is the primary purpose, you can also use this class to allow users with webcams to see themselves and even put themselves into some rather interesting circumstances.

The other aspect of using a webcam with the Flash Player is that any SWF file that tries to access a camera will kick out a Privacy dialog box that lets the user choose whether to allow or deny access to the camera. This Privacy dialog box also lets you choose the camera to be used. More about that in a minute. Finally, although you can connect a number of cameras to your computer, the Camera object will let you display them only one at a time.

Connect your web camera to your computer and have some fun discovering how Flash can make your webcam a communication device.

1. Open a new Flash document. Open the library and create a Video object. Drag it to the stage from the library.

2. Click once on the Video object and give it the instance name of myVid. Set its size to 320 pixels wide by 240 pixels high.

3. Add an Actions layer to the main timeline, open the Actions panel, and enter the following two lines of code into the Script pane:

```
var myCamera:Camera = Camera.getCamera();
myVid.attachCamera(myCamera);
```

The first line retrieves the Camera object using the static Camera.getCamera(); method and gives the camera a name by assigning it to myCamera. The second line simply attaches the feed from the camera to the Video object on the stage using the attachCamera() method of the Video class. That's all you need to get in the game.

4. Go ahead; test the movie. Say hello to the world (see Figure 10-1).

Although you are using a Video *object that is 320 by 240 to play the video feed, you can use any size you want. Just be aware that every time the camera is detected, the* Privacy Settings *dialog box will appear over the SWF file. This means if you have a* Video *object on a stage that is 160 by 120, the user will have a real problem because the* Privacy Settings *dialog box will be larger than the stage. If you do use a web camera, the minimum stage size is 215 by 138 pixels, which is the minimum size required by Flash to display the dialog box.*

Figure 10-1. Hello, world!

You might have noticed the empty parameter in the `Camera.getCamera()` method. It means that Flash is to use the first camera connected to your computer that it finds. If you had three cameras, they would have index values of 0, 1, and 2, which correspond to the name of each camera found in the `Camera.names` property (an `Array`). The only unusual thing about `Camera` index values is that they're strings. If you want to use the second camera, the method is the following:

```
Camera.getCamera("1");
```

Your best bet, though, is to let Flash grab the camera for you. If you haven't been able to get your camera to connect to the Video object, all is not lost. Sometimes there are multiple camera drivers installed, and Flash might have picked the wrong one. To choose the proper driver, test the movie again and follow these steps:

1. Right-click (PC) or Ctrl-click (Mac) on the SWF file to open the Context menu. Choose Settings. The Adobe Flash Player Settings dialog box opens.

2. Along the bottom are four icons. The last two look like a microphone and a camera. Click the camera icon.

3. This is the area in which you can choose your camera. Just click the drop-down menu; when you find your camera, select it and click the Close button (see Figure 10-2).

Figure 10-2. Choose your camera in this dialog box.

277

If you are a Mac user and connect an external iSight camera to your computer, the camera settings might give you a bit of grief. You might see your iSight listed as a choice. If you choose it, the image quality will be absolutely terrible. Instead, choose the generic FireWire camera—IIDC FireWire Video—that will appear in the drop-down menu.

A video box

Video walls are easy to do; let's go in another direction and create a "video box." Here's how:

1. Open a new Flash ActionScript 3.0 document. Set the stage size to 500 pixels wide by 450 pixels high and create a new movieclip named Vid.

2. If it isn't open, open the Symbol editor by double-clicking the movieclip. Add a Video object to the library and drag that object to the stage in the Symbol editor. In the Property Inspector give the Video object the instance name of myVid, set the dimensions of the Video object to 240 pixels wide by 180 pixels high, and set its X and Y coordinates to 0,0.

3. Add a new layer to the movieclip timeline and name it Actions. Select the first frame in the Actions layer, open the Actions panel, and enter these two lines of code:

```
var myCam:Camera = Camera.getCamera();
myVid.attachCamera(myCam);
```

4. Close the Actions panel and click the Scene 1 link to return to the main timeline.

5. Drag two copies of the Vid movieclip to the stage and place them beside each other. Select both clips, open the Transform panel by selecting Window ➤ Transform, and set the width to 130.0%. Before you do the scale, make sure that the Constrain check box is deselected.

6. Select the movieclip on the left and set its vertical Skew value to 45% using the Transform panel. Do the same thing with the movieclip on the right, but set its Skew value to -45. Align the edges of the movieclips as shown in Figure 10-3.

7. Lock Layer 1 and add a new layer named Top. Draw a rectangle in this layer. Select the Free Transform tool and manipulate the rectangle to fit on top of the two movieclips. When you finish, it should look like the box shown in Figure 10-4. Unlock the layers.

8. Select Edit ➤ Select All and convert the selection to a movieclip named Box.

9. With the Free Transform tool, scale the box to about half the size of the height of the stage. Move the box to the lower-left half of the stage.

10. Click once on the box. With the Option (Mac) or Alt (PC) and Shift keys held down, drag a copy of the movieclip to the right and align it with the right edge of the other movieclip. Make another copy; this time drag the copy to the top of the two boxes on the stage.

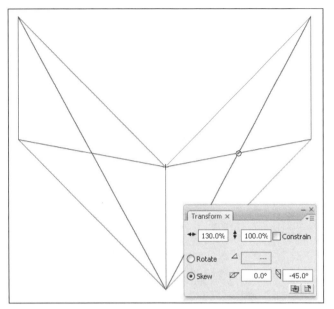

Figure 10-3. Use the Transform panel to scale and skew by the numbers.

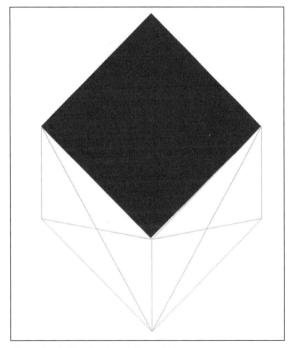

Figure 10-4. The first box is in position.

11. Save and test the movie (see Figure 10-5).

> *If you really want to have some fun, put a bunch of the movieclip boxes on the stage and let the user stack the blocks, using the* startDrag() *and* stopDrag() *methods.*

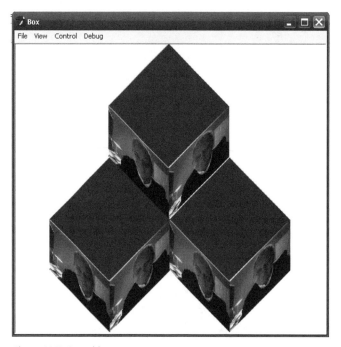

Figure 10-5. Boxed in

Flipping video

As you discovered in the previous exercise, you don't always need to have the video on a flat plane. In this one you keep the video on that plane, but the end result is a sort of kaleidoscopic effect. This is accomplished by simply "flipping" the movieclips containing the Video object.

1. Open the Flip.fla file found in the Chapter 10 exercise folder. Everything is wired up and ready to go with this exercise. All you need to do is to flip the videos.

2. Select the movieclip under Flip Horizontal and select Modify ➤ Transform ➤ Flip Horizontal, as shown in Figure 10-6. You will know the movieclip has flipped because its registration point will move to the upper-right corner from the upper-left corner of the movieclip.

3. Select the movieclip over Flip Vertical and apply a vertical flip transform to the selection.

4. Select the last clip, flip it vertically, and then flip it horizontally.

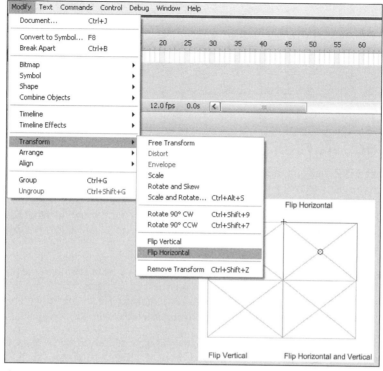

Figure 10-6. A horizontal flip

5. Save and test the movie. If you move around, you get a really interesting distortion, as shown in Figure 10-7.

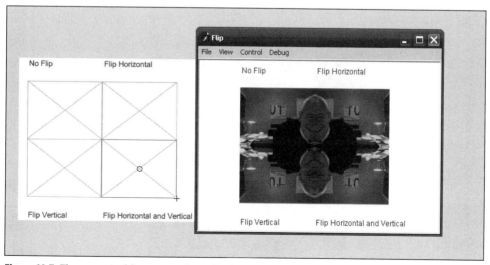

Figure 10-7. The amount of fun you can have should be illegal.

Don't forget that this a movieclip you are using. This means you can bend, twist, rotate, and otherwise launch mayhem on the stage. This example showed you how to create something that looks like a character from Alice in Wonderland. Whip a mask into the movieclip, set it to rotating, and you have turned the movie into a kaleidoscope.

Playing *Blade Runner* in Toronto

A couple of years ago, one of the authors was in New York attending the East Coast version of FlashForward. As he was wandering through the vendor displays, he happened to see an orange booklet put out by Macromedia on one of the vendor's tables: "Web Video with Macromedia Flash." He stuck a copy of the booklet in his pocket and later started flipping through it. What really caught his attention was the page with the interesting title of "No faking it." In particular, this passage flew off the page and into his "creative cortex:"

> *Using Flash it's possible to toss videos around 3D space like a leaf blowing in the wind. Resist the urge. Nothing turns viewers off more than pointless cool effects. That's not to say there aren't great ways to make use of the advanced technology of Flash. Take a picture of Times Square and composite your video over the Sony JumboTron.*

This brings us to the point of this exercise. We suspect we have all looked at the giant pixel boards in our respective cities, or cities we have visited, and thought, "Gee, wouldn't it be cool if I could get myself or a user into that pixel board." Your wait is over. Instead of Times Square, we'll visit the hometown of the authors, Toronto, and wave at everyone from a pixel board on Dundas Square (see Figure 10-8).

Figure 10-8. Screens galore on Dundas Square

Open the DundasSquare.jpg image in the Chapter 10 exercise folder and take a minute or two to plan out the approach to this exercise.

When you first look at the image, a couple of issues immediately arise:

- The areas for the Camera object are not perfectly square. There is some perspective involved.
- There are objects such as street lamps and so on in front of the areas. To maintain the "realism," they simply can't be removed. You have to work around them.

So you have to do the following:

- Make the Camera and Video objects fit the area through the use of Flash's Free Transform tool.
- Keep the objects in front of the videos in place by "masking" the Video or Camera object.
- Create the masks in Adobe Illustrator CS3 because Flash is not exactly an industrial-strength drawing application. This isn't to be interpreted as "dissing" Flash. We just think that the tools in Illustrator give a bit more precision when it comes to tricky angles and curves.
- Place the masks in Flash as graphic symbols.
- Place the masks and the Camera objects into separate movieclips where the mask can be applied.

Now that you know what needs to be done, let's go to work.

> The final file you'll be producing will result in a rather hefty SWF file, which will be quite a "lengthy" download for people with speedy connections. This project, therefore, is best played back from your desktop. If you do want to play this through a web site, we suggest you check out Chapter 13 of Foundation Flash CS3 for Designers from friends of ED. The chapter is dedicated to optimizing Flash movies for web playback.
>
> If you do not have a copy of Illustrator CS3, you can still work along with us. We have included the DundasMask.ai file in the exercise folder. Feel free to use it from step 6 onward.

1. Open Adobe Illustrator CS3 and create a new document. When the new document appears, locate the image named DundasSquare.jpg in the Chapter 10 exercise folder and drag it from the folder onto the Illustrator page. When you release the mouse, the image will drop into its own layer in Illustrator.

2. Select the Magnifying Glass tool and zoom in on the blue sign in the bottom-right corner of the image. There are some features that will have to be accommodated, including the top of a traffic light pole that pokes into the bottom-right corner of the image (see Figure 10-9).

3. Select the Pen tool and click each point of the area where a line changes direction.

Figure 10-9. The lights in the upper-right screen, the perspective in the lower-left screen, and the traffic signal pole in the bottom-right corner have to be accommodated in the mask.

4. When the shape is complete, turn off the stroke around your shape. Then select the Hollow Selection tool, click and drag the points, and manipulate the handles until you have the area covered. When you finish, your shape should resemble that shown in Figure 10-10.

Figure 10-10. The mask shape to be used in Flash

5. At this stage, you can either choose to create a layer in Illustrator for each shape, which you did, or just continue building them until you have the masks in place. Create the remaining masks and save the file. When finished, your image should resemble that shown in Figure 10-11.

Figure 10-11. The final Illustrator image containing all the masks

6. Open the DundasSquare.fla file located in the Chapter 10 exercise folder. When the file opens, create a new layer named Vids.

Life is not a series of straight lines. Things tend to shift their shape (because of perspective) as they recede into the distance. Simply adding the video to a sign and then expecting the viewer to believe that it belongs there is a bit too optimistic. It will look totally out of place. Also, there are obstructions in front of each video's final location. It would look odd to have the video sitting in front of them. The masks created in Illustrator are the key. They match the lines and curves of the area in which the video will be placed. All you have to do is to create the Camera objects and "distort" them to follow the lines of the mask.

We will only be describing how to create the video that will go into Mask01. The remaining screens follow the same technique.

7. Select File ➤ Import ➤ Import to Library. When the Import to Library dialog box opens, select the DundasMask.ai file and click Open to launch the Import "DundasMask.ai" to Library dialog box shown in Figure 10-12.

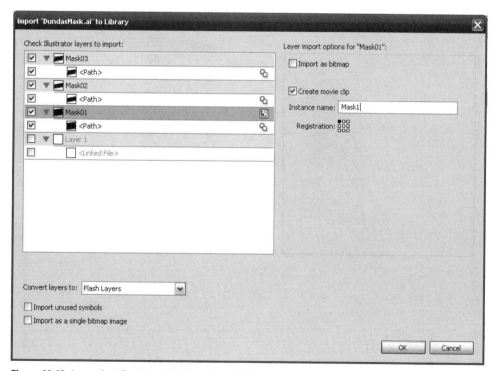

Figure 10-12. Importing Illustrator CS3 layers into Flash

8. Deselect Layer 1. You don't need it because the image is already in the library. Click once on the Mask01 strip and select Create movie clip from the Layer import options for "Mask01" area on the right side of the dialog box. In the Instance name field, enter Mask1. Repeat this step for the Mask02 and Mask03 layers. Click OK to close the dialog box and import the layers into your Flash document.

Preparing the Video objects

With the assets in place, let's get busy and put the masks to work.

1. Double-click the Mask01 movieclip to open it in the Symbol editor.

2. Create a new Video object in the Flash library. When you see the object in the library, create a new layer in the Mask01 movieclip named Video and drag the layer under the mask shape layer.

3. With the Video layer selected, drag a copy of the Video object from the library to the stage. Use the Property Inspector to set its location to 0,0 and give it the instance name of myVid. Now select the Free Transform tool. You'll put the video into "perspective" using the sides of the mask. Click the Video object and reduce its size to a close approximation of the mask.

4. Select the Magnifying Glass tool, or press the M or Z keys on your keyboard, and zoom in on the mask and the Video object. Reselect the Free Transform tool and change the shape of the Video object to roughly follow the edges of the mask. Keep in mind what we told you about this in Chapter 7: you only need to be close because the eye will add the distortion (see Figure 10-13).

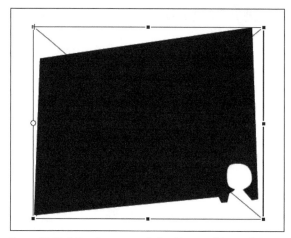

Figure 10-13. "Close" counts only in video masking and the game of horseshoe throwing.

5. Select the layer containing the mask. Right-click (PC) or Ctrl-click (Mac) on the layer name. Select Mask from the drop-down menu. The Video object now takes on the shape of the mask.

6. Add a new layer named Actions. Open the ActionScript editor and enter the following code into the Script pane:

```
var myCam:Camera = Camera.getCamera();
myVid.attachVideo(myCam);
```

7. Close the ActionScript editor and click the Scene 1 link to return to the main timeline.

8. Add a new layer named Video1 and drag a copy of the Mask01 movieclip from the library onto the stage and place it in its correct position over the image. Go ahead and test the file (see Figure 10-14).

Figure 10-14. Live. From Dundas Square in Toronto. It's me!

From here on, it is nothing more than creating the masks and putting them in place using the objects from Illustrator. One of the things we do, though, is to give each mask movieclip a unique name to avoid confusion.

> Another approach to this technique is to create a movieclip containing the Video object and use the movieclip instead of the Video object. In this way, if there is a code change required, you need to change it in only one place: the movieclip.

Another little trick is to simply get the video and the mask sized up against each other in the movieclip. Then you drag the movieclip from the library into the Video layer and move it into position. Thus, you have the black shape to help guide you to line up the object where it is supposed to go. Then you simply double-click the movieclip to open the Symbol editor, apply the mask, and add the code.

Those users without webcams will see the image. The Camera objects are transparent until a webcam is detected, as shown in Figure 10-15.

Figure 10-15. The completed file

Recording and broadcasting video

In late 2006, Adobe released a rather interesting product: the **Flash Media Encoder (FME)**. In late 2007, Adobe realized that it might have something special and released Flash Media Encoder 2 (FME2), which is an update to take advantage of the HD formats (see Chapter 12) now available for playback in the Flash Player.

The real strength of this application lies in its capability to stream or broadcast a live video presentation through a web site. This functionality requires either the use of an FMS or having a Flash Video Streaming Service (FVSS) account. We won't be getting into this rather complicated process because as this book is being written, the Flash Media Server 3 is a beta product and the FLVPlayback component is being "retooled" to accommodate HD playback.

> When Adobe releases these updates in the spring of 2008, well after this book has been printed, be sure to check the book site for addenda to the chapters affected by these changes.

The FME2 allows you to capture your camera output, and what you do with it from there could involve anything in this book. Having said that, there are a number of immediate applications you can use:

- Capturing and broadcasting classes or lectures for students
- Creating video or audio podcasts
- Recording presentations to members of service organizations
- Gathering the family around the computer and sending Aunt Millie in Manchester a greeting from the clan

Let's get started:

1. Point your browser to www.adobe.com/products/flashmediaserver/flashmediaencoder/ and download and install the FME2. (If you use a Mac, you are now out of the game. The FME2 is a PC-only product, which makes sense because the Flash Media Server 3 is also a PC-only product.)

> *Those of you with Intel Macs and who have a PC partition can install the FME.*

2. When the Installer downloads, double-click it to start the installation process. We won't walk you through it because it is very simple. When it finishes installing, you will see the icon shown in Figure 10-16 on your desktop. Double-click the icon to launch the FME2.

3. Attach a webcam to your computer and launch the FME2. When you launch the application, the interface shown in Figure 10-17 appears. Let's take a couple of minutes to walk through the various bits and pieces in the interface.

Figure 10-16. The FME2 desktop shortcut

Figure 10-17. The FME2 interface isn't all that complicated.

The first thing you will notice is the interface is divided into two areas: Input and Output. The two preview areas show what is going into the application on the left and what is going out on the right.

Select the Encoding Options tab and let's work our way through the Input area:

- Preset: This drop-down menu gives you four choices, ranging from Low Bandwidth to Custom. If you select one of the bandwidth choices and make a change, the field will change to Custom. If you find a series of settings that work consistently for you, select File ➤ Save Profile to open the Save As dialog box. You can name and save the file—it is an XML file—and reload it by selecting File ➤ Open Profile.

- Video: Deselect this option to stream only the audio portion of the file.

- Device: This drop-down menu shows you all the cameras detected by the FME2 (see Figure 10-18). For you techies out there, any device recognized by Microsoft DirectShow can be connected to your computer. Adobe has a list of tested devices at www.adobe.com/support/documentation/en/flashmediaencoder/FME_DeviceMatrix.pdf.

Figure 10-18. You can pick your camera.

- Tools icon: This icon looks like a wrench. Click it and the Settings dialog box shown in Figure 10-19 opens. You can use this dialog box to manipulate the image, adjust the color balance, and so on. Click the Camera Control tab and you can (if it is configured) adjust zoom, focus, and other shooting settings. Click OK to accept the changes and close the dialog box.

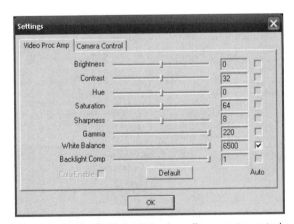

Figure 10-19. The Settings dialog box allows you to control the image capture quality.

- Format: This drop-down menu allows you to choose between the VP6 and H.264 encoding options. Click the Tools button; the Advanced Encoder settings dialog box opens, in which you set key frame frequency, image quality, noise reduction, and so on.

If you select H.264, you can choose Encoding Profile - Baseline, which is the standard for video confer-encing and mobile media. The Level drop-down menu allows you to set a typical frame size, a frame rate, and the maximum data rate. The choices available to you are well beyond the scope of this book, but Apple has posted a rather concise explanation of the codec at http://images.apple.com/quicktime/pdf/H264_Technology_Brief.pdf.

> The formats should tell you that the video created in this application can be played only through the Flash Player 8 and higher.

- Size and fps: Select an output size from the drop-down menu and set the frame rate.
- Crop: Select one or all of the four crop options to trim off unwanted areas of the capture. You can do it by the numbers, click the arrows, or drag the crop handle (it looks like a hollow green box in the Input area) to crop the input.
- Resize: Select this option to expand or shrink the capture.
- Maintain Aspect Ratio: If you selected Resize, choose this option to avoid distortion.
- Timecode: Depending on the input device, it allows you to display the timecode on the video frame (this item might be unavailable). If you can select it, use it to add the SMTPE timecode to the capture.
- Deinterlace: Select this filter, and the FME2 will apply a simple vertical blur to the capture. This will work only if the video's height is greater than 480 pixels and the width is greater than 576 pixels.
- Audio: Deselect this option to produce a video without an audio track.
- Device: Select the audio device that will be used to capture the audio.
- Device tools icon: Click the wrench icon, and the Audio Input Mixer properties dialog box opens. Here you can make rather rudimentary adjustments to the bass and treble.
- Format: You can choose between Mp3 or Nellymoser. We suggest that you stick with the Mp3 format, which is superior to the Nellymoser format used by Flash for voice recordings.
- Sample Rate: Choose an audio sample rate from the drop-down menu. Your choices are 44, 22, and 11 kHz.
- Bit Rate: Choose an audio bitrate from the drop-down menu. Your choices are 48, 40, and 32 kbps.
- Volume: Move this slider to adjust the volume level of the audio file.

Now that you have a handle on what this application can do, let's capture some video. Here's how:

1. Open the FME2 application.
2. Select your capture device. We are using the iSight camera that is built into MacBook Pro.
3. Select VP6 from the Format drop-down menu.
4. Make sure that the Audio area is selected.
5. Choose your microphone. If you don't have an external microphone or headset, just go with the default.

6. In the Output area, select Save to File.

7. Click the Browse button. When the Save As dialog box opens, navigate to a folder where you want the file to be placed.

8. Give the file a name and click the Save button. The path to the video will be shown.

9. To start recording, click the green Start button at the bottom of the Flash Media Encoder.

10. Record your video. When it finishes, click the red Stop button.

If you navigate to the location where the video was saved (for this exercise, we saved a file named Chapter_10.flv to the chapter's complete folder), you can either preview the video in Adobe Bridge CS3 (see Figure 10-20) or in the Adobe Media Player. You can also use it with a Video object or the FLVPlayback component in Flash.

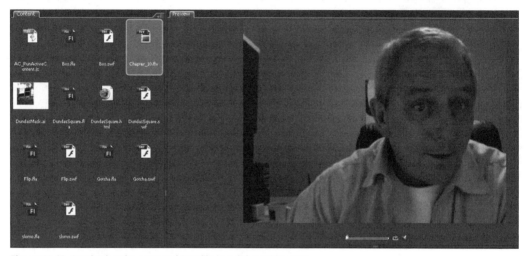

Figure 10-20. Previewing the captured FLV file in Adobe Bridge CS3

Capturing the screen

Chapter 7 introduced you to the Drawing API, which allows you to use ActionScript to draw and fill shapes onscreen that can be used as masks. In this exercise you'll use the BitmapData data class to grab an image from a video. Although you'll use a button to take the screenshot, you can also use a timer to create the shots at regular intervals.

1. Open the BitmapVideo.fla file from the exercise folder. When it opens, as shown in Figure 10-21, you'll see that we essentially constructed the interface for you. The CAPTURE button is what makes all this happen. Click it, and whatever frame is playing in the Video side of the interface will appear in the Captured Image area.

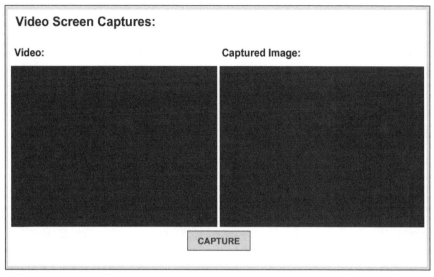

Figure 10-21. We start with a rather simple interface.

2. Click once in the first frame of the Actions layer and open the Actions panel. When the panel opens, click once in the Script pane and enter the following code:

```
import flash.display.BitMap;
import flash.display.BitmapData;

var myVideo:Video = new Video();
myVideo.x = 10;
myVideo.y = 95;
addChild(myVideo);

var nc:NetConnection = new NetConnection();
nc.connect(null);
var ns:NetStream = new NetStream(nc);
myVideo.attachNetStream(ns);

var listener:Object = new Object();
listener.onMetaData = function(md:Object):void{};
ns.client = listener;

ns.play("Cigars.flv");

ns.addEventListener(NetStatusEvent.NET_STATUS, statusHandler);
function statusHandler(event:NetStatusEvent):void{
  if(event.info.code == "NetStream.Buffer.Empty"){
    ns.seek(0);
  }
}
```

We start by importing the `Bitmap` and `BitmapData` classes into the movie. These classes will be used to hold and then display the captured frames from the video. After creating the Video object, we "wire it up" to a NetStream instance, as usual. The NET_STATUS event handler loops the video. In this exercise, we recognize that video is a bunch of images on a video timeline. We'll grab one of these images and store it as a bitmap that will be displayed on the stage when the CAPTURE button is clicked. Let's wire that up.

3. Press Return/Enter twice and enter the following code:

```
var myBitmapData:BitmapData = new BitmapData(320,240,false,0x00333333);

var myBitmap:Bitmap = new Bitmap(myBitmapData);
myBitmap.x = 345;
myBitmap.y = 10;
addChild(myBitmap);

captureBTN.addEventListener(MouseEvent.CLICK, capureBTNClickHandler);
function capureBTNClickHandler(evt:Object):void {
  myBitmapData.draw(myVideo);
}
```

The BitmapData class lets you work with the pixels of a Bitmap object. It isn't named *BitmapPixels* because the pixels contain the data needed to render the bitmap. You can use the methods of the BitmapData class to create variously sized transparent or opaque bitmap images and, as you have discovered earlier in this book, manipulate them in a number of ways when the video plays.

This class is powerful because it lets you separate bitmap-rendering operations from the internal display-updating routines of the Flash Player (which is a fancy way of saying that there is a decrease in the processor hit caused by fairly complex images).

This code block, therefore, starts by creating a `BitmapData` object that is 320 pixels wide by 240 pixels high to match the video's physical dimensions. No opacity, `false`, is applied to the image, and it is filled with a dark grey color: 0x00333333.

> *That color looks a bit odd. Shouldn't it be 0x333333? No—a* BitmapData *image is actually a 32-bit ARGB image, meaning that there are three colors (RGB), but the first value is the Alpha channel. You can also ignore it, meaning that the color would be 0x333333. If you want a semitransparent (50%) initial gray image, it would be 0x80333333 because 80 is hexadecimal for 128, which is half of the 256-value transparency range (0 to 255), and you'd have to change the opacity parameter to* true.

The next code block puts the object on the stage.

The function simply waits for the CAPTURE button to be clicked and, when Flash detects the CLICK, it moves whatever frame of the video is currently showing into the `myBitmapData` object on the stage.

4. Save and test the movie. When you click the button, the image shown in Figure 10-22 appears on the stage. Click the button again and the image changes.

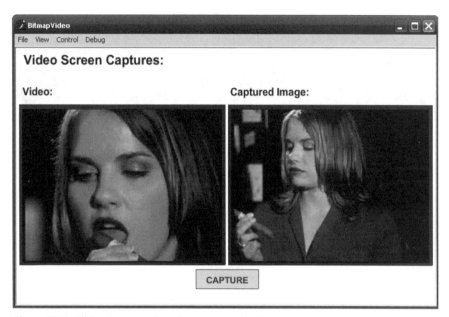

Figure 10-22. Click a button and you have a screenshot.

Capturing webcam content

Now that you know how to capture a frame of a video that is playing, here's how to do the same thing with a webcam. Follow these steps:

1. Open the BitmapWebcam.fla file in the exercise folder.

2. Select the first frame of the Actions layer and open the Actions panel.

3. Click once in line 9 of the Script pane and enter the following:

```
var myCam:Camera = Camera.getCamera();
var myVideo:Video = new Video();
myVideo.attachCamera(myCam);
myVideo.x = 10;
myVideo.y = 10;
addChild(myVideo);
```

This is exactly the same code as that used in the previous exercise. The only change you make is to attach a web camera to the Video object and grab a frame from the camera stream, not an FLV file.

4. Save and test the movie. When you click the CAPTURE button, the image shown in Figure 10-23 is displayed. That handsome mug will be replaced with your handsome mug!

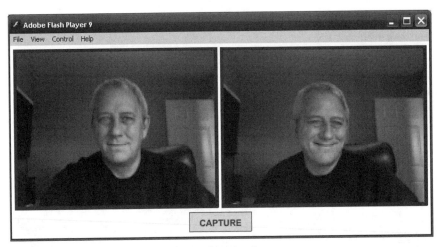

Figure 10-23. Yes, you can create your own photo booth.

Your turn: A little game of "gotcha"

The final exercise will appeal to security freaks. Whenever the camera detects a certain level of motion, it takes a picture.

1. Open the Gotcha.fla file in the Chapter 10 exercise folder, select the first frame of the Actions layer, open the ActionScript editor, and enter the following:

```
import flash.display.Bitmap;
import flash.display.BitmapData;
```

Having imported the Bitmap and BitmapData classes, you can now turn your attention to some motion detection.

2. Press Return/Enter twice and enter the following code:

```
var myBitmaps:Array = new Array();
var myBitmapData:Array = new Array();
for(var i:int = 0; i < 4; i++){
  myBitmapData[i] = new BitmapData(320,240,false,0x00333333)
  myBitmaps[i] = new Bitmap(myBitmapData[i]);
  myBitmaps[i].x = 5 + 165 * i;
  myBitmaps[i].y = 315;
  myBitmaps[i].scaleX = 0.5;
  myBitmaps[i].scaleY = 0.5;
  addChild(myBitmaps[i]);
}

var bitmapCounter:int = 0;
```

The first thing you do is a bit of file management. The images will be sitting on a gray background under the main video. The captures and their backgrounds need to be saved somewhere, and an Array is the solution.

That process starts with the for loop, which limits the number of backgrounds and images that can be displayed at any one time to four. The BitMapData parameters limit the size of the backgrounds to 320 pixels wide and 240 pixels high. It sets their transparency parameter to false and fills each one with a dark gray color.

The remaining six lines place the images over the backgrounds and scale the images to fit. The last line of the for loop is how the images appear on the stage. The final line uses a counter to ensure that only four images appear onscreen at any one time.

With the housekeeping out of the way, let's wire up the webcam.

3. Press Return/Enter twice and enter the following code that initializes the webcam:

```
var myCam:Camera = Camera.getCamera();
myCam.setMotionLevel(70,50);
var myVideo:Video = new Video();
myVideo.attachCamera(myCam);
myVideo.x = 172;
myVideo.y = 10;
addChild(myVideo);
```

That second line of the code is where the magic happens. The Camera class contains a setMotionLevel() method. This method is used to determine how much movement or motion is required to fire an ActivityEvent. That is the purpose of the two parameters. The first parameter (70) is the activity level. If set to 0, you expect no activity (a wheat field); if set to 100, the motion will be constant (a Formula One race). The higher the value, the more motion must be detected to fire the event. If you want to temporarily stop motion detection, it should be set to its maximum of 100.

The second parameter specifies how many milliseconds must elapse without activity before the Flash Player considers activity to have stopped and dispatches the activity event. The default value is 2000 milliseconds (2 seconds). In the example, we really dialed up the sensitivity by reducing the wait time to 50 milliseconds.

4. Press Return/Enter twice and write the code that will capture some images based upon movement:

```
myCam.addEventListener(ActivityEvent.ACTIVITY, motionHandler);
function motionHandler(evt:ActivityEvent):void {
  myBitmapData[bitmapCounter].draw(myVideo);
  bitmapCounter++;
  if (bitmapCounter == 4) {
    bitmapCounter = 0;
  }
}
```

This code block tells Flash what to do when the camera detects motion based upon the parameters used in the setMotionLevel(70,50) method in the previous code block. After the event kicks off, the image is captured and tossed onto the screen under the webcam video that is playing.

5. Save and test the movie. Go ahead, wave at everybody. You will see captures of your movement (see Figure 10-24).

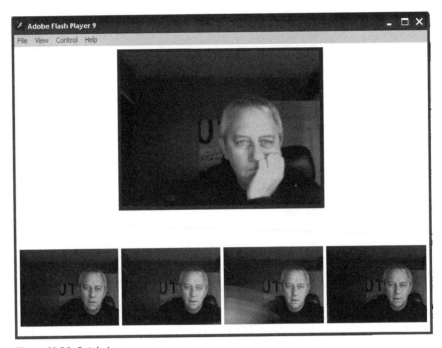

Figure 10-24. Gotcha!

What you've learned

As you have discovered, two simple lines of code make for an outrageous amount of fun. All you need to do is create a Video object on the stage or in a movieclip; then feed a web camera signal into it.

In this chapter, you learned the following:

- How to create a simple webcam feed
- How to place a feed into blocks and then stack them
- How to use a webcam feed to create a kaleidoscope effect
- How to use masking techniques to put the user into the action
- How to capture shots from a video and a webcam
- How to use a webcam to detect motion

In the next chapter, you'll explore the fascinating things you can do with cue points and captions in an FLV file. Turn the page.

Chapter 11

CUE POINTS AND CAPTIONS IN FLASH VIDEO

As you do more and more work with Flash video in your professional life, you'll be called upon to either work with cue points or add captions to a video for the hearing impaired. Until the release of Flash CS3, Flash video was generally regarded as a "nonaccessible" technology. In countries with stringent web accessibility laws governing web sites for those with physical disabilities, adding a video to one of these sites was not easy. This was a major impediment to the adoption of Flash video across government and publicly funded sites.

In fact, the process was just about as appealing as open heart surgery with no anesthetic. It was painful, involving complicated XML, ActionScript, and a huge dose of luck for the captions to be synchronized to the video's audio track. Although there were several proprietary solutions to this dilemma, for many Flash developers and designers it just didn't make sense to lay out the cash for software that might be used only a couple of times. Until an elegant solution hit the market in May 2005, that is. Captionate, which is a really affordable captioning solution, is currently at version 2.19—with a beta of version 3 slotted for sometime in 2008. The product, available at www.buraks.com/captionate, owned the market until Adobe released the current version of Flash and tucked a free captioning component into the application.

If you need to use captions, you first need to master cue points.

What we'll cover in this chapter:

- Embedding cue points into an FLV file
- Using ActionScript to navigate through a video
- Using the FLVPlaybackCaptioning component
- Understanding the relationship between XML, cue points, and Flash
- Learning a technique for using event cue points to launch web pages

Files used in this chapter:

- DisgruntledDan.mov (Chapter11\ExerciseFiles_CH11\Exercise\DisgruntledDan.mov)
- CuePointsEmbedded.fla (Chapter11\ExerciseFiles_CH11\Exercise\ CuePointsEmbedded.fla)
- CuePoints.xml (Chapter11\ExerciseFiles_CH11\Exercise\CuePointsXML\CuePoints.xml)
- ShutEyePopeye.mp4 (Chapter11\ExerciseFiles_CH11\Exercise\CuePointsXML\ ShutEyePopeye.mp4)
- captionsFLV.xml (Chapter11\ExerciseFiles_CH11\Exercise\CaptionComponent\ captionsFLV.xml)
- ThinkAboutIt.flv (Chapter11\ExerciseFiles_CH11\Exercise\CaptionComnponent\ ThinkAboutIt.flv)
- NavigationCuePoints_PrevNext.fla (Chapter11\ExerciseFiles_CH11\Exercise\ NavigationwithCuePoints/NavigationCuePoints_PrevNext.fla)
- DisgruntledDan.flv (Chapter11\ExerciseFiles_CH11\Exercise\ NavigationwithCuePoints/DisgruntledDan.flv)
- NavigationCuePoints_ComboBox.fla (Chapter11\ExerciseFiles_CH11\Exercise\ NavigationwithCuePoints/NavigationCuePoints_ComboBox.fla)
- Authors.mov (Chapter11\ExerciseFiles_CH11\Exercise\YourTurn\Authors.mov)

Cue points explained

For want of a better description, a **cue point** marks a significant point in time within a video. With cue points you can easily navigate to other sections of a video or trigger events in Flash. In fact, cue points have become so important to Flash video that many FLV file–creation applications—Flix, Squeeze, After Effects, and Soundbooth, for example—have this feature built into the application. You need to approach cue point use with a bit of caution: just because they are there is no reason to add them.

Let's assume that you have a 10-second video clip. Because of its short duration, there is no compelling reason to add cue points to this FLV file. In fact, it is a general best practice to not add them to videos that are less than a few seconds in length. Which begs the obvious question: "Okay guys, where do I use cue points?" Glad you asked! You use them in the following situations:

- **Content with defined breaks**: Videos that have been edited into scenes or discrete segments (such as the Disgruntled Dan video you'll be working with in a moment) are ideal because they readily allow the user to navigate through the video without breaking the continuity of the video.

- **A long video**: If the video is longer than 5 minutes, consider letting the user jump through the video at uniform intervals—such as every 30 seconds, 1 minute, or whatever you decide is appropriate. If the video is segmented into scenes like a DVD movie, skip the times and add cue points at the start of each scene.

- **Captions**: If your video needs to be synchronized with other Flash content, captions that appear on or under the video, the only solution available to you is to use cue points.

Cue points are one of the most elemental forms of life in the Flash video food chain. They contain only four pieces of information (a name, a time, a parameters object, and a reference to the Video object or FLVPLayback component) looking for the event to reference a single point in time within a video clip. This is why cue point names should be unique. We won't get into a long and involved discussion on this point other than to say you are only setting yourself up for aggravation if a video contains two cue points named "First."

Still, cue points are really neat because you can associate data with them. Captions are good examples: the text that appears is actually data being fed into a dynamic text box at a specific point in time.

There are actually two types of cue points: external and embedded. **External cue points** live outside of the video. A common example is using an XML document to feed the cue point data into Flash (you'll be doing this later). Another example is using an array in ActionScript to hold the data. The benefit is that the data isn't hard-wired into the FLV file. So if your timing is off, you can fix it very quickly without having to re-encode the video. Finally, you can even use the ActionScript addASCuePoint method to associate cue points with an FLV file. **Embedded cue points** are quite a bit different. These cue points are hardwired into the FLV file when the FLV file is created and can't be subsequently changed or removed.

Regardless of how they are added, you next need to understand there are in fact two "flavors" of cue points: navigation and event. A **navigation cue point** allows the user to move around inside an FLV file. If a series of them are embedded into the FLV file, all users need to do is click the Forward or Back button in the skin and they automatically move to the next or previous cue point. This solution is somewhat awkward because if a cue point hasn't loaded during the Progressive Download method it is unavailable. (It isn't an issue if the content is being streamed through a Flash Media Server.)

An **event cue point** is the exact opposite. These cue points are revealed to ActionScript only through code you write. Let's assume that you want a caption to fade out before the next one appears. You would use an event cue point to let ActionScript know when to start fading the caption.

So much for theory. Let's play with cue points and see what these puppies can do.

Using the Flash CS3 Video Encoder to create cue points

There are a number of applications you can use to add cue points to your video. One of the more common tools is the Video Encoder that ships with Flash. Here's how you can use it to create cue points:

1. Launch the Video Encoder and add the `DisgruntledDan.mov` file from the Chapter 11 exercise folder to the queue. We're using this rather hilarious video created by Dan Purdy, a former student at Humber College in Toronto because Dan broke this video into scenes. Open the video in the QuickTime player and scrub through it to see titles introducing each section of the video (as shown in Figure 11-1).

Figure 11-1. Titles or subtitles in a video are great candidates for cue points.

2. In this exercise, you'll toss in cue points and not worry about data rate. Click the Settings button and, when the Flash Video Encoding Settings dialog box opens, click the Cue Points tab to open the Cue Points panel shown in Figure 11-2. Scrub to the starting out title in the video.

You will notice that, as you scrub the video, the time code is displayed. This time code is critical because it is a major piece of information needed by a cue point. The two boxes in the bottom half of the panel are where the cue points are added, and the box on the right is where you add the Name and Value pairs that can be used by ActionScript. Let's add a cue point at this point in the video.

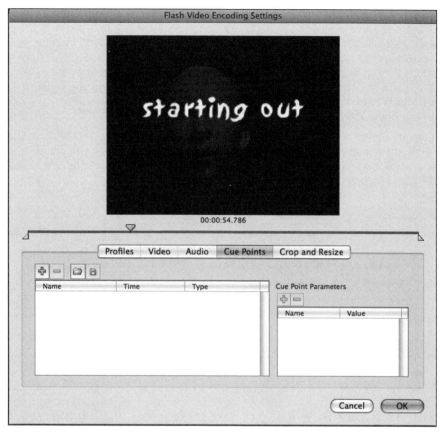

Figure 11-2. Cue points are added in this panel.

3. Click the Add a Cue Point button (it looks like a plus sign), and the first line in the input area lights up. Name the cue point Starting Out. Click once on Event to open the Type drop-down menu. Select Navigation. Congratulations. You have just added a cue point to the FLV file you are about to create (see Figure 11-3).

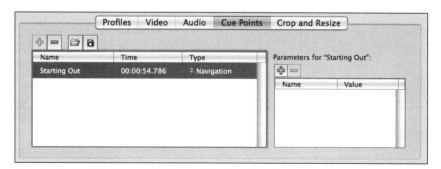

Figure 11-3. A navigation cue point named Starting Out will be added to the FLV file.

4. You are now about to discover the disadvantage of hard wiring or embedding a cue point into a video. Let's assume that the timing is wrong. You want the title to appear and the cue point to be added at 00:00:56.107 instead of its current time. Click once on the time in the input area. No matter how hard you try, you simply can't change the cue point's time. You can change the name and type, but not the time. You have to start over and delete the cue point. Click the Delete Selected Cue Point button (it looks like a minus sign) and restart the process. Don't bother with this right now, but keep in mind that it gets even worse after you encode the FLV file. Any mistakes mean that you have to re-encode the video.

5. Scrub to the titles the new recruits, the big break, and rejection, and add navigation cue points when you see the text. You should now have four navigation cue points, as shown in Figure 11-4. Click the OK button to return to the Encoding queue. Click the Start Queue button; when the encoding finishes, quit the Video Encoder.

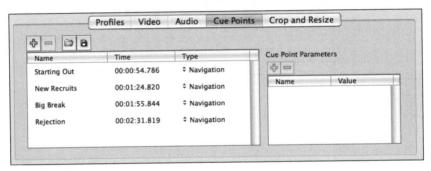

Figure 11-4. The cue points are set.

What do you do if you notice a cue point is wrong after you have encoded the FLV file? Don't panic. As long as you haven't deleted the video from the queue, you can fix the mistake. Simply open the Encoder, choose the video in the queue, and select Edit ➤ Reset Status. *You can now head back to the* Cue Points *panel and make the change.*

6. Launch Flash CS3, create a new document, and add an FLVPlayback component to the stage. Save the file to the same folder as the FLV file you just created.

7. Select the component on the stage and click the Parameters tab in the Property Inspector. Set the source parameter to the FLV file you just created.

8. Scroll up and notice that the cue points have been added to the cuePoints parameter (see Figure 11-5).

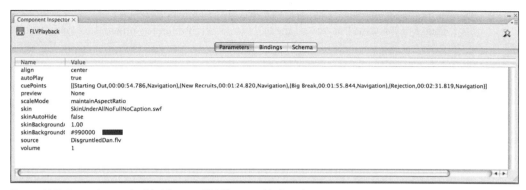

Figure 11-5. Cue points embedded into an FLV file are added to the parameters.

9. Save and test the movie. If you click the Forward and Back buttons in the controls, you can skip forward and backward in the video. What you have just discovered is that the FLVPlayback component, shown in Figure 11-6, automatically finds the cue points when the Forward and Back buttons are clicked.

Figure 11-6. Use the Forward and Back buttons in the skin to navigate between cue points.

ActionScript and cue points

In the previous exercise, you added cue points to an FLV file and then skipped through them using the Forward and Back buttons of the FLVPlayback component. In this exercise you'll let ActionScript play with the cue points. This exercise will display the cue point information you created in the previous exercise in one text box and offer a short explanation of the current scene in another text box. Let's get started:

1. Open the CuePointsEmbedded.fla file found in this chapter's exercise folder. When the file opens, save it to the same location as the FLV file you created in the previous exercise.

2. Select the first frame of the Actions layer and open the Actions panel. Scroll down to line 15 of the code and enter the name of your FLV file.

3. Click once in line 19 and enter the following code:

```
function cuePointHandler(cp:Object):void {
  var key:String;
  var cuePointInfo:String = "";
  for (key in cp) {
    cuePointInfo += key + ": " + cp[key] + "\n";
  }
}
```

You'll start with a function associated with the onCuePoint event from line 12 to get things under way. As you know, you don't really control the FLV file; you use ActionScript to access and/or control the NetStream. This explains why this event is a part of the NetStream class, and you can surmise that cue points actually move along the NetStream.

Although it is primarily used by Flash Media Server 3, the onCuePoint event can be used by Flash, provided that it is attached directly to one of the following objects:

- The object referenced by the client property of a NetStream instance. This explains lines 12 and 13 (listener.onCuePoint = cuePointHandler; ns.client = listener;) of the code.

- An instance of a NetStream subclass. NetStream is a sealed class, which means you cannot add properties or methods to a NetStream object at runtime. However, you can create a subclass of NetStream and define your event handler in the subclass or make the subclass dynamic and add the event handler function to an instance of the subclass.

The rest of the function simply uses a for..in loop to pull the cue point information (name, time, and type) out of the stream, adds it to a string, and puts each bit of information on a separate line—"/n" is a line break—when it is fed into the Cue Point Information text box.

4. Press Return/Enter and enter the following code, which adds the text to the Cue Point Information and Description text boxes:

```
infoTB.text = cuePointInfo;
switch(cp["name"]) {
  case "Starting Out":
    info2TB.text = "Feelings about being a cartoon character.";
    break;
  case "New Recruits":
    info2TB.text = "Observations on the new recruits";
    break;
  case "Big Break":
    info2TB.text = "How Dan got his big break";
    break;
  case "Rejection":
    info2TB.text = "Dan feels rejected";
    break;
```

```
        }
    }
```

The first line of the code is how the cue point's information from the previous step gets added to the Cue Point Information text area that has the instance name of infoTB.

The switch statement looks at the name property of the incoming cue point object (cp), and when the name is encountered through the case statement, the description is added to the Description text box with the instance name of info2TB.

5. Save and test the movie. The text boxes shown in Figure 11-7 are populated with the text from the code. Although this might seem to be an interesting technique with no practical application, it gives you a great opportunity to review or discover any cue points embedded in an FLV file found in a project that contains a number of videos. Another approach is to add a trace() statement for the Cue Point Information; when the information appears in the Output panel, you can copy and paste that information into a text file that can subsequently be saved as an XML document that can (as you will discover later in this chapter) be fed into the Video Encoder.

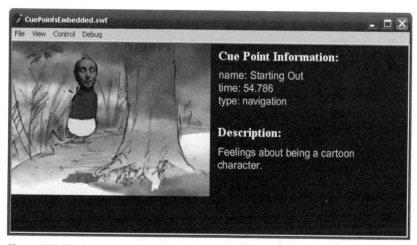

Figure 11-7. Displaying cue point information using ActionScript

Cue points and XML

If you have been carefully reading this chapter, you have deduced that we aren't huge fans of manually adding cue points. Chalk it up to laziness on our part or the fact that we have been involved in digital media for so long that we have become firm believers in this adage: "Let the software do the work." This brings us to the point of this exercise.

When Adobe released Flash CS3 it built a feature into the Flash Video Encoder that allows you to feed the cue points contained in an XML document directly into the Encoder before the FLV file is created. This is a huge time saver. Consider how long it will take to add captions to a video that is five minutes in length and to feed those captions into a text box on the Flash stage. Before you gleefully start writing XML, take a look at the document you will be using in this exercise.

1. Open the CuePoints.xml document found in the CuePointsXML folder of this chapter's exercise folder.

```
<?xml version="1.0" encoding="iso-8859-1"?>
<FLVCoreCuePoints>

  <CuePoint>
    <Time>101000</Time>
    <Type>event</Type>
    <Name>fl.video.caption.2.0.0</Name>
    <Parameters>
      <Parameter>
        <Name>text</Name>
        <Value><![CDATA[<font face="Arial, Helvetica, _sans" size="12">➡
        <i>Popeye:</i> Wha ... Wha... What happened?</font>]]></Value>
      </Parameter>
      <Parameter>
        <Name>endTime</Name>
        <Value>103.85</Value>
      </Parameter>
    </Parameters>
  </CuePoint>

<FLVCoreCuePoints>
```

This is the syntax that must be used. Deviate from it at your own peril. The first line declares the DOC-TYPE, which is optional, but the second line runs the show. It tells Flash that anything between the FLVCoreCuePoints tags counts as a cue point.

Each cue point you will add must be enclosed between <CuePoint> and </CuePoint> tags. The <Time> tag is the start of the cue point, and this number must be expressed in milliseconds. The next tag, <Type>, tells Flash whether the cue point is to be an event or a navigation cue point; and the tag following it, <Name>, is the name of the cue point.

The rules regarding naming are rigid. The <Name> tag must be fl.video.caption.2.0 followed by a series of sequential numbers to guarantee uniqueness. In the sample XML, it starts at fl.video.caption.2.0.0, then fl.video.caption.2.0.1, and so on.

The parameters contain the styling data for the text that will appear in the caption and an end time for the caption. Notice that we used the <i> tag to identify who is speaking by setting the person's name in italics. HTML tags can be used only if they're supported by Flash; a list of them can be found in the documentation by searching on the phrase "supported HTML tags" (make sure that you have the Help panel filtered for "All Books"). The endTime property, which must be expressed in seconds, will be the time when the caption disappears from the screen. Use an integer if you like, but you can go as far as three decimal places to provide millisecond accuracy. Yes, it's odd that time is noted in milliseconds, and endTime is noted in seconds, but "them's the breaks."

Finally, you might optionally contend with using color in captions, and there are a couple of rules involving this as well. If you scroll down to caption 2.0.7, you will see that the text in the caption uses #FF0000, which is a bright red. A couple of lines later, the backgroundColor parameter changes the background color of the caption to 0x01016D, which is a dark blue.

The key is how the colors are identified. Colors are specified by hexadecimal values, but the *indication* that the color is in hex—# or 0x—depends on where a specific color is being stated. The first change to the red uses the pound sign, #, as traditionally used in HTML. Why? Because it appears within HTML-formatted content. The second change—to the dark blue—uses the format for specifying hexadecimal notation in ActionScript: 0x. If you do change the background color of a caption, that color will stick, so all subsequent captions will use this background color. If you need only a single change, as in the example, change the backgroundColor parameter back in the next cue point. In our case, we changed it to black again (0x000000), as seen in caption 2.0.8.

One final point: do your sanity a favor and separate each caption with an empty line or two in the XML. This makes them easier to read and locate. The extra space, called **whitespace**, will be ignored by Flash.

2. Close the XML document and open the Flash Video Encoder. Add ShutEyePopeye.mp4 in the CuePointsXML folder to the Encoding queue.

3. Click the Settings button to open the Flash Video Encoding Settings window. We'll use the default setting for this exercise. Name the file ShutEyePopeye and click the Cue Points tab.

4. When the Cue Points panel opens, you see a Browse button that looks like a file folder. This button is what allows you to embed an XML document into an FLV file. Click the Browse button to open the Load Cue Points File dialog box shown in Figure 11-8. Navigate to the CuePoints.xml document, click Open, and watch the magic happen.

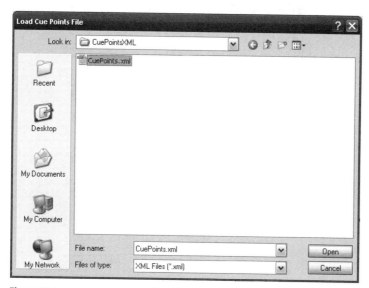

Figure 11-8. Loading cue points found in an XML document

5. When you click Open, Flash gets the XML file and loads it into the Cue Points area of the dialog box. Click the first cue point in the list (see Figure 11-9), and the Name and Value pair for the cue point will show up in the Parameters area. All this information is contained between the <CuePoint> and </CuePoint> tags in the document. Not only that; notice that the milliseconds are translated to *hours:minutes:seconds.millseconds* in the Time area of the cue point. Click OK to return to the queue, and click OK in the queue to encode the video. When you finish, quit the Encoder.

311

Be very careful when creating the XML document. If you have a start time that is later than the end time in another cue point, or if you have added an improperly named tag, the Encoder will kick out an error telling you that the file format is not correct. Unlike ActionScript, it won't tell you what the problem is or where the error is located.

If you're having a hard time figuring out the milliseconds, use the FLVPLayback component's preview parameter or the Encoder. The time code shown under the preview is in milliseconds, and the value you would use for the <Time> parameter would be the number shown without the decimal place. For example, if the time shown in the preview is 5678, that is the value to use.

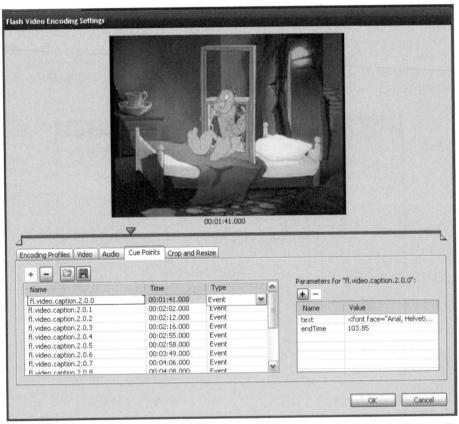

Figure 11-9. How do you add a bunch of cue points easily? Import an XML document into the FLV file.

6. Launch Flash CS3 and create a new ActionScript 3.0 document. When the document opens, drag a copy of the FLVPLayback component to the stage, add a skin, and set the source to the FLV file you just created.

7. Drag a copy of the FLVPlaybackCaptioning component to the pasteboard. This component only needs to be on the stage for it to work its magic.

8. Save and test the movie. The captions appear as the cartoon plays (see Figure 11-10).

As you have seen, the captioning component grabs the cue point information and automatically displays it. Now that you have had a chance to see what this new addition to Flash CS3 can do, let's really dig into it using the FLVPlaybackCaptioning component.

Figure 11-10. The information from the XML document is put to work.

Using the FLVPlaybackCaptioning component

Until the release of the CS3 Studio, Flash video's adoption was hobbled by its sheer inaccessibility to the hearing impaired. The release of the CS3 Studio removed that shackle; yet to this day there really isn't a lot of chatter about captioning in video.

Talk to Flash developers and designers about adding video to their clients' sites and they will claim their clients are resisting it because it is not accessible. Hopefully, this short exercise will put that misconception to rest.

Before you get under way, it is important to realize that this is not exactly a "click/drag" workflow. First you need to create a specific form of XML document. Still, the beauty of XML is the fact that it is external to the Flash SWF file. If your timing is out, simply change the XML. If you find a typo or need to add or remove something, simply change the XML.

Timed text XML for captions

The FLVPlaybackCaptioning component requires you to use a **Timed Text (TT) XML** document. If you open the captionsFLV.xml document, you will see, as shown in the following code, the Timed Text XML code used in this exercise:

```
<?xml version="1.0" encoding="UTF-8"?>
<tt xml:lang="en" xmlns=http://www.w3.org/2006/04/ttaf1➡
xmlns:tts="http://www.w3.org/2006/04/ttaf1#styling">
  <head>
    <styling>
      <style id="1" tts:textAlign="right"/>
      <style id="2" tts:color="transparent"/>
      <style id="3" style="2" tts:backgroundColor="white"/>
      <style id="4" style="2 3" tts:fontSize="20"/>
    </styling>
  </head>
  <body>
    <div xml:lang="en">
      <p begin="00:00:28.00" dur="00:00:02.00">➡
Guy: Hey you forgot this.</p>
      <p begin="00:00:30.50"dur="00:00:01.50">Girl: Wow. </p>
      <p begin="00:00:33.00"dur="00:00:01.5">➡
Girl: Last night was amazing. </p>
      <p begin="00:00:36.00" dur="00:00:01.00" >Guy: Was it?"</p>
      <p begin="00:00:39.00" dur="00:00:01.00">Guy: Really?</p>
      <p begin="00:00:44.50" dur="00:00:04.00">Guy: Mmmmmmmm......</p>
      <p begin="00:00:53.00" dur="00:00:02.50"> ➡
Guy: Just think about it.</p>
      <p begin="00:00:57.00" dur="00:00:03.00"> ➡
Girl: Think about what?</p>
    </div>
  </body>
</tt>
```

If you have written a few XML documents in the past, you see that this format is quite a bit different from what you might be used to—and even from the one used in the previous exercise. This is because the specification for the XML used with the component is the Timed Text captioning specification set by the World Wide Web Consortium. If you use the FLVPlaybackCaptioning component, you must follow this standard.

If you really want to dig into it, the full Timed Text specification is available at www.w3.org/AudioVideo/TT/.

You can set the styling for each caption, and each caption needs a start and an end point. So each caption you write must have a begin attribute, which determines when the caption appears. If you omit the dur or end attribute, the caption will remain onscreen until the next caption appears or until the video ends. In many respects, the dur attribute really represents how long the caption is visible onscreen.

Where did we get those numbers? Quite a few places. You can note the time code on the QuickTime player. You can get the numbers through the FLV Encoder or the preview parameter of the FLVPlayback component. You might even use the software used to create the video in the first place or even Soundbooth CS3.

After you write the XML document, follow these steps to apply the captions to a video:

1. Open a new Flash document and save it to the CaptionComponent folder in the Chapter 11 exercise folder.

2. Drag a copy of the FLVPlayback component to the stage and set its source to ThinkAboutIt.flv in the Parameters panel.

3. Click once in the skin parameter and select SkinUnderPlayCaption.swf. This skin simply contains a Play and a Caption button.

4. Select the layer and name it Video. Add another layer and name it Captions. Drag a copy of the FLVPlaybackCaptioning component to the stage. The component can be anywhere on the stage or the pasteboard, and it will still work.

5. Select the FLVPlaybackCaptioning component on the stage and click the Parameters tab in the Property Inspector. As shown in Figure 11-11, the parameters are as follows:

   - autoLayout: A value of true lets the FLVPlayback component determine the size of the captioning area.

   - captionTargetName: This parameter identifies the movieclip or text field instance used to display the caption on the screen. The default value—auto—means the component will make that decision.

   - flvPlaybackName: This is the instance name of the component, which is handy if you're creating instances of the component at runtime or if there are multiple instances of the component on the stage. If there is only one, as in this example, leave it at auto.

   - showCaptions: If set to false, the captions will not appear until the Caption button on the skin is clicked.

   - simpleFormatting: If your XML document contains no formatting instructions, set this to true. Otherwise, go with the default value, which is false.

   - source: This will be the location of the Timed Text XML document used to supply the captions.

6. Click the source parameter and enter captionsFLV.xml as the value for the parameter (see Figure 11-11). Set the showCaptions value to true. If the XML document is in a location other than the same folder as the video and the SWF file, enter the full path to the document.

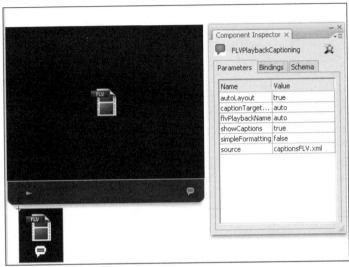

Figure 11-11. The FLVPlaybackCaptioning component on the stage and the component's parameters

7. Save and test the video. The captions will appear, as shown in Figure 11-12. Click the Caption button to turn them off and on.

Figure 11-12. The caption appears over the video.

There obviously is an issue here. What if you are using one of the over skins? In this case, the skin will hide the caption. Another issue: you might not want the caption to appear over the video; you might want to have it appear elsewhere on the screen. Here's how to deal with those two scenarios:

1. Select the Text tool and create a dynamic text box on the stage. Give the text box the instance name of captionTB.

2. Select the captioning component on the stage and open its parameters. Make the following two changes:

   ● captionTargetName: captionTB

   ● autoLayout: false (if you don't make this change, the words will appear in the video)

3. Save and test the movie. The captions will appear where you placed the text box (see Figure 11-13).

Figure 11-13. The caption appears where you place the text box.

> Now that you have seen two ways of embedding cue points contained into an XML document, you might be wondering which technique is the better way to go. The real answer is this: whichever one you choose. If pressed, we find the Timed Text format to be a lot easier and more intuitive, especially when it comes to using the start and end times for the cue points.

Navigating through cue points with ActionScript

As you have gathered, the FLVPlayback component offers you a code-free solution to navigating through an FLV file that is playing. Click the Forward or Back button on the skin, and you are shot over to the next or the previous cue point. This is all well and good, but the extra "weight" of the component is problematic. Surely there must be a way of navigating through an FLV file in a space that is smaller than 52KB? In fact, there is: use ActionScript.

The following two examples show you two methods of accomplishing this task. The first uses two simple buttons on the stage to allow for navigation between the cue points. The second gets a bit heavier, but shows you how you can use a ComboBox component to navigate within an FLV file. Let's get started:

1. Open the NavigationCuePoints_PrevNext.fla file found the Chapter 11 exercise folder. We have placed two buttons on the stage.

2. Select the first frame in the Actions layer and press F9 (Option+F9) to open the Actions panel.

3. Click once in the panel and enter the following familiar code, which sets up the video:

```
var video:Video = new Video();
addChild(video);

var nc:NetConnection = new NetConnection();
nc.connect(null);

var ns:NetStream = new NetStream(nc);
video.attachNetStream(ns);
```

4. Next, it's time to retrieve and store all the embedded cue points. Press Return/Enter twice and type the following code:

```
var videoDuration:Number;
var videoCuePoints:Array = new Array();
var listener:Object = new Object();
listener.onMetaData = metadataHandler;
function metadataHandler(md:Object):void {
  videoDuration = md.duration;
  var i:int;
  for (i = 0; i < md.cuePoints.length; i++) {
    var cuePointData:Object = md.cuePoints[i];
    videoCuePoints.push({name:cuePointData.name, ➥
 time:cuePointData.time});
  }
}
ns.client = listener;

ns.play("DisgruntledDan.flv");
```

We start by creating a series of variables for the data. The important one is the second one: videoCuePoints. The cue points in the video will be placed into an Array.

The function is critical. It starts by finding the duration value in the metadata and adds it to the videoDuration variable declared earlier. The next step is to go back into the metadata and determine how many cue points are in the FLV file: for (i = 0; i < md.cuePoints.length; i++). The metadata object (md) contains a cuePoints array of its own, so the for loop steps through that. Having done that, we loop through the cue points in the FLV file and place the name and time data associated with the cue point into the videoCuePoints array by using the push() method of the Array class. Finally, we tell the NetStream instance what video to play.

5. Having done all the prep work, let's turn our attention to making the buttons functional. Press Return/Enter twice and start to write the code for the Previous button:

```
previousBtn.addEventListener(MouseEvent.CLICK, goBack);
function goBack(evt:MouseEvent):void {
    var i:int;
    for(i=videoCuePoints.length - 1; i >= 0; i--) {
      if (videoCuePoints[i].time < ns.time - 3) {
      ns.seek(videoCuePoints[i].time);
      i = 0;
    } else if (i == 0) {
      ns.seek(0);
    }
  }
}
```

We start by creating the listener for the Previous button. If a mouse click is detected, the goBack() function is executed.

Although it looks complicated, the goBack() function is actually quite simple. We start with a for loop that tells Flash to run through the videoCuePoints array populated by the onMetaData handler.

The conditional statements basically tell Flash to go back to the previous cue point based upon the current time minus three seconds (ns.time - 3), or if all the cue points have been passed, to rewind the video—ns.seek(0);.

6. The Next button is essentially the opposite of the Previous button. Instead of checking to see whether there are cue points behind the current time, you check to see whether there are any ahead of the current time. Press Return/Enter twice and add the following:

```
nextBtn.addEventListener(MouseEvent.CLICK, goForward);
function goForward(evt:MouseEvent):void {
    var i:int;
    for(i=0; i<videoCuePoints.length; i++) {
      If (videoCuePoints[i].time > ns.time) {
      ns.seek(videoCuePoints[i].time);
      i = videoCuePoints.length;
    } else if (i == videoCuePoints.length - 1) {
      ns.seek(videoDuration);
    }
  }
}
```

The key is that first if statement. It checks to see whether there are any cue points beyond the current time in the FLV file. If there aren't, go to the end of the video—ns.seek(videoDuration)—and stay put.

7. Check your code for any errors. If there aren't any, save and test the movie. When you click a button, you move to the previous or next cue point in the FLV file, as shown in Figure 11-14.

```
nextBtn.addEventListener(MouseEvent.CLICK,goForward);
function goForward(evt:MouseEvent) :void {
    // Loop through cue points and find the first cue point
    // after the current position
    var i:int;
    for(i=0; i<videoCuePoints.length; i++)
    {
        if(videoCuePoints[i].time > ns.time)
        {
            ns.seek(videoCuePoints[i].time);
            i = videoCuePoints.length;
        }
        else if(i == videoCuePoints.length - 1)
        {
            // Go to the end
            ns.seek(videoDuration);
        }
    }
}
```

Figure 11-14. Using buttons to navigate between cue points

Using the ComboBox for cue point navigation

Now that you know how to use buttons and/or movieclips to skip through the cue points, here's how to use a ComboBox component to perform the same action:

1. Open the NavigationCuePoints_ComboBox.fla file in the Chapter 11 exercise folder. When it opens, you will see we have given you a blank stage and an Actions layer. If you open the library, you will also see we have added a ComboBox component.

2. Select the first frame in the Actions layer and open the Actions panel.

3. Click once in the first line of the Script pane and enter the following:

```
import fl.controls.ComboBox;
import fl.data.DataProvider;

var video:Video = new Video();
addChild(video);

var nc:NetConnection = new NetConnection();
nc.connect(null);

var ns:NetStream = new NetStream(nc);
video.attachNetStream(ns);
```

```
var moviesCB:ComboBox = new ComboBox();
moviesCB.dropdownWidth = 200;
moviesCB.width = 200;
moviesCB.move(380, 100);
addChild(moviesCB);
```

This code is nothing new. You import the ComboBox and DataProvider classes to be used for wiring up the ComboBox instance and then create and prepare the video. Finally, you create the ComboBox.

4. This time, the onMetaData handler will populate the ComboBox. Press Return/Enter twice and enter the following code:

```
var listener:Object = new Object();
listener.onMetaData = metadataHandler;
function metadataHandler(md:Object):void {
  var videoCuePoints:Array = new Array({label: ➥
"Select a Cue Point", data:""});
  var i:int;
  for (i = 0; i < md.cuePoints.length; i++) {
    var cuePointData:Object = md.cuePoints[i];
    videoCuePoints.push({label: ➥
cuePointData.name , data:cuePointData.time});
  }
  moviesCB.dataProvider = new DataProvider(videoCuePoints);
}
ns.client = listener;

ns.play("DisgruntledDan.flv");
```

As you can see, the metadata object (md) holds the cue points, as in the other example. Inside the for loop, the line videoCuePoints.push({label:cuePointData.name, data:cuePointData.time}); adds the cue point name and time data to a videoCuePoints array declared a few lines prior. The final line associates that array with the ComboBox by way of the dataProvider property. When the user clicks a cue point name in the drop-down menu, the video skips to the time where that cue point appears—but only if you listen for a CHANGE event.

5. Press Return/Enter twice and enter the following code that handles the CHANGE event:

```
moviesCB.addEventListener(Event.CHANGE, changeHandler);
function changeHandler(evt:Event):void {
  if(ComboBox(evt.target).selectedItem.data != ""){
    ns.seek(ComboBox(evt.target).selectedItem.data);
  }
};
```

6. Check for errors; if everything is fine, save and test the movie. When you select an item from the ComboBox, the video starts playing from that cue point (see Figure 11-15).

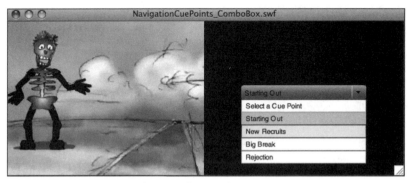

Figure 11-15. Populating a ComboBox with cue points

Your turn: Using event cue points to launch web pages

Most of this chapter dealt with using cue points to navigate through an FLV file or to add a caption to a video. In this exercise, based upon a tutorial done by our tech editor, David Stiller, you'll use event cue points to launch a web page. This isn't as difficult as it might first appear to be. All you need to do is add the URLs to the FLV file and then tell Flash to launch the browser, depending on the cue point currently in play. Here's how:

1. Open the Flash Video Encoder and add the Authors.mov file from the exercise folder to the queue. Click the Cue Points tab.

The video is nothing more than screen shots of the respective web pages. The plan is to allow the user to click the video when an author's page appears. That click will launch the author's home page.

2. Scrub across the video in the Cue Points area and scrub to the point where the first author's name, Tom, appears. Use these settings in the Input area of the panel:
   - Name: Tom
   - Type: Event

3. Click the + button in the Parameters input area and add these parameters to the cue point:
   - Name: url
   - Value: http://www.tomontheweb.ca

4. Add the next two cue points and their Name/Value pairs (see Figure 11-16):
   - Cue Points:
     - Name: Adam
     - Type: Event

- Parameters:
  - Name: url
  - Value: http://www.robinhoodtech.com
- Cue Points:
  - Name: David
  - Type: Event
- Parameters:
  - Name: url
  - Value: http://www.quip.net

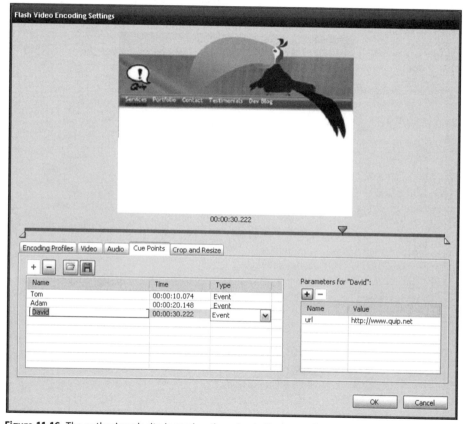

Figure 11-16. The author's web site is used as the value in the cue point's parameters.

5. When you finish, click OK to return to the Encoding queue. Click the Start Queue button to encode the video. When the encoding process finishes, quit the Encoder.

Now that you have an FLV file with the cue points embedded that contain the home pages of the various authors into it, let's put that Name/Value pair to work. Here's how:

1. Launch Flash CS3 and create a new ActionScript 3.0 document.

2. When the new document opens, drag a copy of the FLVPlayback component to the stage. Select the component on the stage and give it the instance name of myVideo in the Property Inspector.

3. Click once on the component. With the component selected, set its source parameter to the FLV file you just created and set the skin parameter to None.

4. Select Modify ➤ Document. When the Document Properties dialog box opens, select Match:Contents and click OK. The stage will shrink to fit the component.

5. Rename Layer 1 to Video. Add a new layer and name it Actions.

With the housekeeping out of the way, let's "wire up" the component.

6. Select the first frame of the Actions layer and open the Actions panel. Click once in the Script pane and enter the following code:

```
import fl.video.MetadataEvent;

var authorSite:String = "";

myVideo.buttonMode = true;

myVideo.addEventListener(Event.COMPLETE, playIt);
function playIt(evt:Event):void {
  myVideo.play();
}

myVideo.addEventListener( MouseEvent.MOUSE_UP, goToSite);
function goToSite(evt:MouseEvent):void {
  if (authorSite != "") {
    navigateToURL(new URLRequest(authorSite), "_blank");
  }
}

myVideo.addEventListener( MetadataEvent.CUE_POINT, getTheSiteInfo);
function getTheSiteInfo(evt:MetadataEvent):void {
  authorSite = evt.info.parameters.url;
}
```

We start by importing the MetadataEvent class, which is part of the video package that manages the component's video-related events. You need to import this class because the Flash Player dispatches a MetadataEvent object when the user requests the FLV file's metadata information packet (NetStream.onMetaData) and when cue points (NetStream.onCuePoint) are encountered in the FLV file. In this case, the Flash Player will encounter cue points. If you don't import this class, Flash won't have a clue what to do when it hits that last function and will kick out a rather nasty error message in the Output panel: 1046: Type was not found or was not a compile-time constant: MetaDataEvent.

The third line of the code turns the usual arrow cursor into a pointer cursor when the mouse hovers over the component. Because FLVPlayback inherits from the MovieClip class, which in turn inherits from Sprite, the component might be thought of as a "movieclip on steroids." So you can use the buttonMode property to make the component interactive.

The magic is contained in those last two functions. The first one uses the navigateToURL() function, which is what opens the author's site in a browser window separate from that containing the SWF file. The second function is how the URL information is pulled out of the cue point's Value parameter. An if statement in the first function only does its thing if the authorSite variable has been populated by the second function.

7. Check your code and then save and test the movie. When you see an author name, click the video. You'll be taken to that author's home page (see Figure 11-17).

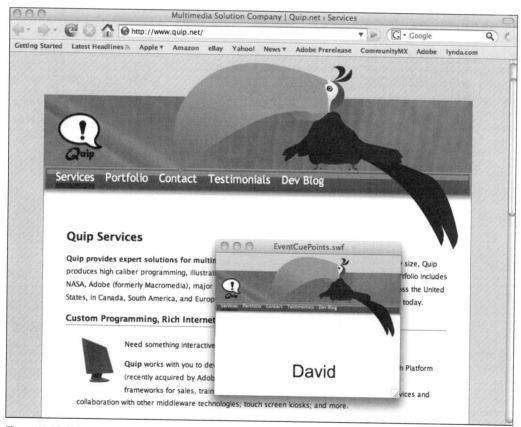

Figure 11-17. Using an event cue point to launch a web page

What you've learned

In this chapter, you undertook a cursory exploration of the power of cue points in video. We hope you have discovered that unleashing this power doesn't require a degree in rocket science.

In this chapter you did the following:

- Learned how to embed cue points in an FLV file using the Flash Video Encoder
- Understood the difference between an event cue point and a navigation cue point
- Discovered how to use components and ActionScript to navigate through an FLV file
- Saw how to use Timed Text XML with the FLVPlaybackCaptioning component
- Embedded an XML document into an FLV file prior to encoding
- Used an event cue point to launch a web page

The word *cursory* is quite appropriate here because there is a lot more than we could show in a single chapter about the use of cue points. Want to add them at runtime? No problem. You can use the addASCuePoint method with the FLVPlayback component to bring this to fruition. Want to navigate through the main timeline or one in a nested movieclip? Play with the last exercise in the chapter to accomplish that task. In many respects, your only limit is your imagination or creativity.

Speaking of creativity, wouldn't it be neat if you could play an FLV file in a cell phone or use the Flash Player to play DVD-quality video through a web browser? Why not? Turn the page to find out.

Chapter 12

GOING SMALL AND GOING BIG WITH FLASH VIDEO

When it comes to Flash video, the past few years have been pretty intense. It seems that Flash video is now a web standard and it is everywhere. From the behemoth known as YouTube to Banner ads, Flash video has become ubiquitous. Still, there were a couple of areas where delivery of video through the Flash Player was, to put it mildly, weak.

There were some very pointed and relevant complaints about the FLV format, especially when compared to DV, its high-resolution cousin. At the same time, devices were becoming viable media players, and the cell phone was becoming yet another medium for the playback of web-delivered video in places such as Japan and Europe. The problem with cell phones was that the video needed to be played back in the device's player, not in the Flash Player. So the video destined for the cell phone had to be saved in a different format (3GP instead of FLV). The Flash Lite Player was simply incapable of managing the FLV format.

In mid-2007, this all changed with the release of the Flash Player 9 beta and Flash Lite 3.0 on Adobe Labs. The Flash Player 9 release allowed us to play video encoded using the H.264 codec (MP4 and MOV files) through the Flash Player. Flash Lite 3.0 allowed us to stream an FLV file into the Flash Lite 3.0 Player using either a Progressive Download or a Flash Media Server (FMS). Both of these products are now on the market and in use.

In many respects, this is an appropriate ending point for the book. Through these two upgrades, Flash video has also grown up, and what the future holds for us is both unknown and exciting.

What we'll cover in this chapter:

- Using Device Central
- Creating a video app for a cell phone using Flash Lite 3.0
- Converting a Flash video to a QuickTime movie
- Playing H.264 and MPEG-4 movies
- Creating full-screen video using the latest iteration of the Flash Player

Files used in this chapter:

- door.flv (Chapter12\ExerciseFiles_CH12\Exercise\Mobile\video\door.flv)
- Particles31.swf (Chapter12\ExerciseFiles_CH12\Exercise\Particles\Particles31.swf)
- Particles31.fla (Chapter12\ExerciseFiles_CH12\Exercise\Particles\Particles31.fla)
- Mobile_03.fla (Chapter12\ExerciseFiles_Ch12\Exercise\Mobile\Mobile_03.fla)
- Particles31.flv (Chapter12\ExerciseFiles_CH12\Exercise\Mobile\video\ Particles31.flv)
- Trip.mp4 (Chapter12\ExerciseFiles_CH12\Exercise\H264\Trip.mp4)
- BigItUp.fla (Chapter12\ExerciseFiles_CH12\Exercise\H264\BigItUp.fla)
- backcountry_bombshells_4min_HD_H264.mp4 (Chapter12\ExerciseFiles_CH12\Exercise\ H264\backcountry_bombshells_4min_HD_H264.mp4)

Going small—playing video on a cell phone

The release of Flash Lite 3.0 suddenly opened up the world of portable video to Flash designers and developers. By "portable," we mean that video can now be streamed into your cell phone and played on demand. Before we get started, though, there are a few things you need to know about this technology that (for all intents and purposes) is still in its infancy:

- FLV files can be streamed into the Flash Lite 3.0 Player. That is the good news. The bad news is that this will take time. Not all handset suppliers will be adding the Flash Lite 3.0 capability to their products. Use Device Central to keep current with which handsets are Flash Lite 3.0– enabled.
- If the FLV file is being streamed from a Flash Media Server, only the Real Time Messaging Protocol (RTMP) used by the Flash Media Server 3 is supported. If you attempt to connect to a Flash Media Server using an HTTP tunneling protocol (RTMPT) or SSL (RTMPS) connection, your connection will default to an RTMP connection.
- Two-way communication between clients, such as a video chat application, is not supported. Only one-way communication—server to device—is supported in Flash Lite 3.0.
- If your device contains a video-recording capability, you can't use the Camera class to record and stream a live video.

- Flash Lite 3.0 does not support the use of Alpha channel video.

- You can't use the FLVPlayback component in Flash CS3, or the FLVPlayback component or video controls that appear in the Components panel, when authoring your video application. The memory requirement for these components is too steep at this time.

Before we get started, this section of the chapter introduces you to using Flash Lite 3.0 to play a video on a cell phone. We will not be examining device video playback or authoring for BREW devices. If you need more information regarding these two subjects, we suggest you spend some time reading the Help menu: Developing Flash Lite 2.x and 3.0 Applications/Working with Video and Images or Developing Flash Lite 2.x and 3.0 Applications/Developing Flash Lite Applications for BREW. We will also not be covering uploading to a server or into the device.

In this first example, you'll jump right into the deep end of the pool and create a small application that plays a video on a cell phone. The next part will use the device's soft keys to play and pause the video, and the final exercise will expand on what you have learned and show you how to play multiple videos using the phone's keypad. Let's get busy:

1. Open Flash CS3 and in the Start Page, select Flash File (Mobile). This will launch Device Central.

2. When Device Central opens (see Figure 12-1), select the Flash Lite category in the Available Devices listing on the left side of the window.

3. Select the Flash Lite 3.0 16 320x240 device. When you do this, the device shown in Figure 12-1 will appear in the New Document area. Select Flash Lite 3.0 from the Player Version drop-down menu.

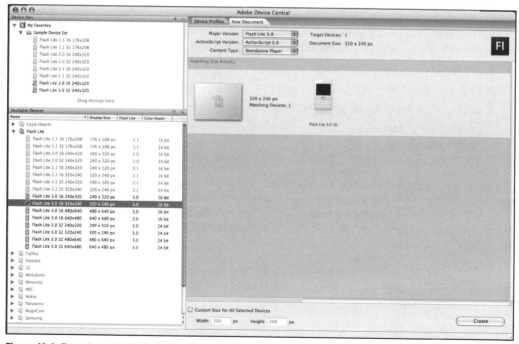

Figure 12-1. Targeting a device in Device Central

4. Select Standalone Player from the Content Type drop-down menu. The device you see is a generic device (because the Flash Lite Player is so new, few devices support it at the time this book was being written). As these devices come into the marketplace, they will appear in subsequent updates of Device Central.

5. Click the Create button. When you do this, Device Central will close and a new Flash document will open. The stage will be resized to fit the screen of the device and the Property Inspector, shown in Figure 12-2, will tell you that you are working with Flash Lite 3.0. Save this file to the Mobile folder in the Chapter 12 exercise folder.

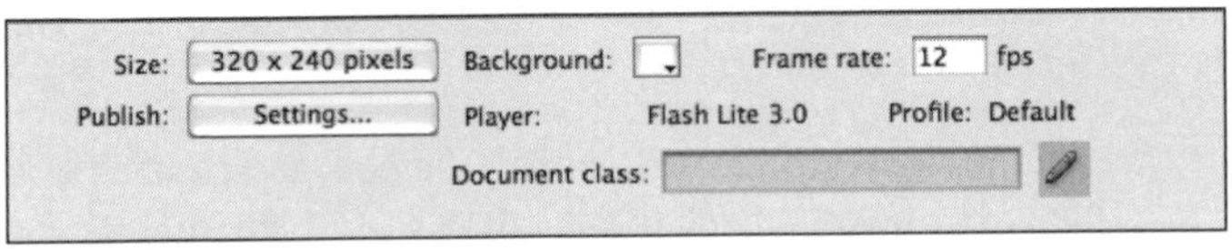

Size:	320 x 240 pixels	Background: ☐	Frame rate: 12 fps
Publish:	Settings...	Player: Flash Lite 3.0	Profile: Default
		Document class:	✏

Figure 12-2. The Property Inspector will change to let you know you are using Flash Lite 3.0.

If you have used previous versions of Flash (Flash MX 2004 or Flash 8), the balance of this exercise will be like a homecoming. The Flash Lite 3.0 Player doesn't use ActionScript 3.0. In fact, this version of the Player marks the movement of the Flash Lite ActionScript to the ActionScript 2.0 standard. This is what makes the playback of FLV files in the Player possible. The ActionScript 2.0 language contains the NetStream and NetConnection classes we have used throughout this book.

Follow these steps to stream a video into a cell phone:

1. Open the Flash library and create a new Video object.

2. Drag the Video object from the library to the stage and give it the instance name of myVideo. In the Property Inspector, set the Video object's width and height to 240 by 180.

3. Add a new layer named Actions.

4. Select the first frame in the Actions layer and open the Actions panel.

5. Click once in the Script pane and enter the following code:

```
_focusRect = false;
fscommand2("SetQuality","high");
fscommand2("Fullscreen","true");
```

The first line turns off the bounding box that appears around a selected object. The next two lines are specific to devices. The second line tells Flash how to treat the content on the screen. The default value—if this line weren't here—is medium. The last line tells Flash to use the entire screen area of the device for the application. Flash uses the two fscommand2() functions to communicate with the device's operating system.

6. Press Return/Enter twice and enter the following code:

```
var nc:NetConnection = new NetConnection();
nc.connect(null);

var ns:NetStream = new NetStream(nc);
myVideo.attachVideo(ns);
ns.play("video/door.flv");
```

You have been doing this throughout the book. The major difference is that ActionScript 2.0 does not need to listen for an FLV file's metadata; it uses the attachVideo() method, not the attachNetStream() method, to connect the stream to the Video object on the stage.

7. Save and test the movie. When you test the movie, Device Central will launch and, as shown in Figure 12-3, the video will play in the interface of the device chosen.

Figure 12-3. When you test the movie, the video plays in the emulator chosen in Device Central.

Controlling video using the soft keys

If you look at the emulator in Figure 12-3, you will see four big keys surrounding the navigation buttons. These keys are called **soft keys**, and we'll use the two keys at the upper right and upper left to pause and play the video. Here's how:

1. Open the project you have been working on, select the layer containing the Video object and add a new layer named text.

2. Click once on the text layer and select the Text tool. Click once on the stage and enter the words Play and Pause.

3. Select the text. In the Property Inspector, apply these settings to the text:

- Font: _serif
- Style: Bold
- Size: 18 points
- Color: Black (#000000)

4. Click once in front of the word Pause and use the spacebar to move it to the right edge of the Video object, as shown in Figure 12-4. This will give the user a visual clue that the two buttons directly under the text can be used to control the video.

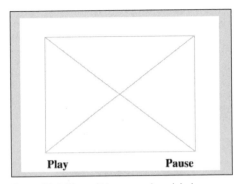

Play   Pause

Figure 12-4. The soft keys are given labels.

5. Click once on the first frame of the Actions layer and open the Actions panel.

6. Click once at the end of line 1, press Return/Enter and enter the following:

```
fscommand2("SetSoftKeys","Play","Pause");
```

You use this line of code to take control of those two keys.The command SetSoftKeys allows you to remap the two keys. The key on the left, SoftKey 1, will be labelled "Play", and the SoftKey on the right will be labelled "Pause".

7. Click once at the end of the code, press Return/Enter, and add the code that will pause the video when it starts to play:

```
ns.pause(true);
```

8. Press Return/Enter twice and add the following objects and functions to control the playback:

```
Key.removeListener(myListener);
var myListener:Object = new Object();
myListener.onKeyDown = function() {
  var keyCode:Number = Key.getCode();
  if (keyCode == ExtendedKey.SOFT1) {
    ns.pause(false);
  } else if (keyCode == ExtendedKey.SOFT2) {
    ns.pause(true);
  }
};
Key.addListener(myListener);
```

This code block starts by removing any existing Listener object that might already be listening for a key press (in device applications with several screens, this is a good habit to get into—it's like clearing the palate before taking another bite). The rest of the code creates the Listener object named myListener, which is nothing more than an Object instance.

The function is fairly uncomplicated. Flash will listen for an onKeyDown event. When it hears it, it gets the code for the key, getCode(), and uses a conditional statement to determine what to do—depending on which key has been pressed. If it is the left soft key, SOFT1, the video is unpaused. If it is the right soft key, the video is paused.

Perfectionists and trivia buffs might be keen to note that the keyCode variable is typed as a Number, and most of the time it will be because Key.getCode() usually returns a numeric value. To make things convenient, ActionScript provides many of the commonly referenced keys as named constants. For example, the device's Enter button (the one surrounded by arrow keys) is represented by the number 13, but you can use Key.ENTER in your conditionals to make the comparison. In this case, keyCode is compared against the constants ExtendedKey.SOFT1 and ExtendedKey.SOFT2, which are strings. ActionScript 2.0 isn't nearly as strict as ActionScript 3.0, and the type mismatch—a string received where a number is expected—goes unnoticed.

9. Save and test the movie. Use your mouse to click the soft keys in the emulator shown in Device Central. The video will load and pause. Click Play to play the video, and click Pause to pause it (see Figure 12-5). As you roll over the soft keys, they change color to indicate they are now active.

Figure 12-5. Soft keys can be used to control a video.

If you like, you can also use the page up and page down keys for the left and right soft keys, respectively. The arrow keys map to the device's arrow keys, Enter/Return is the button in the middle of those arrows, and the keypad number keys match the device number keys.

Now that you know how to use the soft keys to pause and play a video, let's look at how you can use the number keys on the keypad to load a video. Before we do that, we will need to create a MOV file from a Flash file.

Going the other way—Flash to QuickTime

Prior to the release of Flash CS3, converting a Flash movie into a QuickTime file that could be used for broadcast or streaming purposes was a bit of an issue because only the main timeline could be exported. If you had code-driven animations, nested movieclips, or even movieclips in the library that were added to the movie at runtime, you were essentially out of luck.

This has all changed in Flash CS3. About the only thing that won't move into QuickTime is interactivity. To prove it to you, we'll open a movie that uses class files and library content, convert it to a 10-second QuickTime movie, and then add it to the cell phone project.

> The authors are deeply grateful to Seb Lee-Delisle (out of Brighton, UK) for permission to include this project in the book. Seb is the Technical Director of a company named Plug-In Media: www.pluginmedia.net. We first saw this project in late 2007 when one of the authors was attending a Flash conference in Los Angeles. He sat in the audience and was amazed at what Seb could do to create particles in Flash CS3.

We won't explain the code in Seb's project. Instead we'll be using this file to simply show how code-driven animation can now be converted to a QuickTime movie.

Let's go to work:

1. Double-click the Particles31.swf file and open the project in the Flash Player. As you can see in Figure 12-6, you have a number of objects pouring out of the center of the screen. Close the Flash Player.

2. When you opened the Particles folder to launch the SWF file, you might have noticed that there were three files in the folder. The Particle.as file defines a custom Particle class and determines the characteristics of the particles in the SWF file you opened. Double-click Particles31.fla to open the file in Flash. When the file opens, open the Actions panel and you will see how the ActionScript pulls the Spark movieclip out of the library numerous times and puts it in motion. They key here is to understand that there is nothing up our sleeve. We start with a black stage, a movieclip, some ActionScript, and nothing more.

3. Select File ➤ Export ➤ Export Movie to open the Export Movie dialog box. Select QuickTime(*.mov) from the Save as type drop-down menu and click Save.

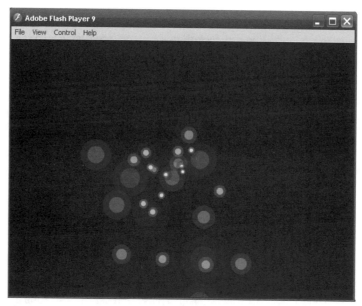

Figure 12-6. We start with a particle shower.

4. Clicking the Save button opens the QuickTime Export Settings dialog box shown in Figure 12-7.

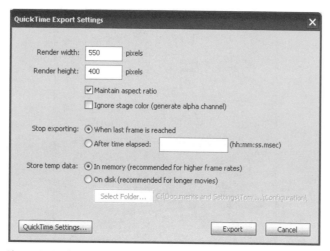

Figure 12-7. The magic starts in the QuickTime Export Settings dialog box.

Here's what each section of this dialog box does:

- Render width: The default value is the width of the stage. You can change this number.
- Render height: The default value is the height of the stage.
- Maintain aspect ratio: Keep this option selected to avoid distorting the content in the movie.
- Ignore stage color (generate alpha channel): This option removes the stage from the video and creates an Alpha channel video that can be used in video editors or even in Flash.
- Stop exporting: When last frame is reached: Select this option if the timeline is used for the animation.
- Stop exporting: After time elapsed: You can enter a duration for the movie if your entire project is ActionScript-driven.
- Store temp data: This is fairly self-explanatory, although we tend to select the On disk option because the hard drive is used as a scratch disk. You can use an external drive if you don't think you have enough space on your hard drive to contain the file.

5. Click the QuickTime Settings button to open the Movie Settings dialog box shown in Figure 12-8.

The Settings area is where you choose the codec used for the conversion. The default, for obvious reasons, is Animation, which is a lossless codec when Compression is set to Best. You can create a smaller MOV file if you select the Video codec from the Compression Settings dialog box.

Click the Settings button in the Sound area and you can change the audio settings for the video.

Figure 12-8. The video codec can be changed in the Movie Settings dialog box.

Unless there is a compelling reason to do so, you really don't need to visit the Movie Settings dialog box because you will be doing the compression in the Flash Video Encoder.

Yes, you can use the Movie Settings dialog box to change the video to the H.264 codec. In this case, the video won't need a side trip to the Encoder. We explain how to use H.264 content later in this chapter.

6. Click the After time elapsed radio button and enter 10 into the input area. This sets the duration of this video to 10 seconds.

7. Click the On disk radio button and click Export. A progress bar shows you the conversion progress. When it finishes, an alert will open, telling you that the process is complete and where to obtain a log file for the conversion.

8. Navigate to the Particles folder and open the QuickTime file. Click the Play button and you have a particle shower video, as shown in Figure 12-9.

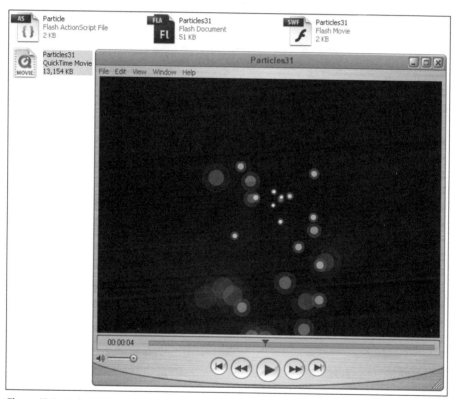

Figure 12-9. Code-driven animations can now become QuickTime videos!

Using the keypad to play multiple videos

In this exercise, you'll create a simple video application that will permit you to use the number 1 or 2 keys on a device's keypad. The videos will be the door.flv file we used earlier and the Particle31.flv file created from the QuickTime movie from the previous exercise. The purpose of this exercise is not to be clever, but to let you discover that it isn't only the soft keys that can be used to control a video file.

Let's get started:

1. Open the `Mobile_03.fla` file found in this chapter's exercise folder. When the file opens, you will see that we have essentially constructed the interface for you (see Figure 12-10). All you will need to do is to write the code.

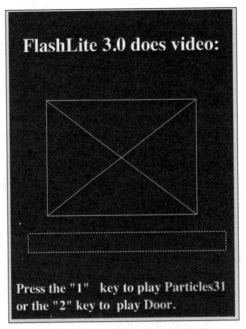

Figure 12-10. We start with a rather simple layout.

2. Select the first frame of the Actions layer and open the ActionScript panel. Click once in the first frame and enter the following:

```
fscommand2("SetSoftKeys", "", "Exit");

var nc = new NetConnection();
nc.connect(null);
var ns:NetStream = new NetStream(nc);
myVideo.attachVideo(ns);

var videos:Array = new Array(
  {path:"video/Particles31.flv", name:"Particles31"},
  {path:"video/door.flv", name:"Door"}
);
```

We start by telling Flash that soft key 2 (the one in the upper right) is the Exit key (notice that the soft key 1 parameter is a blank string, ""; we're not using it here). Although we will be using soft key 2 to tell Flash to Quit the application, there really will be nothing to quit to. Still, it is a good habit to develop.

The remaining lines set the variables for this application. One line creates an Array (a list) named videos that contains a series of objects (the {} brackets are a shortcut for the new Object() constructor). Each object features a property for both the path to the video and the name of the video. By doing this, a single key press will access the video and the video's name, which will appear in the dynamic text field on the stage. If you want to add more videos, it is a simple matter of adding them to the list as a new object.

3. Press Return/Enter twice and add the following:

```
var myListener:Object = new Object();

Key.removeListener(myListener);
myListener.onKeyDown = function():Void {

  var keyCode:Number = Key.getCode();
  var index:Number;
  switch(keyCode) {
    case ExtendedKey.SOFT2:
      fscommand2("quit");
      return;
    case 49:
      index = 0;
      break;
    case 50:
      index = 1;
      break;
  }
  playVideo(videos[index].path, videos[index].name);
};
Key.addListener(myListener);
```

To handle a key press, you need to create an Object instance, define its onKeyDown event, and eventually register that event as a listener for the keyboard, just as we did earlier in this chapter.

The function deals with what happens when the soft key is pressed. Instead of using a series of if() statements, as before, this function uses a switch() statement. Like last time, a keyCode variable is set to the return value of Key.getCode(). If keyCode is soft key 2, the app quits. If it's 49 or 50, a second variable, index, is set to either 0 or 1. What are these? In the arbitrary land of key code assignments, those numbers relate to the 1 and 2 number keys. For a full list of these assignments, see the Keyboard Keys and Key Code Values page in the Learning ActionScript 2.0 in Adobe Flash section of the Help panel. Be aware that the String.fromCharCode() method converts these codes back into normal characters.

After the index variable is set, the final line calls a custom playVideo() function and passes in two parameters, which are determined by the videos array. If index happens to be 0, the first parameter, videos[index].path, retrieves the path property of the first element in the videos array. The second parameter retrieves the name property of the first element.

4. Here's the code for that playVideo() function:

```
function playVideo(file:String, name:String):Void {
    ns.play(file);
    video_txt.text = "Now playing: " + name;
};
```

Pretty simple, really. The incoming file and name parameters correspond to the path and name sent by the key Listener. The file parameter is used in the NetStream.play() method, as invoked on the ns instance. The name parameter is used to update the TextField.text property of the dynamic text field.

5. Check your code. If everything is fine, save and test the file. The videos play when the number key is pressed (see Figure 12-11).

Figure 12-11. Press a number key and a video plays.

Going big—enter H.264

In late August 2007, Adobe made a rather startling announcement: it planned to support the AVC/H.264 video standard in the Flash Player. To help you understand the importance of this announcement, think about many of the projects in this book. The FLV files aren't bad, but because of the lossy nature of the On2 VP6 and Sorenson Squeeze codecs, the video tends to be a bit fuzzy. Living in a world in which HD TV is commonplace, and HD video cameras are accessible to practically everyone, we have gotten used to the crisp image rendered by this format. This format uses the H.264 codec and can now be streamed through the Flash Player and into your web pages.

H.264 is quite common. In fact, you might know it better as MPEG-4. This is an international standard (MPEG-4 H.264) developed by the Motion Pictures Expert Group (MPEG) that is also recognized by the International Standardization Organization (ISO). This is nice to know, but from your perspective, this format has some rather profound implications for you. The biggest one is that video, for all intents and purposes, has become untethered. It is not device-dependent. The file handed to you by your video producer can just as easily be played in a web site as it can on an iPod, Sony Playstation Portable, or HD TV. It also means that thanks to the addition of hardware acceleration and multithreading support to the Flash Player, you can play back video at any resolution and bit rate including the full HD 1080p resolution you can watch on HD TVs (see Figure 12-12).

> *Protected MP4 files such as those you might have downloaded from iTunes or files encrypted by FairPlay will not play through the Flash Player.*

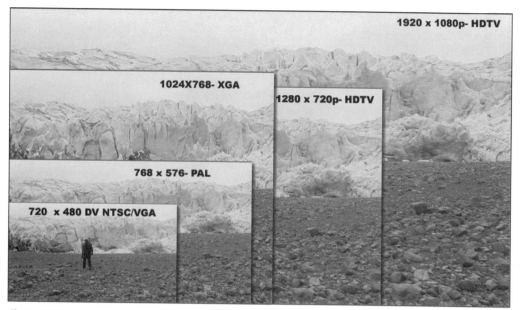

Figure 12-12. Pick a resolution and Flash will play it.

Does this mean that everything we have covered in this book to this very page is irrelevant? Not even close.

First, this format doesn't support alpha transparency. If you need this feature, the On2 VP6 codec is the way to go. You also need to be aware of the fact that H.264 content is processor-heavy. In fact, Adobe recommends that H.264 content is best viewed on dual-core PCs and Macs. Although the market is well on the way to making this transition, it will still be a few years before every computer will be able to manage the heavy lifting required to play this content. Still, don't be terribly surprised if YouTube content starts showing a marked improvement in its quality over the next couple of years. In fact, YouTube quietly switched to the Flash Player 9 in late 2007, and considering that H.264 content can be played only in the Flash Player 9, it doesn't take much deduction to assume that they are gearing up for this as well.

There is one final aspect of the MPEG-4 standard that is quite intriguing. It is a "container" format, which is a techie term for an MPEG-4 file being able to store several types of data on a number of tracks. The format synchronizes and interleaves the data, which means that the audio and video in the container can also include metadata, cover art, subtitles, and so on that can potentially be extracted by Flash. The container can also include multiple video and audio tracks, but for the moment Flash Player 9 will play back only one of each right now and essentially ignore any other tracks.

Now that we have your attention, here are the file formats supported by the Flash Player:

Flash Player 9:

- MP4
- M4v
- MP4V

- FLV
- MOV (H.264 codec only)

Audio:

- M4a
- MP3

Mobile video formats:

- 3GP
- 3G2
- FLV

Playing an H.264 video

Now that you have an idea of what's in store, let's create a small application that plays a video. Just so you really get the point behind the power of this new format, we'll be using a QuickTime MP4 video that is 720 x 480 and weighs in at 113 megabytes.

1. Open a new Flash ActionScript 3.0 document and add a Video object to the stage. Save the file to the H264 folder in the Chapter 12 exercise folder.

2. Change the document size to 848 by 480 and set the stage color to Black (#000000).

3. Select the Video object on the stage. In the Property Inspector change its dimensions to 720 pixels wide and 480 pixels high. Give the Video object the instance name of myVideo.

4. Add a new layer named Actions, select the first frame of the Actions layer, and open the Actions panel.

5. Click once in the Script pane and enter the following:

```
var nc:NetConnection = new NetConnection();
nc.connect(null);
var ns:NetStream = new NetStream(nc);
myVideo.attachNetStream(ns);

var listener:Object = new Object();
listener.onMetaData = function (md:Object):void{};
ns.client = listener

ns.play("Trip.mp4");
```

This is the same code we have been using since Chapter 3. The only major difference is the use of the MP4 file extension instead of FLV.

6. Save the file and publish both the SWF and the HTML files.

7. When the process finishes, open the HTML file just created in a browser, as shown in Figure 12-13. Welcome to the brave new world of HD video in Flash.

Figure 12-13. An MP4 file playing through the Flash Player in a browser

One aspect of Flash video that we have been using quite extensively in this book is error checking and telling Flash what to do when an error is encountered. This time we'll check for a couple of error messages from the NetStream class that are specific to the MP4 format: FileStructureInvalid and NoSupportedTrackFound. The first one (FileStructureInvalid) is kicked out if the file is corrupt or otherwise not supported. The second error message (NoSupportedTrackFound) means that none of the audio or video tracks in the MPEG-4 file is supported. Follow these steps to check for these two issues:

1. Open the project you have been working on. Open the code and add the following highlighted code block:

```
var nc:NetConnection = new NetConnection();
nc.connect(null);
var ns:NetStream = new NetStream(nc);
myVideo.attachNetStream(ns);

var listener:Object = new Object();
listener.onMetaData = function (md:Object):void {};
ns.client = listener

function checkFile(evt:NetStatusEvent):void {
  if (evt.info code == "NetStream.FileStructureInvalid" {
    trace("The MP4 file has an invalid structure.");
```

```
    } else if (evt.info.code == "NetStream.NosSupportedTrackFound") {
      trace("This file contains no supported tracks");
    }
  }
```

```
ns.addEventListener(NetStatusEvent.NET_STATUS,checkFile);
```

```
ns.play("Trip.mp4");
```

Using the metadata in an MPEG-4 file

During the course of preparing the Puppetji files for Chapter 9, we discovered that they contained no metadata, which makes them difficult to work with. The solution was one that Flash video producers, designers, and developers have been using for a few years: inject the metadata into the FLV file. If you face this issue, head over to www.buraks.com/flvmdi/ and pick up a free copy of the FLVMetaData injector.

As you have learned, the onMetaData event is commonly used to obtain and use such information as the video dimensions and duration. This information is also available to the new supported formats.

Because the MPEG-4 format is a container format, you can extract such information as duration, cue points, and dimensions. What makes this even more intriguing is that the potential exists to pull out cover art, subtitles, text, and images from both the H.264 and the MPEG-4 formats.

Still, it is important to note that seek points traditionally used to scrub a video aren't included in the metadata, so you won't be able to use seek points to scrub through an MPEG-4 or H.264 file. There are also a couple of new events that are aimed strictly at the video and audio data in an MPEG-4 file. The onImageData returns GIF, PNG, or JPG data as a ByteArray in ActionScript 3.0. The onTextData event can return such data as subtitles or captions.

In this exercise, we'll create a small application that extracts metadata from a video file:

1. Open the file you have been working on. Delete the Video object from the stage and the library.

2. Change the stage color to Grey (#999999) and add a new layer named MetaOutput.

3. Select the new layer and add a dynamic text object to the stage. Give this object the instance name of metaTxt and, in the Property Inspector set its X and Y positions to 5. Also change the width to 385 and the height to 250.

4. Save the project to the H264 folder.

5. Click the first frame in the Actions layer and enter the following:

```
var myVideo:Video = new Video();
myVideo.x = 300;
myVideo.y = 5;
addChild(myVideo);

var nc:NetConnection = new NetConnection();
nc.connect(null);
```

```
var ns:NetStream = new NetStream(nc);
myVideo.attachNetStream(ns);

var mySound:SoundTransform = ns.soundTransform;
mySound.volume = 0.5;
ns.soundTransform = mySound;

var listener:Object = new Object();
listener.onMetaData = handleMetaData;
ns.client = listener;

ns.addEventListener(NetStatusEvent.NET_STATUS, checkFile);

ns.play("Trip.mp4");

function checkFile(evt:NetStatusEvent):void{
  if (evt.info.code == "NetStream.FileStructureInvalid") {
    trace("The MP4's file structure is invalid.");
  }
  else if (evt.info.code == "NetStream.NoSupportedTrackFound") {
    trace("The MP4 doesn't contain any supported tracks");
  }
}
```

The only new aspect of this code is the discovery that you can also use MP4 files in Video objects created at runtime. Instead of handling the metadata in an anonymous function, this time the function is separate. It's a named function, handleMetaData(), set aside just for sake of illustration (see step 6), so you can examine it on its own.

6. The final step is to use the metadata. It will be placed in the text box on the stage and used to set the size of the Video object. Click once at the end of the checkFile() function. Press Return/Enter twice and add the following function:

```
function handleMetaData(md:Object):void {
  for(var propName:String in md) {
    metaTxt.appendText(propName + " = " + md[propName] + "\n");
  }
  myVideo.width = md.width;
  myVideo.height = md.height;
}
```

This is how the metadata is pulled out of the MP4 file and scooted into the dynamic text box. An onMetaData event kicks off when the Flash Player receives the metadata from the MP4 file. Flash then loops through the metadata using a for..in loop, grabbing it and converting it to a string of property names and values found in the incoming md parameter. This string is then placed into the dynamic text box with the instance name metaTxt. Because of the amount of metadata in the file, each piece of it is placed on its own line in the text box with the escape sequence \n (line feed) and the appendText() method. The function finishes by using the width and height metadata to set the width and the height of the Video object.

7. Check your code and then save and test the movie. The metadata will fill the text box, as shown in Figure 12-14.

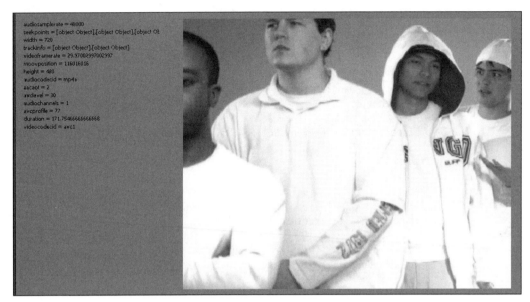

Figure 12-14. Displaying and using the metadata in an MP4 file

Let's think big—really big

Let's face it; most of us have an HD TV sitting at home and/or an HD monitor sitting on our desk. We have become spoiled—we're used to high-definition video and wouldn't mind having the same experience on the Web. Although you can take an FLV file and run it out using the full-screen feature of Flash, until now this wasn't possible with HD content.

In this final exercise of this chapter, we'll show you how to use hardware scaling and acceleration to achieve full-screen HD video. The really cool aspect of hardware scaling is that it isn't limited to H.264 or MPEG-4 files; it can just as easily be applied to larger On2 VP6 files (and even to really large SWF files).

Hardware acceleration is applied through the Flash Player. If you open the HTML file from the previous exercise and right-click (PC) or Ctrl-click (Mac) on the video, the Flash Player dialog box will open. If you click the display settings icon (the one in the lower-left corner), you will see the dialog box shown in Figure 12-15. Select Enable hardware acceleration and you're good to go. The interesting thing about this feature is that it is triggered only when needed. Unchecking the box results in the use of the scaling API used when an FLV file is taken out to full screen. Note that this is available only on Flash Player 9.0.115.0 and higher.

GOING SMALL AND GOING BIG WITH FLASH VIDEO

Figure 12-15. Hardware acceleration is enabled.

In this exercise, you'll create a button that expands the video to full screen. Follow these steps:

1. Open the `BigItUp.fla` file. When the file opens, you will see that the movie consists of nothing more than a button on the screen. If you are coming to HD video for the first time, you might be in for a bit of a shock. If you click on the stage, you will see that the dimensions of the stage are 1465 pixels x 720 pixels. You need the real estate because the video we will be using (`backcountry_bombshells_4min_HD_H264.mp4`) is 1280 x 720.

> The authors want to offer their deep appreciation to Adobe Systems and the Red Bull people for permission to use this video for the exercise. This is the video that was wowing the universe when Adobe announced the addition of H.264 playback through the Flash Player.

Before we start messing with the code, it might not be a bad idea for you to understand how video can be played in full-screen mode. When a button used to go full screen is clicked, the entire Flash stage expands to fill the screen, and any content on the stage is scaled along with it. This is why FLV files look a bit fuzzy when they expand out to the full browser screen.

This latest iteration of the Flash Player does things a bit differently. You can choose to expand the stage, or just a piece of it, by creating a rectangle on the stage. If the rectangle is smaller than the stage, only the rectangle and its contents are scaled to full screen, and hardware acceleration takes over to play the video or the content.

2. Select the first frame of the Actions layer and open the Actions panel. Click once in line 1 of the code and scroll through to see that there really is nothing new here apart from the hole in which you will create the full-screen functionality. You have done all this to this point in the chapter.

3. Click once in line 41. This is where you write the function to create the rectangle used to go full screen. Enter the following code:

```
function goFullScreen(evt:Object):void {
    var scalingRect:Rectangle = new Rectangle(myVideo.x,➥
myVideo.y, myVideo.width, myVideo.height);
    stage.fullScreenSourceRect = scalingRect;
    if (stage.displayState == StageDisplayState.NORMAL) {
      stage.displayState = StageDisplayState.FULL_SCREEN;
    } else {
      stage.displayState = StageDisplayState.NORMAL;
    }
}
```

We create the rectangle and set its size to match that of the Video object. The next line sets the fullScreenSourceRect property of the stage to that of the rectangle just created. The if..else conditional statement is used to check the current state of the stage and to change the stage size from normal to full screen or from full screen back to its original size.

4. Now that we have the rectangle that will be scaled to fit the video, let's "wire up" the button that makes it happen. Click once in line 45 of the Script pane and enter the following:

```
btnBig.addEventListener(MouseEvent.CLICK, goFullScreen);
```

Again, nothing new here. Click once on the button on the stage; the goFullScreen() function you just wrote is executed.

5. Check your code and make sure that you have made no mistakes. When you finish, save the file.

6. Select File ➤ Publish Settings to open the Publish Settings dialog box.

7. Select both the Flash and HTML types. Click the HTML tab at the top of the dialog box to open the HTML Publish Settings.

8. In the Template drop-down menu, select Flash Only - Allow Full Screen, as shown in Figure 12-16. If you select it, you don't need to dig into the Object and Embed tags of the HTML file to make this possible.

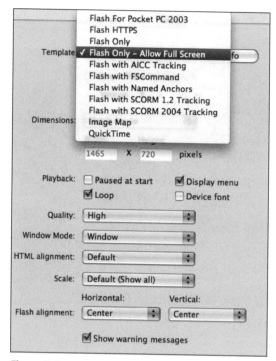

Figure 12-16. Let the software do the work.

9. Click the Formats tab and when you return to the Formats pane, click the Publish button to create the SWF and HTML files.

10. Save the file and open the HTML file in a browser. When you click the Big it Up button, the video expands to full-screen mode, as shown in Figure 12-17. Press Escape to return to the video's original size.

For this to work as expected, you have to have Flash Player 9.0.115.0 or higher installed.

Figure 12-17. Full-screen, high-quality video playing in a browser—who'd a thunk it?

Using the FLVPlayback component to play HD video

In mid-December 2007, Adobe quietly released Update 3 for the Flash Player 9, which updated the Player to version 9.0.115.0. (This might have changed by the time the book is published.) It was odd that the release was so quiet because along with the usual bug fixes and so on, Adobe slipped in an update to the FLVPlayback component that allows you to use this component, instead of a Video object, to play back HD video.

In late January 2008, Adobe also released an updated version of the Flash Media Server (actually it was two versions: Flash Media Interactive Server 3 and Flash Media Streaming Server 3). Apart from eye-popping price drops (have you ever seen the price of software drop to about 10 percent of its previous value and still include an amazing lineup of feature additions?), the FMS 3 lineup includes the capability to stream HD files instead of using the Progressive Download method we have been using throughout this book.

Here's the Executive Summary regarding the differences between Streaming and a Progressive Download. If you use the Progressive Download method, the video file loads into the browser cache and starts playing when enough information is in the cache to start playing the video. A stream doesn't put anything in the browser cache and starts playing as soon as the first bit of information hits the Flash Player.

Included in the Streaming Server is a feature that should appeal to practically everyone thinking of using FMS 3 to stream video. If there was one common "rap" against the FMS, it was the fact it was really hard to learn and required you to master another subset of ActionScript to harness the power of the server. Simply getting a video to stream from the FMS into the Flash Player required you to write both server-side ActionScript and client-side ActionScript. As well, if the files were not in their proper locations, the odds were about 300 percent that the video wouldn't play. This is now a thing of the past thanks to the inclusion of a video on demand (vod) feature in the Streaming Server.

In this exercise, we'll give you the opportunity to try out the vod feature and play an HD video using the FLVPlayback component.

The authors want to thank William Hanna, Dean of the School of Media Studies and Information Technology at the Humber Institute of Technology and Advanced Learning, for permission to use the clip used in this exercise. The clip is taken from a video series (Earley Bird) that was produced by a group of students and graduates known as the Producer's League.

Let's get started:

1. You'll need to install a Developer Edition of FMS 3 on your PC. (There is no Mac version available at this time; FMS 3 comes only in Windows or Linux editions.) Point your browser to www.adobe.com/products/flashmediastreaming and click the Download the free developer edition link on the page.

2. When the download finishes, double-click the Installer and follow the onscreen instructions. If you are curious or a bit nervous about what will be going on during the installation, one of the authors has written a small guide that walks you through the installation process (see www.adobe.com/devnet/flashmediaserver).

3. Navigate to C:\Program Files\Adobe\Flash Media Server 3\applications\vod\media on your PC and copy the Vultures.mp4 file to the media folder found in the vod folder.

   This folder is really cool. The vod service lets you stream any file (FLV, MP4, or MP3) located in this folder without your having to write a line of code to build an application or playing with the server. The other really neat thing is that you can use the Flash CS3 or the Flash 8 FLVPlayback component to play the video.

4. Open a new Flash CS3 document and set the stage size to 854 pixels wide by 520 pixels high.

5. Add an FLVPLayback component to the stage and set its dimensions to 854 pixels wide and 480 pixels high. In the Property Inspector, set the component's X and Y coordinates to 0,0.

6. Click once on the component on the stage to select it and click the Parameters tab in the Property Inspector. Use these settings in Parameters:

   - align: center
   - autoPlay: true
   - cuePoints: None
   - preview: None
   - scaleMode: maintainAspectRatio
   - skin: SkinUnderAllNoCaption.swf
   - skinAuthoHide: false
   - skinBackgroundAlpha: 1.00
   - skinBackgroundColor: #009933

7. Double-click the source parameter. When the Content Path dialog box opens, enter rtmp://localhost/vod/Vultures.mp4 (see Figure 12-18). Make sure that you do not select Match source FLV dimensions or Download FLV for cue points and dimensions.

Figure 12-18. You have to manually enter the path to the video in the Content Path dialog box.

The address uses an RTMP address, not the HTTP address you are familiar with. RTMP is a proprietary protocol developed by Adobe specifically for the FMS. When an RTMP address is detected, Flash is smart enough to figure out where the server is located (in this case, on your computer) and poke into the applications folder to find the vod folder. From there, it is also smart enough to figure out that the video, if it is in the media folder, is in the vod folder.

8. Save the movie and test it. When the SWF file launches, the video starts to play.

> This is a very simple example of the FMS in action. To actually use it to feed a video into a SWF file on a web page, you will need to use the RTMP specifications given to you by your ISP or Flash Video Streaming Service. That, dear reader, is well out of the scope of this book.

What about those of you who don't have an FMS account? No problem:

9. Save the Flash document to the same folder as the Vultures.mp4 file. Open the Content Path dialog box (see Figure 12-19). Simply enter the path to the MP4 file on your computer into the Content Path dialog box.

If your file is destined for playback from your web site, be sure to enter the path http://www.mySite.com/HD/Vultures.mp4 *before you compile the SWF file.*

10. Save and test the movie.

skin	SkinUnderAllNoCaption.swf
skinAutoHide	false
skinBackgroundAlpha	1.00
skinBackgroundColor	#009933
source	E:\Books\FlashVideo_Edition2\956Xch12\Exercise Files_Ch12\Exercise\FLVPlayback\Vultures.mp4
volume	1

Figure 12-19. Enter the path to the video if you don't have access to FMS 3.

Here's where this whole thing gets really cool. Earlier in this chapter, we showed you how to go full screen with HD content. The project you have been using contains a Full Screen button in the skin. Here's how to enable the full-screen feature of the skin:

11. With the Flash movie open, select File ➤ Publish Settings. In the Formats area of the Publish Settings dialog box, select both the Flash (.swf) and HTML (.html) file formats.

12. Click the HTML tab and select Flash Only - Allow Full Screen from the Template drop-down menu.

13. Click the Publish button.

14. Navigate to the folder containing the HTML just generated and double-click it to launch the page in a browser.

15. When the video starts playing, click the Full Screen button. The video and the skin will expand to fill the browser window (see Figure 12-20). How about that? No code!

Figure 12-20. Enter the path to the video if you don't have access to FMS 3.

16. Press Esc to return the video to its regular size.

> Now take a deep breath. As we started digging into the use of these files in Flash, we encountered quite a few issues that we are, for now, chalking up to the sheer newness of this technology with Flash. The other critical aspect of our issues is this: it isn't always Adobe's fault.
>
> The first issue we encountered was a biggie. Several of the videos we used, other than ones supplied by Adobe, didn't work. They were MOV files, MP4 files, and even H.264 files. We found it to be extremely odd because there was no mention of this by Adobe. What we discovered, thanks in part to Adobe's help, was that not all MP4 files are created equal—and that MP4, not MOV, is the format you need to use. Figure 12-21 brings this into sharp focus.

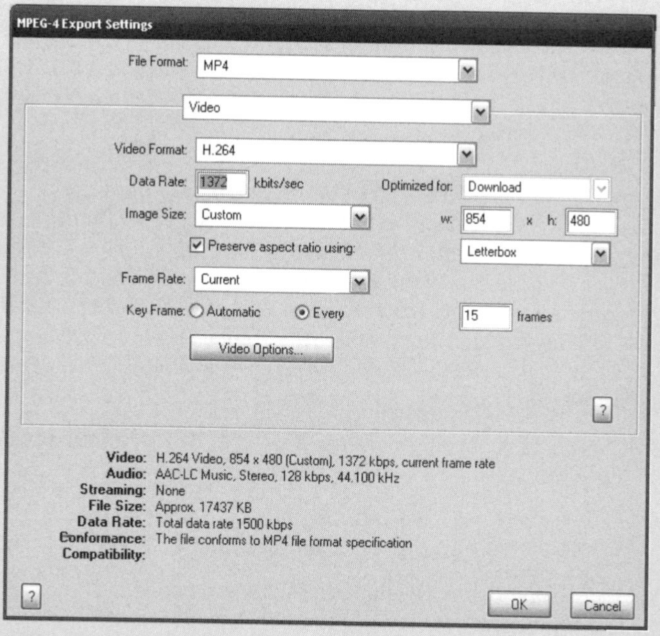

Figure 12-21. The settings used for the Vultures.mp4 video

These are the settings we used to create the Vultures.mp4 *video. Note the use of* H.264 *compression in the* Video Format *drop-down menu. Although H.264 compression is acceptable, MOV files that use the H.264 codec don't always work in Flash (we discovered this with an MOV file). Figure 12-22 shows that this is a MOV file that uses H.264 compression. When we ran it through Flash, the video would not play. Yet, when we re-encoded the video using the settings in Figure 12-21, the video played.*

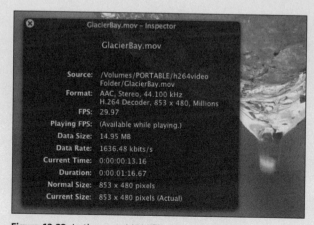

Figure 12-22. In theory, a MOV file with H.264 compression should work.

This raises a rather interesting question. Assuming that not all files are created equal, how do we know which is a "good" movie and which is a "bad" one? The answer is that there is no way to know. You need to make sure that it works by testing it in Flash. If it doesn't play, you need to go back to the source and get a new MP4 file that is properly encoded.

Here are a couple of things that can cause playback failure:

Header information: *All video files contain a header called a moov atom. The location of the moov atom in the file can result in failure. If the moov atom is at the start of the file and you are using a Progressive Download method, the file will play. If it is at the end of the file, where it is placed by Adobe Premiere and After Effects, the entire file has to download before it starts to play. This isn't an issue if you are using FMS 3. If you suspect that this is the case, either use QuickTime Pro to re-encode the video or consider using QTIndexSwapper, which is a small AIR application developed by Renaun Eriickson for this very task. It can be picked up at* http://renaun.com/blog/2007/08/22/234.

Codec choice: *The video codec for the MP4 needs to be H.264, and the audio codec has to be either AAC or MP3.*

AVC profile: *This is the advanced video coding profile used when the file is created. Flash Player 9 supports 66, 77, 100, and 110. It does not support 88, 122, 144, or none.*

Incorrect 4CC: *This is nothing more than a four-character code that is a sequence of four bytes used to identify a data format. The Flash Player supports MP3, MP4a, AVC1, TXG3, GIF, PNG, JPEG, VP60, and VP60A. Thus you might have the correct audio and video codecs along with the right AVC profile and the video still will not play. The Flash Player won't tell you this. You can see a list of all the 4CCs at* http://wiki.multimedia.cx/ index.php?title=QuickTime_container#Video_FOURCCs.

Data rate: *If the data rate is set too high (you can see where it is set in Figure 12-21), there is a real risk that you will experience playback failure.*

What you've learned

It has been quite the chapter. You created Flash applications that allow you to play video on the largest and smallest screen available to you. Along the way, you have learned how to use Device Central to choose and test a device for video playback and explored the new video features of Flash Lite 3.0. You also went in the other direction and used the new video file formats (H.264 and MPEG-4) that can now be used by the latest iteration of the Flash Player.

In this chapter you did the following:

- Learned how to author video applications for a cell phone
- Discovered how to convert a Flash movie to a QuickTime video
- Added H.264 and MPEG-4 video to a Flash movie
- Wrote the ActionScript that allows you to access the metadata in the file
- Created a full-screen video presentation using hardware acceleration in the Flash Player
- Played an MP4 through the FLVPLayback component and used the component's full-screen capability

This brings us to the end of our journey. We hope you enjoyed this exploration of the creative uses and applications of video in Flash. We have come a long way since the release of this book's predecessor: *Foundation Flash 8 Video*. At the time that book was written, video in Flash was just starting to establish itself, and the subtext of that entire book was "this is so new; here are some ideas for what you can do with this technology."

Two years later, Flash video can be played on any Flash-enabled device, ranging from cell phones to monster HD displays. Web playback has been supercharged, and ActionScript 3 lets us do things we only dreamed of in the previous iteration of this book.

The last two paragraphs of that book are still as relevant today as they were in 2006:

"Over the coming months and years, as Adobe makes the integration of its tools even tighter with Flash, the creative possibilities available to you will explode. That should be an immense amount of fun.

Speaking of fun—as we tell anybody that will listen, the amount of fun you can have with Flash video should be illegal. We'll see you in jail!"

INDEX

Numerics

4CC (four-character code), and playback failure, 358
24-bit PNG file, 179

A

accessibility laws governing web sites, 301
ActionScript
  applying filters and blends through, 157–159
  ColorMatrixFilter class, 221–224
  ComboBox for navigating through cue points, 320–322
  creating instance of FLVPlayback component using, 229–232
  cue points and, 307–309
  duration metadata parameter and, 85
  import statements, 201
  looping video using, 236–237
  navigating through cue points with, 317–320
  NetConnection class, 79
  pairing with Video object, 76–79
  playing videos sequentially using, 261–263
  turning blend modes on and off using buttons, 166–170
  turning filters on and off using buttons, 160–166
  video masks and
    creating instance of Video object, 194–197
    creating mask that trims video, 197–200
    draggable mask, creating, 185–186
    drawing with ActionScript, 190–194
    dynamically adding masking object, 189–190
    flashlight effect, adding, 187–188
    overview of, 185
    packages and motion, 204–209
    Tween and easing classes, 200–204
  wiring video player using
    code, 96–100
    loading and playing progress, showing, 102–105
    overview of, 95
    volume level of video, controlling, 100–102
ActionScript 3.0 document, 16

ActionScript editors, 205
Add blend mode for buttons, 98
Adjust Color filter, 152
Adobe
  Bridge CS3, previewing work using, 62
  ExpressInstall, 225–228
  Illustrator images, placing into Flash, 177
  Media Player (AMP), previewing work using, 61–62
Adobe After Effects CS3
  Compression Settings dialog box, 123
  Keylight filter, 116–118
  Output to dialog box, 124
  overview of, 116
  QuickTime file for, 121–124
  Render Queue dialog box
    alpha channel video, creating, 122
    FLV file, creating, 125–126
  Render Settings panel, 122
  Screen Matte properties, 120–121
  View drop-down menu, 119
Adobe Dreamweaver
  adding Flash video to, 243–244
  CommunityMX extension, 227
  EOLAS workaround, 224–225
Adobe Fireworks CS3
  Batch Process dialog box, 214
  creating video player using
    Fireworks symbols and Flash symbols, 93–95
    overview of, 89
    preparing to move from Fireworks to Flash, 91
    wire frame for, 90
  PNG format and, 179
  Save Script button, 216
  scaling images using, 213
Adobe Flash CS3 Video Encoder
  accessing, 1, 10
  Audio tab, 14
  cue points, creating with, 304–307
  Encode Alpha Channel option, 144
  Encoding Settings panel, 11
  Errors dialog box, 15

361